AF557761

Print Media

Print Media

Sanoj Singh

RANDOM PUBLICATIONS
NEW DELHI (INDIA)

Print Media

ISBN 978-93-51111-634-9
© Reserved

All Rights Reserved. No Part of this book may be reproduced in any manner without written permission.

Published in 2015 in India by

RANDOM PUBLICATIONS

4376-A/4B, Gali Murari Lal, Ansari Road
New Delhi-110 002
Phone : +9111-43580356, 011-23289044, 011-43142548
e-mail: sales@randompublications.com,
info@randompublications.com, randomexports@gmail.com

Reprinted 2022

Type Setting by : Friends Media, Delhi-110089
Digitally Printed at: Replika Press Pvt. Ltd.

Preface

Print media are lightweight, portable, disposable publications printed on paper and circulated as physical copies in forms we call books, newspapers, magazines and newsletters. They hold informative and entertaining content that is of general or special interest. They are published either once or daily, weekly, biweekly, monthly, bimonthly or quarterly. Their competitors include electronic, broadcast and Internet media. Today, many books, newspapers, magazines and newsletters publish digital electronic editions on the Internet.

Print media is found in many different forms, from newspapers (the most popular form) and magazines to newsletters, brochures and posters. Other forms of print media, including direct mail marketing, flyers, handbills, banners, billboards and press releases are less popular, but they're still used by industry professionals.

Origin and development of printing Press is an important part of the general history of civilization. Printing has been the principal vehicle for the conveying of ideas during the past 500 years to fully understand political, constitutional, ecclesiastical and economic events, and sociological, philosophical and literary movements one must take into account the influence which the printing press has exerted on them.

Once, newspapers were the main medium for communicating and receiving news. Despite challenges from radio, cinema newsreels and television during the course of the twentieth century, the newspaper industry remained robust and profitable. In the USA alone, more than 56 million newspapers were sold every weekday, and 60 million every Sunday. However, newspaper readership has been in steady decline throughout the 1990s and 2000s, and this trend looks set to continue, especially as younger readers (those in their twenties) are rejecting print-based news in favour of the online variety. Perhaps more significantly for the industry, advertising revenues fell by half between 2000 and 2011.

This work, further, deals with all vital issues, related to print media. For a thorough insight of the existing scenario, possession of this book is but compulsory for all those, concerned with the discipline and profession.

I would like to thank my team for standing beside me throughout my career and writing this book. My special thanks go to "Random Publications" who have published the book.

– Sanoj Singh

Contents

1

Introduction to Printing

Printing is a process for reproducing text and images using a master form or template. The earliest examples include Cylinder seals and other objects such as the Cyrus cylinder and Cylinders of Nabonidus. The earliest known form of woodblock printing came from China dating to before 220 A.D.. Later developments in printing include the movable type, first developed by Bi Sheng in China, and the printing press, a more efficient printing process for western languages with their more limited alphabets, developed by Johannes Gutenberg in the fifteenth century.

Modern printing is done typically with ink on paper using a printing press. Its also frequently done on metals, plastics, cloth and composite materials. On paper it is often carried out as a large-scale industrial process, and is an essential part of publishing and transaction printing.

HISTORY

Woodblock printing

Woodblock printing is a technique for printing text, images or patterns that was used widely throughout East Asia. It originated in China in antiquity as a method of printing ontextiles and later on paper. As a method of printing on cloth, the earliest surviving examples from China date to before 220 A.D.

In East Asia

The earliest surviving woodblock printed fragments are from China and are of silk printed with flowers in three colours from the Han Dynasty (before 220 A.D.), and the earliest example of woodblock printing on paper appeared in the mid-seventh century in China.

By the ninth century, printing on paper had taken off, and the first extant complete printed book containing its date is the Diamond Sutra(British Library) of 868. By the tenth century, 400,000 copies of some sutras and pictures were printed and the Confucian classics were in print. A skilled printer could print up to 2,000 double-page sheets per day.

Printing spread early to Korea and Japan, which also used Chinese logograms, but the technique was also used in Turpan and Vietnamusing a number of other scripts. This technique then spread to Persia and Russia. This technique was transmitted to Europe from China, via the Islamic world, and by around 1400 was being used on paper for old master prints and playing cards. However, Arabs never used this to print the Quran because of the limit of Islam doctrine.

In the Middle East

Block printing, called *tarish* in Arabic was developed in Arabic Egypt during the ninth-tenth centuries, mostly for prayers and amulets. There is some evidence to suggest that these print blocks were made from non-wood materials, possibly tin, lead, or clay. The techniques employed are uncertain, however, and they appear to have had very little influence outside of the Muslim world. Though Europe adopted woodblock printing from the Muslim world, initially for fabric, the technique of metal block printing remained unknown in Europe. Block printing later went out of use in Islamic Central Asia after movable type printing was introduced from China.

In Europe

Block printing first came to Europe as a method for printing on cloth, where it was common by 1300. Images printed on cloth for religious purposes could be quite large and elaborate, and when paper became relatively easily available, around 1400, the medium transferred very quickly to small woodcut religious images and playing cards printed on paper. These prints were produced in very large numbers from about 1425 onward.

Around the mid-fifteenth-century, *block-books*, woodcut books with both text and images, usually carved in the same block, emerged as a cheaper alternative to manuscripts and books printed with movable type. These were all short heavily illustrated works, the bestsellers of the day, repeated in many different block-book versions: the Ars moriendi and the Biblia pauperum were the most common. There is still some controversy among scholars as to whether their introduction preceded or, the majority view, followed the introduction of movable type, with the range of estimated dates being between about 1440 and 1460.

Movable-type printing

Movable type is the system of printing and typography using movable pieces of metal type, made by casting from matrices struck by letterpunches. Movable type allowed for much more flexible processes than hand copying or block printing. Around 1040, the first known movable type system was created in China by Bi Sheng out ofporcelain. Sheng used clay type, which broke easily, but Wang Zhen later carved a more durable type from wood by 1298 C.E., and developed a complex system of revolving tables and number-association with written Chinese characters that made typesetting and printing more efficient. Still, the main method in use there remained woodblock printing (xylography), which "proved to be cheaper and more efficient for printing Chinese, with its thousands of characters".

Copper movable type printing originated in China at the beginning of twelfth century. It was used in large-scale printing of paper money issued by the Northern Song dynasty.

Around 1230, Koreans invented a metal type movable printing using bronze. The Jikji, published in 1377, is the earliest known metal printed book. Types-casting was used, adapted from the method of casting coins. The character was cut in beech wood, which was then pressed into a soft clay to form a mould and bronze poured into the mould and the type was finally polished.

Around 1450, Johannes Gutenberg introduced what is regarded as the first modern movable type system in Europe, along with innovations in casting the type based on a matrix and hand mould. Gutenberg was the first to create his type pieces from an alloy of lead, tin, and antimony – the same components still used today.

The Printing press

Johannes Gutenberg's work on his printing press began in approximately 1436 when he partnered with Andreas Dritzehen – a man he had previously instructed in gem-cutting – and Andreas Heilmann, the owner of a paper mill. It was not until a 1439 lawsuit against Gutenberg that an official record exists; witness testimony discussed type, an inventory of metals (including lead) and his type mold.

Compared to woodblock printing, movable type page setting and printing using a press was faster and more durable. The metal type pieces were sturdier and the lettering more uniform, leading to typography and fonts. The high quality and relatively low price of theGutenberg Bible (1455) established the superiority of movable type for western languages, and printing presses rapidly spread across Europe, leading up to the Renaissance, and later all around the world. Today, practically all movable type printing ultimately derives from Gutenberg's innovations to movable type printing, which is often regarded as the most important invention of the second millennium.

Rotary printing press

The rotary printing press was invented by Richard March Hoe in 1843. It uses impressions curved around a cylinder to print on long continuous rolls of paper or other substrates. Rotary drum printing was later significantly improved by William Bullock.

CONVENTIONAL PRINTING TECHNOLOGY

All printing process are concerned with two kinds of areas on the final output:

1. Image of printing areas,
2. Non-image or non-printing areas

After the information has been prepared for production (the prepress step), each printing process has definitive means of separating the image from the non-image areas.

Conventional printing has four types of process:

1. Planographics, in which the printing and non-printing areas are on the same plane surface and the difference between them is maintained chemically or by physical properties, the examples are: offset lithography, collotype, and screenless printing.
2. Relief, in which the printing areas are on a plane surface and the non printing areas are below the surface, examples: flexography and letterpress.
3. Intaglio, in which the non-printing areas are on a plane surface and the printing area are etched or engraved below the surface, examples: steel die engraving, gravure
4. Porous, in which the printing areas are on fine mesh screens through which ink can penetrate, and the non-printing areas are a stencil over the screen to block the flow of ink in those areas, examples: screen printing, stencil duplicator.

Offset press

Offset printing is a widely used printing technique where the inked image is transferred (or "offset") from a plate to a rubber blanket, then to the printing surface. When used in combination with the lithographic process, which is based on the repulsion of oil and water, the offset technique employs a flat (planographic) image carrier on which the image to be printed obtains ink from ink rollers, while the non-printing area attracts a film of water, keeping the non-printing areas ink-free.

Currently, most books and newspapers are printed using the technique of offset lithography.

Other printing techniques

The other significant printing techniques include:

- Flexography used for packaging, labels, newspapers
- Hot wax dye transfer
- Inkjet used typically to print a small number of books or packaging and also, to print a variety of materials from high quality papers simulating offset printing, to floor tiles; Inkjet is also used to apply mailing addresses to direct mail pieces

- Laser printing (Toner Printing) mainly used in offices and for transactional printing (bills, bank documents). Laser printing is commonly used by direct mail companies to create variable data letters or coupons.
- Pad printing popular for its unusual ability to print on complex three-dimensional surfaces
- Relief print, (mainly used for catalogues)
- Rotogravure mainly used for magazines and packaging
- Screen-printing for T-shirts to floor tiles
- Intaglio - Used mainly for high value documents such as Currencies.
- Thermal printing - Popular in the 1990s for Fax printing. Used today for airline baggage tags and in Supermarket deli counters.

Gravure

Gravure printing is an intaglio printing technique, where the image to be printed is made up of small depressions in the surface of the printing plate. The cells are filled with ink and the excess is scraped off the surface with a doctor blade, then a rubber-covered roller presses paper onto the surface of the plate and into contact with the ink in the cells. The printing cylinders are usually made from copper plated steel, which is subsequently chromed, and may be produced by digital engraving or laser etching.

Gravure printing is used for long, high-quality print runs such as magazines, mail-order catalogues, packaging, and printing onto fabric and wallpaper. It is also used for printing postage stamps and decorative plastic laminates, such as kitchen worktops.

IMPACT OF GERMAN MOVABLE TYPE PRINTING PRESS

Quantitative aspects

It is estimated that following the innovation of Gutenberg's printing press, the European book output rose from a few million to around one billion copies within a span of less than four centuries.

Religious impact

Samuel Hartlib, who was exiled in Britain and enthusiastic about social and cultural reforms, wrote in 1641 that "the art of printing will so spread knowledge that the common people, knowing their own rights and liberties, will not be governed by way of oppression". Both churchmen and governments were concerned that print allowed readers, eventually including those from all classes of society, to study religious texts and politically sensitive issues by themselves, instead of having their thinking mediated by the religious and political authorities. In the Muslim world, printing, especially in Arabic scripts, was strongly opposed throughout the early modern period, though sometimes printing in Hebrew or Armenian script was permitted. Thus the first movable type printing in the Ottoman Empire was in Hebrew in 1493. According to an imperial ambassador to Istanbul in the middle of the sixteenth century, it was a sin for the Turks to print religious books.

In 1515, Sultan Selim I issued a decree under which the practice of printing would be punishable by death. At the end of the sixteenth century, Sultan Murad III permitted the sale of non-religious printed books in Arabic characters, yet the majority were imported from Italy. Ibrahim Muteferrika established the first press for printing in Arabic in the Ottoman Empire, against opposition from the calligraphers and parts of the Ulama. It operated until 1742, producing altogether seventeen works, all of which were concerned with non-religious, utilitarian matters. Printing did not become common in the Islamic world until the 19th century.

Jews were banned from German printing guilds; as a result Hebrew printing sprang up in Italy, beginning in 1470 in Rome, then spreading to other cities including Bari, Pisa, Livorno, and Mantua. Local rulers had the authority to grant or revoke licenses to publish Hebrew books, and many of those printed during this period carry the words 'con licenza de superiori' (indicating their printing having been licensed by the censor) on their title pages.

It was thought that the introduction of the printing medium 'would strengthen religion and enhance the power of monarchs.' The majority of books were of a religious nature, with the church and crown regulating the content. The consequences of printing 'wrong' material were extreme. Meyrowitz used the example of William Carter who in 1584 printed a pro-Catholic pamphlet in Protestant-dominated England. The consequence of his action was hanging.

The widespread distribution of the Bible 'had a revolutionary impact, because it decreased the power of the Catholic Church as the prime possessor and interpretor of God's word.'

Social impact

Print gave a broader range of readers access to knowledge and enabled later generations to build directly on the intellectual achievements of earlier ones without the changes arising within verbal traditions. Print, according to Acton in his lecture *On the Study of History* (1895), gave "assurance that the work of the Renaissance would last, that what was written would be accessible to all, that such an occultation of knowledge and ideas as had depressed the Middle Ages would never recur, that not an idea would be lost".

Print was instrumental in changing the nature of reading within society.

Elizabeth Eisenstein identifies two long term effects of the invention of printing. She claims that print created a sustained and uniform reference for knowledge as well as allowing for comparison between incompatible views. (Eisenstein in Briggs and Burke, 2002: p21)

Asa Briggs and Peter Burke identify five kinds of reading that developed in relation to the introduction of print:

1. *Critical reading:* Due to the fact that texts finally became accessible to the general population, critical reading emerged because people were given the option to form their own opinions on texts
2. *Dangerous Reading:* Reading was seen as a dangerous pursuit because it was considered rebellious and unsociable especially in the case of women, because reading could stir up dangerous emotions such as love and that if women could read, they could read love notes
3. *Creative reading:* Printing allowed people to read texts and interpret them creatively, often in very different ways than the author intended
4. *Extensive Reading:* Print allowed for a wide range of texts to become available, thus, previous methods of intensive reading of texts from start to finish, began to change and with texts being readily available, people began reading on particular topics or chapters, allowing for much more extensive reading on a wider range of topics
5. *Private reading:* Became linked to the rise of individualism because before print, reading was often a group event, where one person would read to a group of people and with print, literacy rose as did availability of texts, thus reading became a solitary pursuit

The invention of printing also changed the occupational structure of European cities. Printers emerged as a new group of artisans for whom literacy was essential, although the much more labour-intensive occupation of the scribe naturally declined. Proof-correcting arose as a new occupation, while a rise in the amount of booksellers and librarians naturally followed the explosion in the numbers of books.

DIGITAL PRINTING

By 2005, Digital printing accounts for approximately 9 per cent of the 45 trillion pages printed annually around the world.

Printing at home, an office, or an engineering environment is subdivided into:

- Small format (up to ledger size paper sheets), as used in business offices and libraries
- Wide format (up to 3' or 914mm wide rolls of paper), as used in drafting and design establishments.

Some of the more common printing technologies are:

- Blueprint – and related chemical technologies
- Daisy wheel – where pre-formed characters are applied individually
- Dot-matrix – which produces arbitrary patterns of dots with an array of printing studs
- Line printing – where formed characters are applied to the paper by lines

- Heat transfer – such as early fax machines or modern receipt printers that apply heat to special paper, which turns black to form the printed image
- Inkjet – including bubble-jet, where ink is sprayed onto the paper to create the desired image
- Electrophotography – where toner is attracted to a charged image and then developed
- Laser – a type of xerography where the charged image is written pixel by pixel using a laser
- Solid ink printer – where cubes of ink are melted to make ink or liquid toner

Vendors typically stress the total cost to operate the equipment, involving complex calculations that include all cost factors involved in the operation as well as the capital equipment costs, amortization, etc. For the most part, toner systems are more economical than inkjet in the long run, even though inkjets are less expensive in the initial purchase price.

Professional digital printing (using toner) primarily uses an electrical charge to transfer toner or liquid ink to the substrate onto which it is printed. Digital print quality has steadily improved from early colour and black and white copiers to sophisticated colour digital presses such as the Xerox iGen3, the Kodak Nexpress, the HP Indigo Digital Press series, and the InfoPrint 5000. The iGen3 and Nexpress use toner particles and the Indigo uses liquid ink. The InfoPrint 5000 is a full-colour, continuous forms inkjet drop-on-demand printing system. All handle variable data, and rival offset in quality. Digital offset presses are also called direct imaging presses, although these presses can receive computer files and automatically turn them into print-ready plates, they cannot insert variable data.

Small press and fanzines generally use digital printing. Prior to the introduction of cheap photocopying the use of machines such as the spirit duplicator, hectograph, andmimeograph was common.

3D PRINTING

3D printing is a form of manufacturing technology where objects are created using three-dimensional files and 3D printers. Objects are created by laying down or building up layers of material. As of 2012, some companies such as Sculpteo or Shapeways are proposing online solutions for 3D printing.

GANG RUN PRINTING

Gang run printing is a method in which multiple printing projects are placed on a common paper sheet in an effort to reduce printing costs and paper waste. Gang runs are generally used with sheet-fed printing presses and CMYK process colour jobs, which require four separate plates that are hung on the plate cylinder of the press. Printers use the term "gang run" or "gang" to describe the practice of placing many print projects on the same oversized sheet. Basically, instead of running one postcard that is 4 x 6 as an individual job the printer would place 15 different postcards on 20 x 18 sheet therefore using the same amount of press time the printer will get 15 jobs done in the roughly the same amount of time as one job.

PRINTED ELECTRONICS

Printed electronics is the manufacturing of electronic devices using standard printing processes. Printed electronics technology can be produced on cheap materials such as paper or flexible film, which makes it an extremely cost-effective method of production. Since early 2010, the printable electronics industry has been gaining momentum and several large companies, including Bemis Company and Illinois Tool Works have made investments in printed electronics and industry associations including OE-A and FlexTech Alliance are contributing heavily to the advancement of the printed electronics industry.

HISTORY OF PRINTING

The history of printing goes back to the duplication of images by means of stamps in very early times. The use of round seals for rolling an impression into clay tablets goes back to early Mesopotamian civilization before 3000 BCE, where they are the most common works of art to survive, and feature complex and beautiful images.The printing press is considered one of the most important inventions in history. This device has made it possible for books, newspapers, magazines, and other reading materials to be produced in great numbers, and it plays an important role in promoting literacy among the masses. It was developed based on early principles of printing, and it has undergone many modifications over the years to meet the needs of people in different eras. In both China and Egypt, the use of small stamps for seals preceded the use of larger blocks. In Europe and India, the printing of cloth certainly preceded the printing of paper or papyrus. This was also the case in China. The process is essentially the same - in Europe special presentation impressions of prints were often printed on silk until the seventeenth century.

WOODBLOCK PRINTING

Block printing is a technique for printing text, images or patterns used widely throughout East Asia both as a method of printing on textilesand later, under the influence of Buddhism, on paper. As a method of printing on cloth, the earliest surviving examples from China date to about 220. *Ukiyo-e* is the best known type of Japanese woodblock art print. Most European uses of the technique on paper are covered by the art term woodcut, except for the block-books produced mainly in the fifteenth century.

In China

The world's earliest woodblock printed fragments to survive are from China and are of silk printed with flowers in three colours from theHan Dynasty (before AD 220). The technology of printing on cloth in China was adapted to paper under the influence of Buddhism which mandated the circulation of standard translations over a wide area, as well as the production of multiple copies of key texts for religious reasons. It reached Europe, via the Islamic world, and by around 1400 was being used on paper for old master prints andplaying cards. The oldest wood-block printed book is the *Diamond Sutra*. It carries a date on 'the 13th day of the fourth moon of the ninth year of the Xiantong era' (*i.e.* 11 May 868). A number printed *dhâraG-î*-s, however, predate the *Diamond Sûtra* by about two hundred years.

In India

In Buddhism, great merit is thought to accrue from copying and preserving texts. The fourth-century master listed the copying of scripture as the first of ten essential religious practices. The importance of perpetuating texts is set out with special force in the longer Sukhâvatîvyûha Sûtra which not only urges the devout to hear, learn, remember and study the text but to obtain a good copy and to preserve it.

This 'cult of the book' led to techniques for reproducing texts in great numbers, especially the short prayers or charms known as *dhâraG-î*-s. Stamps were carved for printing these prayers on clay tablets from at least the seventh century, the date of the oldest surviving examples. Especially popular was the *Pratîtyasamutpâda Gâthâ*, a short verse text summing up Nâgârjuna's philosophy of causal genesis or dependent origination. Nagarjuna lived in the early centuries of the current era and the Buddhist Creed, as the *Gâthâ* is frequently called, was printed on clay tablets in huge numbers from the sixth century. This tradition was transmitted to China and Tibet with Buddhism. Printing text from woodblocks does not, however, seem to have been developed in India.

In Europe

Block printing was practised in Christian Europe as a method for printing on cloth, where it was common by 1300. Images printed on cloth for religious purposes could be quite large and elaborate, and when paper became relatively easily available, around 1400, the medium transferred very quickly to small woodcut religious images and playing cardsprinted on paper. These prints were produced in very large numbers from about 1425 onwards.

Around the mid-century, *block-books*, woodcut books with both text and images, usually carved in the same block, emerged as a cheaper alternative to manuscripts and books printed with movable type. These were all short heavily illustrated works, the bestsellers of the day, repeated in many different block-book versions: the Ars moriendi and theBiblia pauperum were the most common. There is still some controversy among scholars as to whether their introduction preceded or, the majority view, followed the introduction of movable type, with the range of estimated dates being between about 1440–1460.

Stencil

Stencils may have been used to colour cloth for a very long time; the technique probably reached its peak of sophistication in Katazome and other techniques used on silks for clothes during the Edo period in Japan. In Europe, from about 1450 they were very commonly used to colour old master prints printed in black and white, usually woodcuts. This was especially the case with playing-cards, which continued to be coloured by stencil long after most other subjects for prints were left in black and white. Stenciling back in the 27th century BC was different. They used colour from plants and flowers such as indigo (which extracts blue). Stencils were used for mass publications, as the type didn't have to be hand-written.

MOVABLE TYPE

Around 1040, the world's first known movable type system was created in China by Bi Sheng out of porcelain. He also developed wooden movable type, but it was abandoned in favour of clay movable types due to the presence of wood grains and the unevenness of the wooden type after being soaked in ink. Neither movable type system was widely used, one reason being the enormous Chinese character set. Metal movable type began to be used in Korea during theGoryeo Dynasty (around 1230). Jikji was printed during the Goryeo Dynasty in 1377, it is the world's oldest extant book printed with movable metal type.

It is traditionally summarized that Johannes Gutenberg, of the German city of Mainz, developed European movable type printing technology around 1439 and in just over a decade, the European age of printing began. However, the details show a more complex evolutionary processspread over multiple locations. Also, Johann Fust and Peter Schöffer experimented with Gutenberg in Mainz.

Compared to woodblock printing, movable type page-setting was quicker and more durable. The metal type pieces were more durable and the lettering was more uniform, leading to typography and fonts. The high quality and relatively low price of the Gutenberg Bible(1455) established the superiority of movable type, and printing presses rapidly spread across Europe, leading up to the Renaissance, and later all around the world. Today, practically all movable type printing ultimately derives from Gutenberg's movable type printing, which is often regarded as the most important invention of the second millennium.

Gutenberg is also credited with the introduction of an oil-based ink which was more durable than previously used water-based inks. Having worked as a professional goldsmith, Gutenberg made skillful use of the knowledge of metals he had learned as a craftsman.

Gutenberg was also the first to make his type from an alloy of lead, tin, and antimony, known as type metal, printer's lead, or printer's metal, which was critical for producing durable type that produced high-quality printed books, and proved to be more suitable for printing than the clay, wooden or bronze types used in East Asia. To create these lead types, Gutenberg used what some considered his most ingenious invention, a special matrix wherewith the moulding of new movable types with an unprecedented precision at short notice became feasible. Within a year of printing the Gutenberg Bible, Gutenberg also published the first coloured prints.

The invention of the printing press revolutionized communication and book production leading to the spread of knowledge. Rapidly, printing spread from Germany by emigrating German printers, but also by foreign apprentices returning home. A printing press was built in Venice in 1469, and by 1500 the city had 417 printers.

In 1470 Johann Heynlin set up a printing press in Paris. In 1473 Kasper Straubepublished the Almanach cracoviense ad annum 1474 in Kraków. Dirk Martens set up a printing press in Aalst (Flanders) in 1473. He printed a book about the two lovers of Enea Piccolomini who became Pope Pius II. In 1476 a printing press was set up in England byWilliam Caxton. Belarusian Francysk Skaryna printed the first book in Slavic language on August 6, 1517. The Italian Juan Pablos set up an imported press in Mexico City in 1539. The first printing press in Southeast Asia was set up in the Philippines by the Spanish in 1593. The Rev. Jose Glover intended to bring the first printing press to England's American colonies in 1638, but died on the voyage, so his widow, Elizabeth Harris Glover, established the printing house, which was run by Stephen Day and became The Cambridge Press.

The Gutenberg press was much more efficient than manual copying and still was largely unchanged in the eras of John Baskerville andGiambattista Bodoni, over 300 years later. By 1800, Lord Stanhope had constructed a press completely from cast iron, reducing the force required by 90 per cent while doubling the size of the printed area. While Stanhope's "mechanical theory" had improved the efficiency of the press, it still was only capable of 250 sheets per hour. German printer Friedrich Koenig would be the first to design a non-manpowered machine—using steam. Having moved to London in 1804, Koenig soon met Thomas Bensley and secured financial support for his project in 1807. Patented in 1810, Koenig had designed a steam press "much like a hand press connected to a steam engine." The first production trial of this model occurred in April 1811.

Flat-bed printing press

A printing press is a mechanical device for applying pressure to an inked surface resting upon a medium (such as paper or cloth), thereby transferring an image. The systems involved were first assembled in Germany by the goldsmith Johannes Gutenberg in the mid-15th century. Printing methods based on Gutenberg's printing press spread rapidly throughout first Europe and then the rest of the world, replacing most block printing and making it the sole progenitor of modern movable type printing. As a method of creating reproductions for mass consumption, The printing press has been superseded by the advent of offset printing.

Johannes Gutenberg's work in the printing press began in approximately 1436 when he partnered with Andreas Dritzehen—a man he had previously instructed in gem-cutting—and Andreas Heilmann, owner of a paper mill. It was not until a 1439 lawsuit against Gutenberg that official record exists; witnesses testimony discussed type, an inventory of metals (including lead) and his type mold.

Others in Europe were developing movable type at this time, including goldsmith Procopius Waldfoghel of France and Laurens Janszoon Coster of the Netherlands. They are not known to have contributed specific advances to the printing press.

PRINTING HOUSES

Early printing houses (near the time of Gutenberg) were run by "master printers." These printers owned shops, selected and edited manuscripts, determined the sizes of print runs, sold the works they produced, raised capital and organized distribution. Some master printing houses, like that ofAldus Manutius, became the cultural center for literati such as Erasmus.

- *Print shop apprentices:* Apprentices, usually between the ages of 15 and 20, worked for master printers. Apprentices were not required to be literate, and literacy rates at the time were very low, in comparison to today. Apprentices prepared ink, dampened sheets of paper, and assisted at the press. An apprentice who wished to learn to become a compositor had to learn Latin and spend time under the supervision of a journeyman.
- *Journeyman printers:* After completing their apprenticeships, *journeyman* printers were free to move employers. This facilitated the spread of printing to areas that were less print-centred.
- *Compositors:* Those who set the type for printing.
- *Pressmen:* The person who worked the press. This was physically labour intensive.

The earliest-known image of a European, Gutenberg-style print shop is the *Dance of Death* by Matthias Huss, at Lyon, 1499. This image depicts a compositor standing at a compositor's case being grabbed by a skeleton. The case is raised to facilitate his work. At the right of the printing house a bookshop is shown.

Financial aspects

Court records from the city of Mainz document that Johannes Fust was, for some time, Gutenberg's financial backer.

By the sixteenth century jobs associated with printing were becoming increasingly specialized. Structures supporting publishers were more and more complex, leading to this division of labour. In Europe between 1500 and 1700 the role of the Master Printer was dying out and giving way to the bookseller—publisher. Printing during this period had a stronger commercial imperative than previously. Risks associated with the industry however were substantial, although dependent on the nature of the publication.

Bookseller publishers negotiated at trade fairs and at print shops. Jobbing work appeared in which printers did menial tasks in the beginning of their careers to support themselves.

1500–1700: Publishers developed several new methods of funding projects:

1. Cooperative associations/publication syndicates—a number of individuals shared the risks associated with printing and shared in the profit. This was pioneered by the French.
2. Subscription publishing—pioneered by the English in the early 17th century. A prospectus for a publication was drawn up by a publisher to raise funding. The prospectus was given to potential buyers who signed up for a copy. If there were not enough subscriptions the publication did not go ahead. Lists of subscribers were included in the books as endorsements. If enough people subscribed a reprint might occur. Some authors used subscription publication to bypass the publisher entirely.
3. Installment publishing—books were issued in parts until a complete book had been issued. This was not necessarily done with a fixed time period. It was an effective method of spreading cost over a period of time. It also allowed earlier returns on investment to help cover production costs of subsequent installments.

The *Mechanick Exercises*, by Joseph Moxon, in London, 1683, was said to be the first publication done in installments.

Publishing trade organizations allowed publishers to organize business concerns collectively. Systems of self-regulation occurred in these arrangements. For example, if one publisher did something to irritate other publishers he would be controlled by peer pressure. Such systems are known as cartels, and are in most countries now considered to be in restraint of trade. These arrangements helped deal with labour unrest among journeymen, who faced difficult working conditions. Brotherhoods predated unions, without the formal regulations now associated with unions.

In most cases, publishers bought the copyright in a work from the author, and made some arrangement about the possible profits. This required a substantial amount of capital in addition to the capital for the physical equipment and staff. Alternatively, an author who had sufficient money would sometimes keep the copyright himself, and simply pay the printer for the production of the book.

ROTARY PRINTING PRESS

A rotary printing press is a printing press in which the impressions are carved around a cylinder so that the printing can be done on long continuous rolls of paper, cardboard,plastic, or a large number of other substrates. Rotary drum printing was invented by Richard March Hoe in 1843 and patented in 1847, and then significantly improved by William Bullock in 1863.

Intaglio

Intaglio is a family of printmaking techniques in which the image is incised into a surface, known as the matrix or plate. Normally, copper or zinc plates are used as a surface, and the incisions are created by etching, engraving, drypoint, aquatint ormezzotint. Collographs may also be printed as intaglio plates. To print an intaglio plate the surface is covered in thick ink and then rubbed with tarlatan cloth to remove most of the excess. The final smooth wipe is usually done by hand, sometimes with the aid of newspaper or old public phone book pages, leaving ink only in the incisions. A damp piece of paper is placed on top and the plate and paper are run through a printing press that, through pressure, transfers the ink from the recesses of the plate to the paper.

Lithography (1796)

Invented by Bavarian author Aloys Senefelder in 1796, lithography is a method for printing on a smooth surface. Lithography is a printing process that uses chemical processes to create an image. For instance, the positive part of an image would be a hydrophobic chemical, while the negative image would be water.

Thus, when the plate is introduced to a compatible ink and water mixture, the ink will adhere to the positive image and the water will clean the negative image. This allows for a relatively flat print plate which allows for much longer runs than the older physical methods of imaging (*e.g.*, embossing or engraving). High-volume lithography is used today to produce posters, maps, books, newspapers, and packaging — just about any smooth, mass-produced item with print and graphics on it. Most books, indeed all types of high-volume text, are now printed using offset lithography.

In offset lithography, which depends on photographic processes, flexible aluminum, polyester, mylar or paper printing plates are used in place of stone tablets. Modern printing plates have a brushed or roughened texture and are covered with a photosensitive emulsion. A photographic negative of the desired image is placed in contact with the emulsion and the plate is exposed to ultraviolet light. After development, the emulsion shows a reverse of the negative image, which is thus a duplicate of the original (positive) image. The image on the plate emulsion can also be created through direct laser imaging in a CTP (Computer-To-Plate) device called a platesetter. The positive image is the emulsion that remains after imaging. For many years, chemicals have been used to remove the non-image emulsion, but now plates are available that do not require chemical processing.

COLOUR PRINTING

Chromolithography became the most successful of several methods of colour printing developed by the 19th century; other methods were developed by printers such as Jacob Christoph Le Blon, George Baxter and Edmund Evans, and mostly relied on using severalwoodblocks with the colours. Hand-colouring also remained important; elements of the official British Ordnance Survey maps were coloured by hand by boys until 1875. Chromolithography developed from lithography and the term covers various types of lithography that are printed in colour.

The initial technique involved the use of multiple lithographic stones, one for each colour, and was still extremely expensive when done for the best quality results. Depending on the number of colours present, a chromolithograph could take months to produce, by very skilled workers. However much cheaper prints could be produced by simplifying both the number of colours used, and the refinement of the detail in the image. Cheaper images, like the advertisement illustrated, relied heavily on an initial black print (not always a lithograph), on which colours were then overprinted. To make an expensive reproduction print as what was once referred to as a "'chromo'", a lithographer, with a finished painting in front of him, gradually created and corrected the many stones using proofs to look as much as possible like the painting in front of him, sometimes using dozens of layers.

Alois Senefelder, the inventor of lithography, introduced the subject of coloured lithography in his 1818 *Vollstaendiges Lehrbuch der Steindruckerey (A Complete Course of Lithography)*, where he told of his plans to print using colour and explained the colours he wished to be able to print someday. Although Senefelder recorded plans for chromolithography, printers in other countries, such as France andEngland, were also trying to find a new way to print in colour. Godefroy Engelmann of Mulhouse in France was awarded a patent on chromolithography in July 1837, but there are disputes over whether chromolithography was already in use before this date, as some sources say, pointing to areas of printing such as the production of playing cards.

Screenprinting (1907)

Screenprinting has its origins in simple stencilling, most notably of the Japanese form (katazome), used who cut banana leaves and inserted ink through the design holes on textiles, mostly for clothing. This was taken up in France. The modern screenprinting process originated from patents taken out by Samuel Simon in 1907 in England. This idea was then adopted in San Francisco, California, by John Pilsworth in 1914 who used screenprinting to form multicolour prints in a subtractive mode, differing from screenprinting as it is done today.

Flexography

Flexography (also called "surface printing"), often abbreviated to "flexo", is a method of printing most commonly used for packaging (labels, tape, bags, boxes, banners, and so on).

A flexo print is achieved by creating a mirrored master of the required image as a 3D relief in a rubber or polymer material. A measured amount of ink is deposited upon the surface of the printing plate (or printing cylinder) using an anilox roll. The print surface then rotates, contacting the print material which transfers the ink.

Originally flexo printing was basic in quality. Labels requiring high quality have generally been printed Offset until recently. In the last few years great advances have been made to the quality of flexo printing presses.

The greatest advances though have been in the area of PhotoPolymer Printing Plates, including improvements to the plate material and the method of plate creation. —usually photographic exposure followed by chemical etch, though also by direct laser engraving.

Photocopier (1960s)

Xerographic office photocopying was introduced by Xerox in the 1960s, and over the following 20 years it gradually replaced copies made by Verifax, Photostat, carbon paper,mimeograph machines, and other duplicating machines. The prevalence of its use is one of the factors that prevented the development of the paperless office heralded early in the digital revolution.

Thermal printer

A thermal printer (or direct thermal printer) produces a printed image by selectively heating coated thermochromic paper, or thermal paper as it is commonly known, when the paper passes over the thermal print head. The coating turns black in the areas where it is heated, producing an image.

Laser printer (1969)

The laser printer, based on a modified xerographic copier, was invented at Xerox in 1969 by researcher Gary Starkweather, who had a fully functional networked printer system working by 1971. Laser printing eventually became a multibillion-dollar business for Xerox.

The first commercial implementation of a laser printer was the IBM model 3800 in 1976, used for high-volume printing of documents such as invoices and mailing labels. It is often cited as "taking up a whole room," implying that it was a primitive version of the later familiar device used with a personal computer. While large, it was designed for an entirely different purpose. Many 3800s are still in use.

The first laser printer designed for use with an individual computer was released with the Xerox Star 8010 in 1981. Although it was innovative, the Star was an expensive ($17,000) system that was only purchased by a small number of laboratories and institutions. After personal computers became more widespread, the first laser printer intended for a mass market was the HP LaserJet 8ppm, released in 1984, using a Canon engine controlled by HP software. The HP LaserJet printer was quickly followed by other laser printers from Brother Industries, IBM, and others.

Most noteworthy was the role the laser printer played in popularizing desktop publishing with the introduction of the Apple LaserWriter for the Apple Macintosh, along with Aldus PageMaker software, in 1985. With these products, users could create documents that would previously have required professional typesetting.

Dot matrix printer (1970)

A dot matrix printer or impact matrix printer refers to a type of computer printer with a print head that runs back and forth on the page and prints by impact, striking an ink-soaked cloth ribbon against the paper, much like a typewriter. Unlike a typewriter or daisy wheel printer, letters are drawn out of a dot matrix, and thus, varied fonts and arbitrary graphics can be produced. Because the printing involves mechanical pressure, these printers can create carbon copies and carbonless copies.

Each dot is produced by a tiny metal rod, also called a "wire" or "pin", which is driven forward by the power of a tiny electromagnet or solenoid, either directly or through small levers (pawls). Facing the ribbon and the paper is a small guide plate (often made of an artificial jewel such as sapphire or ruby [2]) pierced with holes to serve as guides for the pins. The moving portion of the printer is called the print head, and when running the printer as a generic text device generally prints one line of text at a time. Most dot matrix printers have a single vertical line of dot-making equipment on their print heads; others have a few interleaved rows in order to improve dot density.

Inkjet printer

Inkjet printers are a type of computer printer that operates by propelling tiny droplets of liquid ink onto paper.

Dye-sublimation printer

A dye-sublimation printer (or dye-sub printer) is a computer printer which employs a printing process that uses heat to transfer dye to a medium such as a plastic card, printer paper or poster paper. The process is usually to lay one colour at a time using a ribbon that has colour panels. Most dye-sublimation printers use CMYO colours which differs from the more recognised CMYK colours in that the black dye is eliminated in favour of a clear overcoating. This overcoating (which has numerous names depending on the manufacturer) is effectively a thin laminate which protects the print from discolouration from UV light and the air while also rendering the print water-resistant. Many consumer andprofessional dye-sublimation printers are designed and used for producing photographic prints.

Digital press (1993)

Digital printing is the reproduction of digital images on a physical surface, such as common or photographic paper or paperboard-cover stock, film, cloth, plastic, vinyl, magnets,labels etc.

It can be differentiated from litho, flexography, gravure or letterpress printing in many ways, some of which are:

- Every impression made onto the paper can be different, as opposed to making several hundred or thousand impressions of the same image from one set of printing plates, as in traditional methods.
- The Ink or Toner does not absorb into the substrate, as does conventional ink, but forms a layer on the surface and may be fused to the substrate by using an inline fuser fluid with heat process(toner) or UV curing process(ink).
- It generally requires less waste in terms of chemicals used and paper wasted in set up or makeready(bringing the image "up to colour" and checking position).
- It is excellent for rapid prototyping, or small print runs which means that it is more accessible to a wider range of designers and more cost effective in short runs.

Frescography (1998)

Frescography is a method for reproduction/creation of murals using digital printingmethods. The frescography is based on digitally cut-out motifs which are stored in adatabase. CAM software programmes then allow to enter the measurements of a wall or ceiling to create a mural design with low resolution motifs. Since architectural elements such as beams, windows or doors can be integrated, the design will result in an accurately and tailor-fit wall mural. Once a design is finished, the low resolutionmotifs are converted into the original high resolution images and are printed on canvas by Wide-format printers. The canvas then can be applied to the wall in a wall-paperhanging like procedure and will then look like on-site created mural.

3D printing

Three-dimensional printing is a method of converting a virtual 3D model into a physical object. 3D printing is a category of rapid prototyping technology. 3D printers typically work by 'printing' successive layers on top of the previous to build up a three dimensional object. 3D printers are generally faster, more affordable and easier to use than other additive fabrication technologies.

TECHNOLOGICAL DEVELOPMENTS

Woodcut

Woodcut is a relief printing artistic technique in printmaking in which an image is carved into the surface of a block of wood, with the printing parts remaining level with the surface while the non-printing parts are removed, typically with gouges. The areas to show 'white' are cut away with a knife or chisel, leaving the characters or image to show in 'black' at the original surface level. The block is cut along the grain of the wood (unlike wood engraving where the block is cut in the end-grain). In Europe beechwood was most commonly used; in Japan, a special type of cherry wood was popular.

Woodcut first appeared in ancient China. From 6th century onward, woodcut icons became popular and especially flourished in Buddhist texts. Since the 10th century, woodcut pictures appeared in inbetweenings of Chinese literature, and some banknotes, such as Jiaozi (currency). Woodcut New Year picture are also very popular with the Chinese.

In China and Tibet printed images mostly remained tied as illustrations to accompanying text until the modern period. The earliest woodblock printed book, the Diamond Sutracontains a large image as frontispiece, and many Buddhist texts contain some images. Later some notable Chinese artists designed woodcuts for books, the individual print develop in China in the form of New Year picture as an art-form in the way it did in Europe and Japan.

In Europe, Woodcut is the oldest technique used for old master prints, developing about 1400, by using on paper existing techniques for printing on cloth. The explosion of sales of cheap woodcuts in the middle of the century led to a fall in standards, and many popular prints were very crude. The development of hatching followed on rather later than inengraving. Michael Wolgemut was significant in making German woodcut more sophisticated from about 1475, and Erhard Reuwich was the first to use cross-hatching (far harder to do than in engraving or etching). Both of these produced mainly book-illustrations, as did various Italian artists who were also raising standards there at the same period. At the end of the century Albrecht Dürer brought the Western woodcut to a level that has never been surpassed, and greatly increased the status of the *single-leaf* (*i.e.* an image sold separately) woodcut.

Engraving

Engraving is the practice of incising a design onto a hard, flat surface, by cutting grooves into it. The result may be a decorated object in itself, as when silver, gold or steel are engraved, or may provide an intaglio printing plate, of copper or another metal, for printing images on paper, which are called engravings. Engraving was a historically important method of producing images on paper, both in artistic printmaking, and also for commercial reproductions and illustrations for books and magazines. It has long been replaced by photography in its commercial applications and, partly because of the difficulty of learning the technique, is much less common in printmaking, where it has been largely replaced by etching and other techniques. Other terms often used for engravings are *copper-plate engraving* and *Line engraving*. These should all mean exactly the same, but especially in the past were often used very loosely to cover several printmaking techniques, so that many so-called engravings were in fact produced by totally different techniques, such as etching.

In antiquity, the only engraving that could be carried out is evident in the shallow grooves found in some jewellery after the beginning of the 1st Millennium B.C. The majority of so-called engraved designs on ancient gold rings or other items were produced by chasing or sometimes a combination of lost-wax casting and chasing. In the European Middle Ages goldsmiths used engraving to decorate and inscribe metalwork. It is thought that they began to print impressions of their designs to record them. From this grew the engraving of copper printing plates to produce artistic images on paper, known as old master prints in Germany in the 1430s. Italy soon followed. Many early engravers came from a goldsmithing background. The first and greatest period of the engraving was from about 1470 to 1530, with such masters as Martin Schongauer,Albrecht Dürer, and Lucas van Leiden.

Etching

Etching is the process of using strong acid or mordant to cut into the unprotected parts of a metal surface to create a design in intaglio in the metal (the original process—in modern manufacturing other chemicals may be used on other types of material). As an intaglio method of printmaking it is, along with engraving, the most important technique for old master prints, and remains widely used today.

Halftoning

Halftone is the reprographic technique that simulates ones it is continuous tone imagery through the use of equally spaced dots of varying size. 'Halftone' can also be used to refer specifically to the image that is produced by this process.

The idea of halftone printing originates from William Fox Talbot. In the early 1850s he suggested using "photographic screens or veils" in connection with a photographic intaglioprocess.

Several different kinds of screens were proposed during the following decades, but the first half-tone photo-engraving process was invented by Canadians George-Édouard Desbarats and William Leggo Jr.[3] On October 30, 1869, Desbarats published the *Canadian Illustrated News* which became the world's first periodical to successfully employ this photo-mechanical technique; featuring a full page half-tone image of His Royal Highness Prince Arthur, from a photograph by Notman.[4] Ambitious to exploit a much larger circulation, Debarats and Leggo went to New York and launched the *New York Daily Graphic* in March 1873, which became the world's first illustrated daily.

The first truly successful commercial method was patented by Frederic Ives of Philadelphia in 1881. But although he found a way of breaking up the image into dots of varying sizes he did not make use of a screen. In 1882 the German George Meisenbach patented a halftone process in England. His invention was based on the previous ideas of Berchtold and Swan. He used single lined screens which were turned during exposure to produce cross-lined effects. He was the first to achieve any commercial success withrelief halftones.

Xerography

Xerography (or electrophotography) is a photocopying technique developed by Chester Carlson in 1938 and patented on October 6, 1942. He received U.S. Patent 2,297,691for his invention. The name xerography came from the Greek radicals*xeros* (dry) and*graphos* (writing), because there are no liquid chemicals involved in the process, unlike earlier reproduction techniques like cyanotype.

In 1938 Bulgarian physicist Georgi Nadjakov found that when placed into electric field and exposed to light, some dielectrics acquire permanent electric polarization in the exposed areas.[5] That polarization persists in the dark and is destroyed in light. Chester Carlson, the inventor of photocopying, was originally a patent attorney and part-time researcher and inventor.

His job at the patent office in New York required him to make a large number of copies of important papers. Carlson, who was arthritic, found this a painful and tedious process. This prompted him to conduct experiments with photoconductivity. Carlson experimented with "electrophotography" in his kitchen and in 1938, applied for a patent for the process. He made the first "photocopy" using a zinc plate covered with sulfur. The words "10-22-38

Astoria" were written on a microscope slide, which was placed on top of more sulfur and under a bright light. After the slide was removed, a mirror image of the words remained. Carlson tried to sell his invention to some companies, but because the process was still underdeveloped he failed. At the time multiple copies were made using carbon paper or duplicating machines and people did not feel the need for an electronic machine. Between 1939 and 1944, Carlson was turned down by over 20 companies, including IBM and GE, neither of which believed there was a significant market for copiers.

OFFSET PRINTING

Offset printing or web offset printing is a commonly used printing technique in which the inked image is transferred (or "offset") from a plate to a rubber blanket, then to the printing surface. When used in combination with the lithographic process, which is based on the repulsion of oil and water, the offset technique employs a flat (planographic) image carrier on which the image to be printed obtains ink from ink rollers, while the non-printing area attracts a water-based film (called "fountain solution"), keeping the non-printing areas ink-free. The modern "web" process feeds a large reel of paper through a large press machine in several parts, typically for several metres, which then prints continuously as the paper is fed through.

Development of the offset press came in two versions: In 1875 by Robert Barclay of England for printing on tin, and in 1904 by Ira Washington Rubel of the United States for printing on paper.

HISTORY

Lithography was initially created to be an inexpensive method of reproducing artwork. This printing process was limited to use on flat, porous surfaces because the printing plates were produced from limestone. In fact, the word 'lithograph' historically means "An image from stone." or "Print from stone." Tin cans were popular packaging materials in the 19th century, but transfer technologies were required before the lithographic process could be used to print on the tin.

The first rotary offset lithographic printing press was created in England and patented in 1875 by Robert Barclay. This development combined mid-19th century transfer printing technologies and Richard March Hoe's 1843 rotary printing press—a press that used a metal cylinder instead of a flat stone. The offset cylinder was covered with specially treated cardboard that transferred the printed image from the stone to the surface of the metal. Later, the cardboard covering of the offset cylinder was changed to rubber, which is still the most commonly used material.

As the 19th century closed and photography became popular, many lithographic firms went out of business. Photoengraving, a process that used halftone technology instead of illustration, became the primary aesthetic of the era. Many printers, including Ira Washington Rubel of New Jersey, were using the low-cost lithograph process to produce copies of photographs and books. Rubel discovered in 1901—by forgetting to load a sheet—that when printing from the rubber roller, instead of the metal, the printed page was clearer and sharper. After further refinement, the Potter Press printing Company in New York produced a press in 1903. By 1907 the Rubel offset press was in use in San Francisco.

The Harris Automatic Press Company also created a similar press around the same time. Charles and Albert Harris modeled their press "on a rotary letter press machine."

It was originally named 'Offset' as the printer was very rarely accurate when printing.

MODERN OFFSET PRINTING

Offset lithography is one of the most common ways of creating printed matter. A few of its common applications include: newspapers, magazines, brochures, stationery, and books. Compared to other printing methods, offset printing is best suited for economically producing large volumes of high quality prints in a manner that requires little maintenance. Many modern offset presses use computer to plate systems as opposed to the older computer to film work flows, which further increases their quality.

Advantages of offset printing compared to other printing methods include:

- Consistent high image quality. Offset printing produces sharp and clean images and type more easily than, for example, letterpress printing; this is because the rubber blanket conforms to the texture of the printing surface.
- Quick and easy production of printing plates.
- Longer printing plate life than on direct litho presses because there is no direct contact between the plate and the printing surface. Properly developed plates used with optimized inks and fountain solution may achieve run lengths of more than a million impressions.
- Cost. Offset printing is the cheapest method for producing high quality prints in commercial printing quantities.
- A further advantage of offset printing is the possibility of adjusting the amount of ink on the fountain roller with screw keys. Most commonly, a metal blade controls the amount of ink transferred from the ink trough to the fountain roller. By adjusting the screws, the gap between the blade and the fountain roller is altered, leading to the amount of ink applied to the roller to be increased or decreased in certain areas. Consequently the density of the colour in the respective area of the image is modified. On older machines the

screws are adjusted manually, but on modern machines the screw keys are operated electronically by the printer controlling the machine, enabling a much more precise result.

Disadvantages of offset printing compared to other printing methods include:

- Slightly inferior image quality compared to rotogravure or photogravure printing.
- Propensity for anodized aluminum printing plates to become sensitive (due to chemical oxidation) and print in non-image/background areas when developed plates are not cared for properly.
- Time and cost associated with producing plates and printing press setup. As a result, very small quantity printing jobs may now use digital offset machines.

THE OFFSET PRINTING PROCESS

The most common kind of offset printing is derived from the photo offset process, which involves using light-sensitive chemicals andphotographic techniques to transfer images and type from original materials to printing plates. In current use, original materials may be an actual photographic print and typeset text. However, it is more common — with the prevalence of computers and digital images — that the source material exists only as data in a digital publishing system.

Offset Lithographic printing on to a web (reel) of paper is commonly used for printing of newspapers and magazines for high speed production.

In this process, ink is transferred from the ink duct to the paper in several steps:

1. The ink duct roller delivers ink from the ink duct to the ink pyramid, also called the *Ink Train*.
2. The ductor roller, sometimes called a vibrator roller due to its rapid back and forth motion, transfers ink from the duct roller to the first distribution roller. It is never in contact with both rollers at the same time.
3. The distribution rollers evenly distribute the ink. The first distribution roller picks up the ink from driving rollers, and the last distribution rollers transfer the ink to the form rollers.
4. The transfer rollers transfer ink between the ink-absorbing and ink-delivering driving rollers.
5. Driving rollers roll against the distribution rollers and either absorb or deliver ink, depending on their placement.
6. Ink form rollers transfer ink from the last distribution rollers on to the printing plate.
7. The printing plate transfers the ink to the offset cylinder (typically called the *blanket cylinder*) usually covered with a rubber "blanket."

8. The paper is then pressed against the blanket cylinder by the impression cylinder, transferring the ink onto the paper to form the printed image.

Process printing

The actual process of printing is quite involved. One of the most important functions in the process is pre-press production. This stage makes sure that all files are correctly processed in preparation for printing. This includes converting to the proper CMYK colour model, finalizing the files, and creating plates for each colour of the job to be run on the press.

Every printing technology has its own identifying marks, as does offset printing. In text reproduction, the type edges are sharp and have clear outlines. The paper surrounding the ink dots is usually unprinted. The halftone dots are always hexagonal though there are different screening methods.

Variations

- *Blanket-to-blanket:* A printing method in which there are two blanket cylinders through which a sheet of paper is passed and printed on both sides. Blanket-to-blanket presses are considered a perfecting press because they print on both sides of the sheet at the same time. Since the blanket-to-blanket press has two blanket cylinders, making it possible to print on both sides of a sheet, there is no impression cylinder. The opposite blanket cylinders act as an impression cylinder to each other when print production occurs. There are also two plate cylinders on the press.
- *Blanket-to-steel:* A printing method similar to a sheet offset press; except that the plate and cylinder pressures are quite precise. Actual squeeze between plate and blanket cylinder is optimal at.005"; as is the squeeze or pressure between the blanket cylinder and the substrate. Blanket-to-steel presses are considered one-colour presses. In order to print the reverse side, the web is turned over between printing units by means of turning bars. The method can be used to print business forms, computer letters, and direct mail advertising.
- *Variable-size printing:* A printing process that uses removable printing units, inserts, or cassettes for one-sided and blanket-to-blanket two-sided printing.
- *Keyless offset:* A printing process that is based on the concept of using fresh ink for each revolution by removing residual inks on the inking drum after each revolution. It is suitable for printing newspapers.
- *Dry Offset Printing:* A printing process which uses a metal backed photopolymer relief plate, similar to a letterpress plate, but, unlike letterpress printing where the ink is transferred directly from the

plate to the substrate, in dry offset printing the ink is transferred to a rubber blanket before being transferred to the substrate. This method is used for printing on injection moulded rigid plastic buckets, tubs, cups and flowerpots.

PLATES

- *Metal plates:* The plates used in offset printing are thin, flexible, and usually larger than the paper size to be printed, and are usually made of aluminum, although sometimes they are made of multimetal, paper, or plastic.
- *Polyester plates:* These are much cheaper and can be used in place of aluminum plates for smaller formats or medium quality jobs, as their dimensional stability is lower.

Computer-to-plate (CTP)/ direct-to-plate (DTP)

Computer-to-plate (CTP) is a newer technology that allows the imaging of metal or polyester plates without the use of film. By eliminating the stripping, compositing, and traditional plate making processes, CTP altered the printing industry, which led to reduced prepress times, lower costs of labour, and improved print quality.

Most CTP systems used thermal CTP or violet technologies. Both technologies has the same characteristics in term of quality and plate durability (longer runs). However the often violet CTP systems are cheaper than thermal ones, and thermal CTP systems do not need to be operated under yellow light.

Thermal CTP involves the use of thermal lasers to expose and/or remove areas of coating while the plate is being imaged. This depends on whether the plate is negative, or positive working. These lasers are generally at a wavelength of 830 nanometers, but vary in their energy usage depending on whether they are used to expose or ablate material. Violet CTP lasers have a much lower wavelength, 405–410 nanometers.

Violet CTP is "based on emulsion tuned to visible light exposure."

- Another process is CTCP (computer to conventional plate) system in which conventional offset plates can be exposed, making it an economical option.

SHEET-FED OFFSET

Sheet-fed refers to individual sheets of paper or rolls being fed into a press via a suction bar that lifts and drops each sheet onto place. A lithographic ("litho" for short) press uses principles of lithography to apply ink to a printing plate, as explained previously. Sheet-fed litho is commonly used for printing of short-run magazines, brochures, letter headings, and general commercial (jobbing) printing. In sheet-fed offset, "the printing is carried out on single sheets of paper as they are fed to the press one at a time." Sheet-fed presses use mechanical registration to relate each sheet to one another to ensure that they are reproduced with the same imagery in the same position on every sheet running through the press.

Perfecting press: A perfecting press, also known as a duplex press, is one that can print on both sides of the paper at the same time. Web and sheet-fed offset presses are similar in that many of them can also print on both sides of the paper in one pass, making it easier and faster to print duplex.

Offset duplicators: Small offset lithographic presses that are used for fast, good quality reproduction of one- and two-colour copies in sizes up to 12" by 18". Popular models were made by A.B. Dick, Multilith, and the Chief and Davidson lines made by A.T.F./Davidson. Offset duplicators are made for fast and quick printing jobs; printing up to 12,000 impressions per hour. They are able to print business forms, letterheads, labels, bulletins, postcards, envelopes, folders, reports, and sales literature.

Feeder system: The feeder system is responsible for making sure paper runs through the press correctly.This is where the substrate is loaded and then the system is correctly set up to the certain specifications of the substrate to the press.

Printing/inking system: The Printing Unit consists of many different systems. The dampening system is used to apply dampening solution to the plates with water rollers. The inking system uses rollers to deliver ink to the plate and blanket cylinders to be transferred to the substrate. The plate cylinder is where the plates containing all of the imaging are mounted. Finally the blanket and impression cylinders are used to transfer the image to the substrate running through the press.

Delivery system: The delivery system is the final destination in the printing process while the paper runs through the press. Once the paper reaches delivery, it is stacked for the ink to cure in a proper manner. This is the step in which sheets are inspected to make sure they have proper ink density and registration.

Slur: Production or impact of double image in printing is known as 'slur'.

WEB-FED OFFSET

Web-fed refers to the use of rolls (or "webs") of paper supplied to the printing press. Offset web printing is generally used for runs in excess of five or ten thousand impressions. Typical examples of web printing include newspapers, newspaper inserts/ads, magazines, direct mail, catalogs, and books. Web-fed presses are divided into two general classes: "cold" or "non-heatset," and "heatset" offset web presses; the difference being how the inks that are used dry. Cold web offset printing dries through absorption into the paper, while heatset utilizes drying lamps or heaters to cure or "set" the inks. Heatset presses can print on both coated (slick) and uncoated papers, while coldset presses are restricted to uncoated paper stock, such as newsprint. Some coldset web presses can be fitted with heat dryers, or ultraviolet lamps (for use with UV-curing inks). It is also possible to add a drier to a cold-set press. This can enable a newspaper press to print colour pages heatset and black and white pages coldset.

Web offset presses are beneficial in long run printing jobs, typically press runs that exceed ten or twenty thousand impressions. Speed is a determining factor when considering the completion time for press production; some web presses print at speeds of 3,000 feet per minute or faster. In addition to the benefits of speed and quick completion, some web presses have the inline ability to cut, perforate, and fold. Heatset web offset: This subset of web offset printing uses inks which dry by evaporation in a dryer typically positioned just after the printing units. This is typically done on coated papers, where the ink stays largely on the surface, and gives a glossy high contrast print image after the drying. As the paper leaves the dryer too hot for the folding and cutting that are typically downstream procedures, a set of "chill rolls" positioned after the dryer lowers the paper temperature and sets the ink.

The speed at which the ink dries is a function of dryer temperature and length of time the paper is exposed to this temperature. This type of printing is typically used for magazines, catalogs, inserts and other medium-to-high volume, medium-to-high quality production runs.

Coldset web offset: This is also a subset of web offset printing, typically used for lower quality print output. It is typical of newspaper production. In this process, the ink dries by absorption into the underlying paper. A typical coldset configuration is often a series of vertically arranged print units and peripherals. As newspapers seek new markets, which often imply higher quality (more gloss, more contrast), they may add a heatset tower (with a dryer) or use UV (ultraviolet) based inks which "cure" on the surface by polymerisation rather than by evaporation or absorption.

WEB-FED VERSUS SHEET-FED

Sheet-fed presses offer several advantages. Because individual sheets are fed through, a large number of sheet sizes and format sizes can be run through the same press. In addition, waste sheets can be used for make-ready (which is the testing process to ensure a quality print run). This allows for lower cost preparation so that good paper is not wasted while setting up the press, for plates and inks. Waste sheets do bring some disadvantages as often there are dust and offset powder particles that transfer on to the blankets and plate cylinders, creating imperfections on the printed sheet. This method produces the highest quality images. Web-fed presses, on the other hand, are much faster than sheet-fed presses, with speeds in excess of 20,000 cut-offs per hour. (Cut-off is the paper that has been cut off a reel or web on the press. The length of each sheet is equal to the cylinder's circumference.) The speed of web-fed presses makes them ideal for large runs such as newspapers, magazines, and comic books. However, web-fed presses have a fixed cut-off, unlike rotogravure or flexographic presses, which are variable.

INKS

Offset printing uses inks that, compared to other printing methods, are highly viscous. Typical inks have a dynamic viscosity of 40–100 Pa·s.

There are many types of paste inks available for utilization in offset lithographic printing and each have their own advantages and disadvantages. These include heat-set, cold-set, and energy-curable (or EC), such as ultraviolet- (or UV-) curable, and electron beam- (or EB-) curable. Heat-set inks are the most common variety and are "set" by applying heat and then rapid cooling to catalyze the curing process. They are used in magazines, catalogs, and inserts. Cold-set inks are set simply by absorption into non-coated stocks and are generally used for newspapers and books but are also found in insert printing and are the most economical option. Energy-curable inks are the highest-quality offset litho inks and are set by application of light energy.

They require specialized equipment such as inter-station curing lamps, and are usually the most expensive type of offset litho ink:

- Letterset inks are mainly used with offset presses that do not have dampening systems and uses imaging plates that have a raised image.
- Waterless inks are heat-resistant and are used to keep silicone-based plates from showing toning in non-image areas. These inks are typically used on waterless Direct Imaging presses.
- Single Fluid Inks are newer ink that uses a process allowing lithographic plates on a lithographic press without using a dampening system during the process.

Ink/water balance

Ink and water balance is an extremely important part of offset printing. If ink and water are not properly balanced, the press operator may end up with many different problems affecting the quality of the finished product, such as emulsification (the water overpowering and mixing with the ink). This leads to scumming, catchup, trapping problems, ink density issues and in extreme cases the ink not properly drying on the paper; resulting in the job being unfit for delivery to the client. With the proper balance, the job will have the correct ink density and should need little further adjustment except for minor ones. An example would be when the press heats up during normal operation, thus evaporating water at a faster rate. In this case the machinist will gradually increase the water as the press heats up to compensate for the increased evaporation of water. Printing machinists generally try to use as little water as possible to avoid these problems.

Fountain solution

Fountain solution is the water-based (or "aqueous") component in the lithographic process that moistens the non- image area of the plate in order to keep ink from depositing (and thus printing). Historically, fountain solutions were acid-based and made with gum arabic, chromates and/or phosphates, and magnesium nitrate. Alcohol is added to the water to lower the surface tension and help cool the press a bit so the ink stays stable so it can set and dry fast. While the acid fountain solution has improved in the last several decades, neutral and alkaline fountain solutions have also been developed. Both of these chemistries rely heavily on surfactants/emulsifiers and phosphates and/or silicates to provide adequate cleaning and desensitizing, respectively. Since about 2000, alkaline-based fountain solutions have become less common due to the inherent health hazards of high pH and the objectionable odour of the necessary microbiological additives. Acid-based fountain solutions are still the most common variety and yield the best quality results by means of superior protection of the printing plate, lower dot gains, and longer plate life. Acids are also the most versatile; capable of running with all types of offset litho inks. However, because these products require more active ingredients to run well than do neutrals and alkalines, they are also the most expensive to produce. However, neutrals and, to a lesser degree, alkalines are still an industry staple and will continue to be used for most newspapers and many lower-quality inserts. In recent years alternatives have been developed which do not use fountain solutions at all (waterless printing).

IN INDUSTRY

Offset lithography became the most popular form of commercial printing from the 1950s ("offset printing"). Substantial investment in the larger presses required for offset lithography was needed, and had an effect on the shape of the printing industry, leading to fewer, larger, printers. The change made a greatly increased use of colour printingpossible, as this had previously been much more expensive. Subsequent improvements in plates, inks, and paper have further refined the technology of its superior production speed and plate durability. Today, lithography is the primary printing technology used in the U.S. and most often as offset lithography.

Today, offset lithography is "responsible for over half of all printing using printing plates". The consistent high quality of the prints and the volume of prints created for their respective cost makes commercial offset lithography very efficient for businesses, especially when many prints must be created. Odour free offset printing is the newest technology.

2

Printing Techniques

INTRODUCTION

There are many different print techniques out there to make your printed piece stand out. Although some of these processes can be expensive and/or difficult to do, they truly make a difference in your final product. We show you some techniques below:

EMBOSSING/DEBOSSING

Embossing and dembossing are similar processes that create a different result. Both processes involve making a metal plate and a counter. The plate is mounted on a press and the paper is stamped between the plate and counter. This force of pressure pushes the stock into the plate, creating the impression. Embossing produces a raised impression on your paper stock, while debossing creates a depressed impression.

Fig. Emboss

Fig. Deboss

VARNISH

A varnish is a liquid coating applied to a printed surface to add an intensified chosen finish. The types of varnishes are gloss, matte, silk/satin, UV and spot UV. Whichever look you are going for in your piece, you can transform it with these coatings.

Fig. Spot UV Varnish

Die Cutting

Die cut involves cutting irregular shapes in paper or paperboard using a die. A die can be used in printing for cutting, scoring, stamping, embossing and debossing. Dies are normally custom pieces, but your printer will usually have some standard dies (such as for rounded corners) available if you don't need a custom template

Foil Stamping

To get the gold/silver stamp, a foil layer is affixed to a certain material by a heating process. This is quite similar to uv-spot printing.

Fig. Silver Foil Stamp

Thermography

Thermography produces raised printing similar in appearance to engraving, but using a different process. In thermography, a special powder is added to the ink that is to be printed on the paper. The printed piece is heated, causing the powder and ink mixture to dry, which in turn results in a raised effect on the paper.

Letterpress

Letterpress is the oldest printing process. In this method, a surface with raised letters is inked and pressed to the surface of the printing substrate to reproduce an image in reverse. Typically, metal type has been used, but other possibilities include carved wood or stone blocks. Most popularly used on wedding invitations, this process can also be used to create unique business cards as well as other custom printed products.

Fig. Bell'Invito Letterpress Stationary

Silk Screen Printing

Screen printing is a printing technique that uses a woven mesh to support an ink-blocking stencil. The attached stencil forms open areas of mesh that allows ink to transfer onto the material. A roller is moved across the screen stencil, forcing or pumping ink past the threads of the woven mesh in the open areas.

Fig. The Silk Screen Process in action

METHODS OF PRINTING

LETTERPRESS

The first ever press was a Letterpress. It basically uses stamps to grab ink and place it on the paper (or other material). Think of a typewriter, but doing whole pages in one press. Of course, this took long to do as each page was setup before by hand and manually placing these letter stamps in place. As time went on, full page stamps were created instead to make the process easier (though still inefficient compared to other methods). Today however, the Letterpress is not used much as it is not an efficient and far too expensive method of printing.

Offset Lithography

This method of printing is the most common used today. It is also one of the oldest. It works on the principle that water and oil (ink) don't mix. Using metal or polyester sheets (called plates), image and non-image areas are burned onto the plate using light to expose the image areas. this plate is attached onto a cylinder that as it goes around on the press, picks up water onto the non image areas. since water and oil don't mix, when the plate comes into contact with the ink, it only sticks to where the water isn't, our image area. The plate then comes into contact with a rubber sheet (called a blanket) and it transfers the image. The blanket them rotates around and presses to image into the paper. This is where the offset term comes from. While other methods can be done with offset theories, the Offset Lithography is so common that when someone refers to offset printing, this is what they mean.

Flexography

This is traditionally used to print labels. If you look at a bottle of pop, the plastic or cellophane label on it was likely done by flexography. It is the packaging industry who primarily uses flexography. The idea behind flexography is similar to a Letterpress where it uses a stamp, but this one is created with rubber etched with tiny grooves that pick up ink. The rubber stamp (plate) wrapped around a cylinder which rotates and picks up ink from a reservoir then presses it into the printing material. This is often done on plastics, tissues, labels, stickers and cardboard.

Gravure

This is a method usually used in printing long runs of magazines. Much like flexography, gravure printing has a cylinder that picks up ink in tiny etched grooves and places it on the paper. The difference is, gravure doesn't use a plate. Its grooves are actually etched into the cylinder. This allows it to last much longer and can be used for more impressions (contacts with the paper/material) before it wears out.

Screen Printing

This is still a common method of printing. It is often used on all the odd materials. Solid letters on plastics, T-shirts and clothing materials, a lot of signs and others use screen printing. The idea behind screen prints is basically a screened material such as silk or nylon is stretched across a frame and fastened into place.

A stencil, cut my hand or made electronically, is placed over that screen to block out non- printing areas. Ink (often rubber based) is placed inside the frame and scrapped across the stencil with a rubber squeegee. The ink goes through the screen and onto the material.

Digital Printing

There are several way to do digital printing. Many methods try to reproduce the effects of the previously described styles. There are inkjet, laser and toner, and magnetic digital printers. In inkjet, the ink cartridge holds liquid ink that is released in tiny sprays onto the paper. It makes several dots, that when viewed without a magnifying glass creates the illusion of your image. Laser and toner method uses a laser to charge the paper in certain areas which will attract toner of cymk colours to it. It then goes through a fuser which melts the toner into the paper. Magnetic works in much the same way but instead of electrical charges, it uses magnetic ones. It also passes through a fuser to melt the toner on.

This is all just touching the tip of the iceberg for each of these methods. This is just a rough summary of what these printing methods are all about. If you are interested in learning more, the internet has all the information you could want about this. Printing is considered the greatest invention of the second millennium and is a major reason why we are where we are today.

USING SPECIAL PRINTING TECHNIQUES

Designers nowadays learn their craft in design schools that mainly teach using computers. This educational style makes us sometimes forget of more practical and physical sides of graphic design, like printing techniques for example.

Of course, knowing the basics of typography, layout rules, colour management, illustration, or any other skill that graphic designers use on a daily basis is a must. Nevertheless, some printing techniques can help you to take your work from good to great. Adding that extra touch will sometimes be costly, but it will definitely make your designs better.

You should also not use these techniques without knowing what you are doing, otherwise you could end up with the opposite of what you want: extra cost and no added value, sometimes it could even degrade your work. So take some time to read about each technique, and maybe investigate further before you are going to use one of these options.

LETTERPRESS

Starting in the 15th century, letterpress has been the regular printing technique until the 19th century. The process of letterpress printing demands much more work than modern techniques, the printer needs to compose and lock movable type into the bed of a press, then ink it and press it on paper. It is a set of skills that not many workers still get nowadays, but it can give beautiful results.

Fig. Composed Movable Type

When using wooden blocks for printing, usually chosen for larger formats like posters, the ink will often have a nice texture that gives it a handmade feeling. With metal letters, you will get a slight embossing in your paper that gives some depth to your design. In both cases, the craftmanship that is necessary for printing will be visible on the final outcome, especially if you use some nice papers. After being discarded to use more modern printing techniques, letterpress has become popular again and is often used by graphic designers for smaller scale print work, such as business cards or wedding invitations. There is even an iPad application dedicated to recreate the letterpress experience, Letter M Press.

Fig. Letterpress Printed Summer Promo

DIE CUT

Die cutting, while not a printing technique per se, can turn an average design into a beautiful piece of work. Like printing, the process involves a press, but this time for cutting the paper with various shapes. The shapes can be regular or custom-made.

Most print shops will have some standard dies (the piece used for the cutting) for the shapes that are used more often, but if you want to get more creative you will have to get a custom die created specifically for your design. This is obviously more costly, but it allows you to cut pretty much any shapes within the limits of the technology.

Die cut is often used to give business cards a different shape, but it can be used on pretty much anything: postcards, brochures, catalogue front pages to reveal the next page, book covers,...

Fig. Die Cut Card

VARNISH

Varnish is a thin layer that is often used to give a gloss finish to your print and helps to protect the printing underneath. I said often, because there are different types of varnish, gloss is just the most popular.

The varnishing process takes place after the printing work is done, and comes before folding, cutting or packaging. Technically speaking, there are two types of varnishes, oil or water based. In both cases it takes quite long to dry, but that's not really the graphic designer's problem.

When speaking of the rendering, there are more types of varnishes:

- *Gloss:* That gives a glossy finish to the surface.
- *Matte:* That gives a non-glossy, smooth finish.

- *Silk:* A finish that looks like a compromise between the glossy and matte varnishes.
- *UV:* A technique that uses ultraviolet process to give an extra-glossy and very reflective finish.

Any of these varnishes will give a nice look to your printed designs, but in my opinion the best use of varnish is to use partial varnish. Spraying the varnish partially will make only a part of your design more reflective, attracting the viewer's attention to these parts of the design.

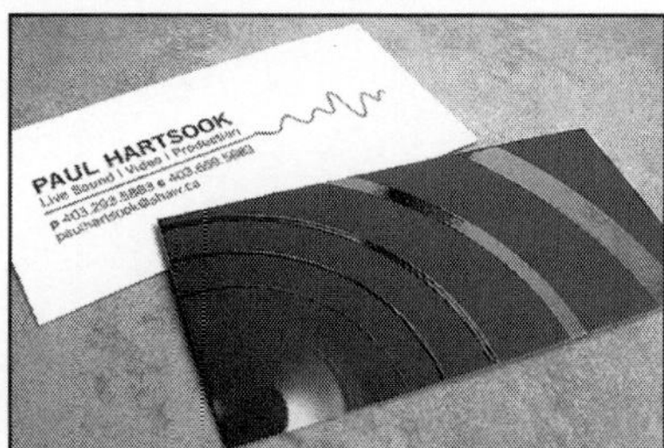

Fig. Business Card of Paul Hartsook Using a Partial Varnish

Embossing

Embossing, or debossing for the opposite effect (but it uses the same technique), is the process of raising a pattern against the background (while debossing sinks the pattern). This technique creates relief in your printed work and gives it a third dimension.

There are two ways to create embossings: stamp embossing and dry embossing. Stamp embossing is done by stamping an image on paper, then adding powder and applying heat on it. For dry embossing, it is done by tracing a stencil with a stylus over paper. Embossing and debossing are definitely techniques that your clients will love, so you should ask for some samples at your print shop to let the client see it for himself and convince him to spend the extra bucks for it.

Fig. Embossing Sample

Lamination

Lamination can be achieved in two ways: it can be a film added on your printed work, or it can be done with a liquid that dries and forms a tough surface.

In both case the result is a water-resistant surface that becomes more glossy, with vibrant colours.

For example, lamination can be used in book covers, to reinforce it, or when designing menus for restaurants. Any printed design that needs to be more resistant to water, the weather or things like that, is a good bet for lamination.

Foil

Foil printing, commonly called foil stamping, is the application of a silver or gold pigment foil. It can also be made with other kind of pigments, but it's less frequent. That technique can help you to create much more shiny and unique designs that you couldn't do with regular colours. Fashion catalogues use it more than others, but you can get creative with it.

Fig. Foil Sample

Serigraphy

Serigraphy, also known as silkscreen printing, is a printing technique that uses a woven mesh to support an ink-blocking stencil to receive a desired image. It existed for centuries, but in modern society it was popularized in the sixties by Andy Warhol with his prints of Marilyn Monroe or Chairman Mao.

It is still used quite often for small quantity prints, packaging or more artistic posters. One of the big advantages of serigraphy is that you can print on other surfaces than regular paper, allowing you to create some things that are impossible with other printing techniques.

Thermographic Printing

Thermographic printing, or thermography, is a process that lets you create some raised printing, a bit like in engraving. A powder is added to a slow drying ink to create the raised printing effect. Done right, thermographic printing can make your designs look very classy.

MOVABLE TYPE

The world's first known movable type system for printing was created in

China around 1040 A.D. by Bi Sheng (990–1051) during the Northern Song Dynasty (960–1127); When this technology spread to Korea during the Goryeo Dynasty in 1234, they made the metal movable-type system for printing. This led to the printing of the Jikji in 1377, the oldest extant movable metal print book. The diffusion of both movable-type systems was, however, limited: They were expensive, and required an enormous amount of labour involved in manipulating the thousands of ceramic tablets, or in the case of Korea, metal tablets required for scripts based on the Chinese writing system, which have thousands of characters.

Around 1450, Johannes Gutenberg invented an improved movable type mechanical printing system in Europe, along with innovations in casting the type based on a matrix and hand mould. The more limited number of characters needed for European languages was an important factor. Gutenberg was the first to create his type pieces from an alloy of lead, tin, and antimony—the same components still used today.

For alphabetic scripts, movable-type page setting was quicker and more durable than woodblock printing. The metal type pieces were more durable and the lettering was more uniform, leading to typography and fonts. The printing press was especially efficient for limited alphabets. The high quality and relatively low price of the Gutenberg Bible (1455) established the superiority of movable type in Europe and the use of printing presses spread rapidly. The printing press may be regarded as one of the key factors fostering the Renaissance and due to its effectiveness, its use spread around the globe.

The 19th-century invention of hot metal typesetting and its successors caused movable type to decline in the 20th century.

PRECURSORS TO MOVABLE TYPE

Letter punch and coins

The technique of imprinting multiple copies of symbols or glyphs with a master *type* punch made of hard metal first developed around 3000 BC inancient Sumer. These metal punch types can be seen as precursors of the letter punches adapted in later millennia to printing with movable metal type. Cylinder seals were used in Mesopotamia to create an impression on a surface by rolling the seal on wet clay. They were used to "sign" documents and mark objects as the owner's property. Cylinder seals were a related form of early typography capable of printing small page designs in relief (*cameo*) on wax or clay—a miniature forerunner of rotogravure printing used by wealthy individuals to seal and certify documents. By 650 BC the ancient Greeks were using larger diameter punches to imprint small page images onto coins and tokens.

The designs of the artists who made the first coin punches were stylized with a degree of skill that could not be mistaken for common handiwork—salient and very specific types designed to be reproduced *ad infinitum*. Unlike the first typefaces used to print books in the 13th century, coin types were neither combined nor printed with ink on paper, but "published" in metal—a more durable medium—and survived in substantial numbers. As the portable face of ruling authority, coins were a compact form of standardized knowledge issued in large editions, an early mass medium that stabilized trade and civilization throughout the Mediterranean world of antiquity.

Seals and stamps

Seals and stamps may have been precursors to movable type. The uneven spacing of the impressions on brick stamps found in theMesopotamian cities of Uruk and Larsa, dating from the 2nd millennium BC, has been conjectured by some archaeologists as evidence that the stamps were made using movable type. The enigmatic Minoan Phaistos Disc of 1800–1600 BC has been considered by one scholar as an early example of a body of text being reproduced with reusable characters: it may have been produced by pressing pre-formed hieroglyphic "seals" into the soft clay. A few authors even view the disc as technically meeting all definitional criteria to represent an early incidence of movable-type printing. Recently it has been alleged by Jerome Eisenberg that the disk is a forgery.

Woodblock printing

Following the invention of paper in the Han Dynasty, writing materials became more portable and economical than the bones, shells, bamboo slips, metal or stone tablets, silk, etc. previously used. Yet copying books by hand was still labour-consuming. Not until the Xiping Era (172-178 AD), towards the end of the Eastern Han Dynasty did sealing print and monotype appear. It was soon used for printing designs on fabrics, and later for printing texts. Woodblock printing worked as follows.

First, the neat hand-copied script was stuck on a relatively thick and smooth board, with the front of the paper, which was so thin that it was nearly transparent, sticking to the board, and characters showing in opposite, so distinctly that every stroke could be easily recognized. Then, carvers cut the parts with no character off the board with knives, so that the characters were cut in relief, completely different from those cut in intaglio. When printing, the bulging characters would have some ink spread on them and be covered by paper. With workers' hands moving on the back of paper gently, characters would be printed on the paper.

By the Song Dynasty, woodblock printing came to its heyday. Although woodblock printing played an influential role in spreading culture, there remained some apparent drawbacks. Firstly, carving the printing plate required considerable time, labour and materials; secondly, it was not convenient to store these plates; and finally, it was difficult to correct mistakes. With woodblock printing, one printing plate could be used for tens of hundreds of books, playing a magnificent role in spreading culture. Yet carving the plate was time and labour consuming. Huge books cost years of effort. The plates needed a lot of storage space, and were often damaged by deformation, worms and corrosion. If books had a small print run, and were not reprinted, the printing plates would become nothing but waste; and worse, if a mistake was found, it was difficult to correct it without discarding the whole plate.

HISTORY OF MOVABLE TYPE

Prior to the development of metal movable type, most printing was done using blocks carved from wood. Woodblock printing was used extensively in East Asia, and created the world's first print culture.

Ceramic movable type in China

Bi Sheng (990–1051) developed the first known movable-type system for printing in China around 1040 AD during the Northern Song dynasty, using ceramic materials. As described by the Chinese scholar Shen Kuo (1031–1095):

When he wished to print, he took an iron frame and set it on the iron plate. In this he placed the types, set close together. When the frame was full, the whole made one solid block of type. He then placed it near the fire to warm it. When the paste [at the back] was slightly melted, he took a smooth board and pressed it over the surface, so that the block of type became as even as a whetstone.

For each character there were several types, and for certain common characters there were twenty or more types each, in order to be prepared for the repetition of characters on the same page. When the characters were not in use he had them arranged with paper labels, one label for each rhyme-group, and kept them in wooden cases.

If one were to print only two or three copies, this method would be neither simple nor easy. But for printing hundreds or thousands of copies, it was marvelously quick. As a rule he kept two forms going. While the impression was being made from the one form, the type was being put in place on the other. When the printing of the one form was finished, the other was then ready. In this way the two forms alternated and the printing was done with great rapidity.

In 1193, Zhou Bida, an officer of Southern Song Dynasty, made a set of clay movable-type method according to the method described by Shen Kuo in his *Dream Pool Essays*, and printed his book *Notes of The Jade Hall*.

The claim that Bi Sheng's clay types were *fragile* and "not practical for large-scale printing" and "short lived" was refuted by facts and experiments. Bao Shicheng (1775–1885) wrote that baked clay moveable type was "as hard and tough as horn"; experiments show that clay type, after being baked in an oven, becomes hard and difficult to break, such that it remains intact after being dropped from a height of two metres onto a marble floor. Korea could have tried clay movable type, but with little success, probably due to misinterpration of Shen Kua's description "as thin as coin", which likely referred to the depth of the character matrix, not the total length of the moveable type body. The length of clay movable types in China was 1 to 2 centimetres, not 2mm, thus hard as horn.

There has been an ongoing debate regarding the success of ceramic printing technology as there have been no printed materials found with ceramic movable types. However, it is historically recorded to have been used as late as 1844 in China from the Song dynasty through the Qing dynasty.

Wooden movable type in China

Bi Sheng (990–1051) also pioneered the use of wooden movable type around 1040 AD, as described by the Chinese scholar Shen Kuo (1031–1095). However, this technology was abandoned in favour of clay movable types due to the presence of wood grains and the unevenness of the wooden type after being soaked in ink.

In 1298, Wang Zhen, a Yuan dynasty governmental official of Jingde County, Anhui Province, China, re-invented a method of making movable wooden types. He made more than 30,000 wooden movable types and printed 100 copies of *Records of Jingde County*, a book of more than 60,000 Chinese characters. Soon afterwards, he summarized his invention in his book *A method of making moveable wooden types for printing books*. Although the wooden type was more durable under the mechanical rigours of handling, repeated printing wore the character faces down, and the types could only be replaced by carving new pieces.

This system was later enhanced by pressing wooden blocks into sand and casting metal types from the depression in copper, bronze, iron or tin. This new method overcame many of the shortcomings of woodblock printing. Rather than manually carving an individual block to print a single page, movable type printing allowed for the quick assembly of a page of text. Furthermore, these new, more compact type fonts could be reused and stored. The set of wafer-like metal stamp types could be assembled to form pages, inked, and page impressions taken from rubbings on cloth or paper. In 1322, a Fenghua county officer Ma Chengde in Zhejiang, made 100,000 wooded movable types and printed 43 volume *Daxue Yanyi*. Wooden movable types were used continually in China. Even as late as 1733, a 2300-volume *Wuying Palace Collected Gems Edition* was printed with 253500 wooden movable type on order of the Yongzheng Emperor, and completed in one year.

A number of books printed in Tangut script during the Western Xia (1038–1227) period are known, of which the Auspicious Tantra of All-Reaching Union that was discovered in the ruins of Baisigou Square Pagoda in 1991 is believed to have been printed sometime during the reign of Emperor Renzong of Western Xia (1139–1193). It is considered by many Chinese experts to be the earliest extant example of a book printed using wooden movable type.

The logistical problems of handling the several thousand logographs (required for full literacy in Chinese language) posed a particular difficulty. It was faster to carve one woodblock per page than to composit a page from so many different types. However, if one used movable type to produce multiple copies of the same document, the speed of printing would increase relatively.

Metal movable type in China

Bronze movable type printing was invented in China no later than the 12th century, according to at least 13 material finds in China, in large scale bronze plate printing of paper money and formal official documents issued by Jin (1115–1234) and Southern Song (1127–1279) dynasties with embedded bronze metal types for anti counterfeit markers. Such paper money printing might date back to the 11th-century *jiaozi* of Northern Song (960–1127).

The typical example of this kind of bronze movable type embedded copper-block printing is a printed "check" of Jin Dynasty with two square holes for embedding two bronze movable type characters, each selected from 1000 different characters, such that each printed paper money has different combination of markers. A copper block printed paper money dated between 1215–1216 in the collection ofLuo Zhenyu's *Pictorial Paper Money of the Four Dynasties*, 1914, shows two special characters one called *Ziliao*, the other called *Zihao*for the purpose of preventing counterfeit; over the *Ziliao* there is a small character printed with movable copper type, while over the*Zihao* there is an empty square hole, apparently the associated copper metal type was lost. Another sample of Song dynasty money of the same period in the collection of Shanghai Museum has two empty square holes above *Ziliao* as well as *Zihou*, due to lost of the two copper movable types. Song dynasty bronze block embedded with bronze metal movable type printed paper money was issued in large scale and in circulation for a long time.

In the 1298 book *Zao Huozi Yinshufa* of the Yuan dynasty (1271–1368) official Wang Zhen, there is mention of tin movable type, used probably since the Southern Song dynasty (1127–1279), but this was largely experimental. It was unsatisfactory due to its incompatibility with the inking process.

During the Mongol Empire (1206–1405), printing using movable type spread from China to Central Asia. The Uyghurs of Central Asia used movable type, their script type adopted from the Mongol language, some with Chinese words printed between the pages, a strong evidence that the books were printed in China.

During the Ming Dynasty (1368–1644), Hua Sui in 1490 used bronze type in printing books. In 1574 the massive 1000 volume encyclopaedia Imperial

Readings of the Taiping Era were printed with bronze movable type. In 1725, the Qing Dynasty government made 250,000 bronze movable-type characters and printed 64 sets of the encyclopedic *Gujin Tushu Jicheng, Complete Collection of Illustrations and Writings from the Earliest to Current Times*). Each set consisted of 5040 volumes, making a total of 322,560 volumes printed using movable type.

Metal movable type in Korea

The transition from wood type to metal type occurred in 1234 during the Goryeo Dynasty of Koreaand is credited to Choe Yun-ui. A set of ritual books, *Sangjeong Gogeum Yemun* were printed with the movable metal type in 1234. Examples of this metal type are on display in the Asian Reading Room of the Library of Congress in Washington, D.C. The oldest extant movable metal print book is the Jikji, printed in Korea in 1377.

The techniques for bronze casting, used at the time for making coins (as well as bells and statues) were adapted to making metal type. The following description of the Korean font casting process was recorded by the Joseon dynasty scholar Seong Hyeon(1439–1504):

At first, one cuts letters in beech wood. One fills a trough level with fine sandy [clay] of the reed-growing seashore. Wood-cut letters are pressed into the sand, then the impressions become negative and form letters [molds]. At this step, placing one trough together with another, one pours the molten bronze down into an opening. The fluid flows in, filling these negative molds, one by one becoming type. Lastly, one scrapes and files off the irregularities, and piles them up to be arranged.

A potential solution to the linguistic and cultural bottleneck that held back movable type in Korea for 200 years appeared in the early 15th century—a generation before Gutenberg would begin working on his own movable-type invention in Europe—when King Sejong the Great devised a simplified alphabet of 24 characters (hangul) for use by the common people, which could have made the typecasting and compositing process more feasible. Adoption of the new alphabet was stifled by the Korea's cultural elite, who were *"...appalled at the idea of losing Chinese, the badge of their elitism."*

Proliferation of movable type was also obstructed by a "Confucian prohibition on the commercialization of printing" restricted the distribution of books produced using the new method to the government. The technique was restricted to use by the royal foundry for official state publications only, where the focus was on reprinting Chinese classics lost in 1126 when Korea's libraries and palaces had perished in a conflict between dynasties.

In the early 13th century, however, the Koreans invented a form of movable type that has been described by the French scholar Henri-Jean Martin as '[extremely similar] to Gutenberg's'.

Metal movable type in Europe

Johannes Gutenberg of Mainz, Germany is acknowledged as the first to invent a metal movable-type printing system in Europe, theprinting press. Gutenberg was a goldsmith familiar with techniques of cutting punches for making coins from moulds. Between 1436 and 1450 he developed hardware and techniques for casting letters from matrices using a device called the hand mould. Gutenberg's key invention and contribution to movable-type printing in Europe, the hand mould was the first practical means of making cheap copies of letterpunches in the vast quantities needed to print complete books, making the movable-type printing process a viable enterprise.

Before Gutenberg, books were copied out by hand on scrolls and paper, or printed from hand-carved wooden blocks. It was extremely time-consuming; even a small book could take months to complete, and the carved letters or blocks were very flimsy and the susceptibility of wood to ink gave such blocks a limited lifespan.

Gutenberg and his associates developed oil-based inks ideally suited to printing with a press on paper, and the first Latin typefaces. His method of casting type may have been different from the hand mould used in subsequent decades. Detailed analysis of the type used in his 42-line Bible has revealed irregularities in some of the characters that cannot be attributed to ink spread or type wear under the pressure of the press. Scholars conjecture that the type pieces may have been cast from a series of matrices made with a series of individual stroke punches, producing many different versions of the same glyph. It has also been suggested that the method used by Gutenberg involved using a single punch to make a mould, but the mould was such that the process of taking the type out disturbed the casting, creating variants and anomalies, and that the punch-matrix system came into use possibly around the 1470s. This raises the possibility that the development of movable type in the West may have been progressive rather than a single innovation.

Gutenberg's movable-type printing system spread rapidly across Europe, from the single Mainz printing press in 1457 to 110 presses by 1480, of which 50 were in Italy. Venice quickly became the center of typographic and printing activity. Significant were the contributions ofNicolas Jenson, Francesco Griffo, Aldus Manutius, and other printers of late 15th-century Europe. Despite some conjectures, there is no evidence that movable type from the East ever reached Europe.

TYPE-FOUNDING

Type-founding as practiced in Europe and the west consists of three stages.

Punchcutting: If the glyph design includes enclosed spaces (counters) then a counterpunch is made. The counter shapes are transferred in relief (cameo) onto the end of a rectangular bar of mild steel using a specialized engraving tool called a graver. The finished counterpunch is hardened by heating and quenching (tempering), or exposure to a cyanide solution (case hardening).

The counterpunch is then struck against the end of a similar rectangular steel bar—the letterpunch—to impress the counter shapes as recessed spaces (intaglio). The outer profile of the glyph is completed by scraping away with a graver the material outside the counter spaces, leaving only the stroke or lines of the glyph. Progress towards the finished design is checked by successive *smoke proofs*; temporary prints made from a thin coating of carbon deposited on the punch surface by a candle flame. The finished letter punch is finally hardened to withstand the rigours of reproduction by striking.

One counterpunch and one letterpunch are produced for every letter or glyph making up a complete font:

- *Matrix:* The letterpunch is used to strike a blank die of soft metal to make a negative letter mould, called a matrix.
- *Casting:* The matrix is inserted into the bottom of a device called a *hand mould*. The mould is clamped shut and molten type metal alloy consisting mostly of lead and tin, with a small amount of antimony for hardening, is poured into a cavity from the top. Antimony has the rare property of expanding as it cools, giving the casting sharp edges. When the type metal has sufficiently cooled, the mould is unlocked and a rectangular block approximately 4 centimeters long, called a *sort*, is extracted. Excess casting on the end of the sort, called the *tang*, is later removed to make the sort the precise height required for printing, known as "type height".

The type-height was quite different in different countries, the Monotype Corporation Limited in London UK produced moulds in various heights:

- *0.918 inches:* United Kingdom, Canada, USA
- *0.928 inches:* France, Germany, Swiss and most other European Countries
- *0.933 inches:* Belgium height
- *0.9785 inches:* Dutch height

A Dutch printers manual mentions a tiny difference between French and German Height:

- 62.027 points Didot = 23.30 mm = English height
- 62.666 points Didot = 23.55 mm = French height
- 62.685 points Didot = 23.56 mm = German height
- 66.047 points Didot = 24.85 mm = Dutch Height

Tiny differences in type-height will cause quite bold images of characters.

TYPESETTING

Modern, factory-produced movable type was available in the late 19th century. It was held in the printing shop in a *job case*, a drawer about 2 inches high, a yard wide, and about two feet deep, with many small compartments for the various letters and ligatures. The most popular and accepted of the job case designs in America was the California Job Case, which took its name from the Pacific coast location of the foundries that made the case popular.

Traditionally, the capital letters were stored in a separate drawer or case that was located above the case that held the other letters; this is why capital letters are called "upper case" characters while the non-capitals are "lower case".

Compartments also held spacers, which are blocks of blank type used to separate words and fill out a line of type, such as *em* and *en*quads (*quadrats*, or spaces. A *quadrat* is a block of type whose face is lower than the printing letters so that it does not itself print.). An em space was the width of a capital letter "M" – as wide as it was high – while an en space referred to a space half the width of its height (usually the dimensions for a capital "N").

Individual letters are assembled into words and lines of text with the aid of a composing stick, and the whole assembly is tightly bound together to make up a page image called a *forme*, where all letter faces are exactly the same height to form a flat surface of type. The forme is mounted on a printing press, a thin coating of viscous ink is applied and impressions made on paper under great pressure in the press. "Sorts" is the term given to special characters not freely available in the typical type case, such as the "@" mark, etc.

METAL TYPE COMBINED WITH OTHER METHODS

Sometimes it is erroneously stated that printing with metal type replaced the earlier methods. In the industrial era printing methods would be chosen to suit the purpose. For example, when printing large scale letters in posters etc. the metal type would have proved too heavy and economically unviable. Thus, large scale type was made as carved wood blocks as well as ceramics plates. Also in many cases where large scale text was required, it was simpler to hand the job to a sign painter than a printer. Images could be printed together with movable type if they were made as woodcuts or wood engravings as long as the blocks were made to the same type height. If intagliomethods, such as copper plates, were used for the images, then images and the text would have required separate print runs on different machines.

LETTERPRESS PRINTING

Letterpress printing is a technique of relief printing using a printing press. A worker composes and locksmovable type into the bed of a press, inks it, and presses paper against it to transfer the ink from the type which creates an impression on the paper.

In practice, letterpress also includes other forms of relief printing with printing presses, such as wood engravings, photo-etched zinc "cuts" (plates), and linoleum blocks, which can be used alongside metal type in a single operation, as well as stereotypes and electrotypes of type and blocks. With certain letterpress units it is also possible to join movable type with slugs cast using hot metal typesetting.

Letterpress printing was the normal form of printing text from its invention by Johannes Gutenberg in the mid-15th century until the 19th century and remained in wide use for books and other uses until the second half of the 20th century. Letterpress printing remained the primary way to print and distribute information until the twentieth century, when offset printing was developed, which largely supplanted its role in printing books and newspapers. More recently, letterpress printing has seen a revival in an artisanal form.

HISTORY

Johannes Gutenberg is credited with the invention, in about 1440, of modern movable type printing from individually cast, reusable letters set together in a form (frame or chase). He also invented a wooden printing press, based on the extant wine press, where the type surface was inked with leather covered ink balls and paper laid carefully on top by hand, then slid under a padded surface and pressure applied from above by a large threaded screw.

Later metal presses used a knuckle and lever arrangement instead of the screw, but the principle was the same. Ink rollers made ofcomposition made inking faster and paved the way for further automation.

Industrialization

With the advent of industrial mechanisation, inking was carried out by rollers that passed over the face of the type, then moved out of the way onto an ink plate to pick up a fresh film of ink for the next sheet. Meanwhile, a sheet of paper slid against a hinged platen, which then rapidly pressed onto the type and swung back again as the sheet was removed and the next sheet inserted. As the fresh sheet of paper replaced the printed paper, the now freshly-inked rollers ran over the type again. Fully automated 20th-century presses, such as the Kluge and "Original" Heidelberg Platen (the "Windmill"), incorporated pneumatic sheet feed and delivery.

Rotary presses were used for high-speed work. In the oscillating press, the form slid under a drum around which each sheet of paper got wrapped for the impression, sliding back under the inking rollers while the paper was removed and a new sheet inserted. In a newspaperpress, a papier-mâché mixture called a flong was used to make a mould of the entire form of type, then dried and bent, and a curved metal plate cast against it. The plates were clipped to a rotating drum and could print against a continuous reel of paper at the enormously high speeds required for overnight newspaper production. This invention helped aid the high demand for knowledge during this time period.

NORTH AMERICAN HISTORY

Canada

Letterpress printing was introduced in Canada in 1752 in Halifax, Nova Scotia by John Bushell in the newspaper format. ((This paper was named the Halifax Gazette and became Canada's first newspaper. Bushell apprenticed under Bartholomew Green in Boston. Green moved to Halifax in 1751 in hopes of starting a newspaper, as it did not exist in the area. Two weeks and a day after the press he was going to use for this new project arrived in Halifax, Green died. Upon receiving word about what happened, Bushell moved to Halifax and continued what Green had started. The Halifax Gazette was first published on March 23, 1752, making Bushell the first letterpress printer in Halifax, and eventually Canada. There is only one known surviving copy which was found in Massachusetts Historical Society.

United States

One of the first forms of letterpress printing in the United States was Publick Occurrences Both Forreign and Domestick started by Benjamin Harris. This was the first form of a newspaper with multiple pages in the Americas. The first publication of Publick Occurrences Both Forreign and Domestick was September 25, 1690.

REVIVAL AND RISE OF 'CRAFT' LETTERPRESS

Letterpress started to become largely out-of-date in the 1980's because of the rise of computers and new self-publishing print and publish methods. Many printing establishments went out of business from the 1980's to 1990's and sold their equipment after computers replaced letterpress's abilities more efficiently. Letterpress recently has had a rebirth in popularity because of the "allure of hand-set type" and the differences today between traditional letterpress and computerized printed text. Letterpress is unique and different from standard printing formats that we are currently used to. Letterpress commonly features a relief impression of the type, although this was considered bad printing in traditional letterpress. Letterpress's goal before the recent revival of letterpress was to not show any impression. The type touched the paper slightly to leave a transfer of ink, but did not leave an impression. An example of this former technique would be newspapers. Contemporary letterpress has a distinct goal of showing the impression of type, to distinctly note that it is letterpress. Since its revival letterpress is largely has been used for fine art and stationary as its traditional use for newspaper printing is no longer relevant for use.

Contemporary letterpress is considered a craft as it involves using a skill and is made by hand. A small amount of high-quality art and hobby letterpress printing remain across North America. This fine letterpress work is crisper than offset litho because of its impression into the paper, giving greater visual definition to the type and artwork, although it is not what letterpress traditionally was meant for. Today, many of these small letterpress shops survive by printing fine editions of books or by printing upscale invitations and stationery. These methods often use presses that require the press operator to feed paper one sheet at a time by hand. These printmakers are just as likely to use new printing methods as old, for instance by printing photopolymer plates (used in modern rotary letterpress) on restored 19th century presses.

Martha Stewart's influence

Letterpress publishing has recently undergone a revival in the USA, Canada, and the UK, under the general banner of the 'Small Press Movement'. Renewed interest in letterpress was fueled by Martha Stewart Weddings magazine, which began using pictures of letterpress invitations in the 1990s. In 2004 they state "Great care is taken in choosing the perfect wedding stationery — couples ponder details from the level of formality to the flourishes of the typeface.

The method of printing should be no less important, as it can enliven the design exquisitely. That is certainly the case with letterpress.". In regards to having printed letterpress invitations, The beauty and texture became appealing to brides who began wanting letterpress invitations instead of engraved, thermographed, or offset-printed invitations. At the same time, presses were being discarded by commercial print shops, and became affordable and available to artisans throughout the country. Popular presses are, in particular, Vandercook cylinder proof presses andChandler and Price platen presses. In the UK there is particular affection for the Arab press, built by Josiah Wade in Halifax.

Education

The movement has been helped by the emergence of a number of organizations that teach letterpress such as Columbia College Chicago's Center for Book and Paper Arts, Art Center College of Design and Armory Center for the Arts both in Pasadena, Calif., New York's Center for Book Arts, Studio on the Square and The Arm NYC, the Wells College Book Arts Center in Aurora, New York, the San Francisco Center for the Book, Bookworks, Seattle's School of Visual Concepts, Olympia's The Evergreen State College, Black Rock Press, North Carolina State University, Washington D.C's Corcoran College of Art and Design, Penland School of Crafts, the Minnesota Center for Book Arts, the International Printing Museum in Carson, CA, Western Washington University in Bellingham, WA, Old Dominion University in Norfolk, VA, and the Bowehouse Press at VCU in Richmond, VA.

Economical Materials

Affordable copper, magnesium and photopolymer platemakers and milled aluminum bases have allowed letterpress printers to produce type and images derived from digital artwork, fonts and scans. Economical plates have encouraged the rise of "digital letterpress" in the 21st century, allowing a small number of firms to flourish commercially and enabling a larger number of boutique and hobby printers to avoid the limitations and complications of acquiring and composing metal type. At the same time there has been a renaissance in small-scale type foundries to produce new metal type on Monotype equipment, Thompson casters and the original American Type Founders machines.

PROCESS

The process of letterpress printing consists of several stages: composition, imposition and lock-up, and printing. In a small shop, all would occur in a single room, whereas in larger printing plants, such as with urban newspapers and magazines, each might form a distinct department with its own room, or even floor.

Composition

Fig. Tools for composing by hand: block of type tied up, a composing stick, a bodkin, and string, all resting in a type galley.

Composition, or typesetting, is the stage where pieces of movable type are assembled to form the desired text. The person charged with composition is called a "compositor".

Traditionally, as in manual composition, it involves selecting the individual type letters from a type case, placing them in a composing stick, which holds several lines, then transferring those to a larger type galley.

By this method the compositor gradually builds out the text of an individual page letter by letter. In mechanical typesetting, it may involve using a keyboard to select the type, or even cast the desired type on the spot, as in hot metal typesetting, which are then added to a galley designed for the product of that process.

After a galley is assembled to fill a page's worth of type, the type is tied together into a single unit so that it may be transported without falling apart. From this bundle a galley proof is made, which is inspected by a proof-reader to make sure that the particular page is accurate.

Imposition

Broadly, imposition or imposing is the process by which the tied assemblages of type are converted into a "form" ("forme") ready to use on the press. A person charged with imposition is a *stoneman*, doing their work on a large, flat *imposition stone* (though some later ones were also of iron).

More specifically, imposition is the technique of arranging the various pages of type with respect to one another (this is its modern sense). Depending on page size and the sheet of paper used, several pages may be printed at once on a single sheet. After printing, these are cut and trimmed before folding or binding. In these steps, the imposition process ensures that the pages face the right direction and in the right order with the right margins.

Low-height pieces of wood or metal furniture are added to make up the blank areas of a page. The printer uses a mallet to level the type and blocks to ensure the printing surface is flat.

Lock-up is the final step before printing. The printer removes the cords that hold the type together, and turns the quoins with a key or lever to "lock" the entire complex of type, blocks, furniture, and chase (frame) into place—creating what is called a *form* or *forme*. The printer takes the finished form to the printing press, and proofs it again for errors before starting the printing run.

Printing

The working of the printing process depends on the type of press used, as well as any of its associated technologies (which varied by time period).

Hand presses generally required two people to operate them: one to ink the type, the other to work the press. Later mechanized jobbing presses require a single operator to feed and remove the paper, as the inking and pressing are done automatically.

The completed sheets are then taken to dry and for finishing, depending on the variety of printed matter being produced. With newspapers, they are taken to a folding machine. Sheets for books are sent for bookbinding.

VARIANTS ON THE LETTERPRESS

The invention of ultra-violet curing inks has helped keep the rotary letterpress alive in areas like self-adhesive labels. There is also still a large amount of flexographic printing, a similar process, which uses rubber plates to print on curved or awkward surfaces, and a lesser amount of relief printing from huge wooden letters for lower-quality poster work. Rotary letterpress machines are still used on a wide scale for printing self-adhesive and non-self-adhesive labels, tube laminate, cup stock, etc. The printing quality achieved by a modern letterpress machine with UV curing is on par with flexo presses.

It is more convenient and user friendly than a flexo press. It uses water-wash photopolymer plates, which are as good as any solvent-washed flexo plate. Today even CtP (computer-to-plate) plates are available making it a full-fledged, modern printing process. Because there is no anilox roller in the process, the make-ready time also goes down when compared to a flexo press. Inking is controlled by keys very much similar to an offset press. UV inks for letterpress are in paste form, unlike flexo.

Various manufacturers produce UV rotary letterpress machines, *viz.* Dashen, Nickel, Taiyo Kikai, KoPack, Gallus, etc.—and offer hot/cold foil stamping, rotary die cutting, flatbed die cutting, sheeting, rotary screen printing, adhesive side printing, and inkjet numbering. Central impression presses are more popular than inline presses due to their ease of registration and simple design. Printing of up to nine colours plus varnish is possible with various online converting processes.

CRAFTSMANSHIP

Fig. Wooden blocks for English printing

The process requires a high degree of craftsmanship, but in the right hands, letterpress excels at fine typography. It is used by many small presses that produce fine, handmade, limited-edition books, artists' books, and high-end ephemera such as greeting cards andbroadsides. Setting type by hand has become less common with the invention of the photopolymer plate.

To bring out the best attributes of letterpress, printers must understand the capabilities and advantages of what can be a very unforgiving medium. For instance, since most letterpress equipment prints only one colour at a time, printing multiple colours can be challenging. The inking system on letterpress equipment is less precise than on offset presses, posing problems for some graphics. Detailed, white (or "knocked out") areas, such as small, serif type, or very fine halftone surrounded by fields of colour can fill in with ink and lose definition. However, a skilled printer overcomes most of these problems.

However, a letterpress provides the option of a wider range of paper, including handmade, organic, and tree-free. Letterpress printing provides a wide range of production choices. The classic feel and finish of letterpress papers takes printing back to an era of quality and craftsmanship. Even the smell of the ink, more apparent on a letterpress-printed page than with offset, may appeal to collectors.

While less common in contemporary letterpress printing, it is possible to print halftoned photographs, via photopolymer plates. However, letterpress printing's strengths are crisp lines, patterns, and typography.

Creating artwork

Creating files for letterpress is similar to conventional printing with these exceptions:

- *Ink Colour:* Files are created using spot colours, not CMYK or RGB. A spot colour is specified for each colour to use. Typically one or two colours are used.
- *Paper Colour:* Dark ink on a light paper gives the best image. Inks are translucent and the paper colour shows through. For light colours on dark paper, printers use foil stampingor engraving instead of letterpress. To build up colour density, letterpress pieces can be run through the press two times using the same colour.
- *Screens:* Gray-scale images can be used if made with a coarse screen (85 line or less). A second colour should be used instead of screening a colour in most cases.
- *Thickness:* Art must be above ¼ point and with no hairlines.
- *Fonts:* Type must be five points or larger for best results. For reversed type the point size should be 12 point or larger, as smaller type with its thin stroke can fill in, or plug. An outline stroke is often applied to allow for ink gain.
- *Solids:* Letterpress solids print differently than conventionally printed lithographic solids. While letterpress does lay down a thick film of ink, the process tends to show the texture of the sheet. Also, solid areas do not give the appearance of depth that fine type and thin lines do. Solid areas can also cause the paper to ripple, especially on thinner sheets.
- *Registration:* Letterpress does register well, however, it does not have the capabilities of modern offset printing. Trapping and key lines do not work well in letterpress printing. A blank area should be incorporated between colours. Black and very dark colours may be overprinted over lighter colours.
- *Depth:* The type depth is dependent on the paper. Typically, letterpress papers are thick and soft so the type creates a deep

impression. When making fold-over items, the printer typically backs off the pressure to avoid embossing the backside of the piece.

- *Image and File Prep:* Letterpress excels at line copy and type, so vector images work well. Crop marks should be shown as a register colour. Images need to bleed (extend past the trim line).
- *Die cut, Emboss and Scores:* These effects work well with most Letterpress paper. Images to emboss or die cut are called out in a different colour layer (typically magenta). Scores are typically indicated with a cyan line. Any intricate shapes or patterns should be reviewed with the printer. For thick cover stocks many printers use a "kiss cut" (partially through the stock) rather than a score.
- *Envelopes:* It is best to print on the flap of a ready-made envelope. Other areas of the ready-made envelopes can be printed, but bruising can occur on the other side of the envelope.

CURRENT INITIATIVES

Several dozen colleges and universities around the United States have either begun or re-activated programmes teaching letterpress printing in fully equipped facilities. In many cases these letterpress shops are affiliated with the college's library or art department, and in others they are independent, student-run operations or extracurricular activities sponsored by the college. Many are included in degree programmes. The College and University Letterpress Printers' Association (CULPA) was founded in 2006 by Abigail Uhteg at the Maryland Institute College of Art to help these schools stay connected and share resources.

The current renaissance of letterpress printing has created a crop of hobby press shops that are owner-operated and driven by a love of the craft. Several larger printers have added an environmental component to the venerable art by using only wind-generated electricity to drive their presses and plant equipment. Notably, a few small boutique letterpress shops are using only solar power.

In London, St Bride Library houses a large collection of letterpress information in its collection of 50,000 books: all the classic works on printing technique, visual style, typography, graphic design, calligraphy and more. This is one of the world's foremost collections and is located off Fleet Street in the heart of London's old printing and publishing district. In addition, regular talks, conferences, exhibitions and demonstrations take place.

The St Bride Institute, Edinburgh College of Art, Central Saint Martins College of Art and Design, The Arts University Bournemouth, Plymouth University, University for the Creative Arts Farnham and London College of Communication, run short courses in letterpress as well as offering these facilities as part of their Graphic Design Degree Courses.

The Hamilton Wood Type and Printing Museum in Two Rivers, Wisconsin houses one of the largest collections of wood type and wood cuts in the world inside one of the Hamilton Manufacturing Company's factory buildings. Also included are presses and vintage prints. The museum hold many workshops and conferences throughout the year and regularly welcomes groups of students from Universities from across the United States.

In 2011 John Bonadies and Jeff Adams created a virtual letterpress that runs on an iPad (and later the Mac) and replicates each step of the letterpress process. LetterMpresswas funded from a Kickstarter campaign enabling the developers to collect and digitize wood type from around the world. The app's press is modeled after a Vandercook SP-15 (considered to be a top-of-the-line proof press in its time, and coveted by artists and designers today).

PHOTOTYPESETTING

Phototypesetting was a method of setting type, rendered obsolete with the popularity of the personal computer and desktop publishingsoftware, that used a photographic process to generate columns of type on a scroll of photographic paper. Typesetters used a machine called a phototypesetter, which would quickly project light through a film negative image of an individual character in a font, through a lens that would magnify or reduce the size of the character onto photographic paper, which would collect on a spool in a light-tight canister. The photographic paper or film would then be fed into a processor, a machine that would pull the paper or film strip through two or three baths of chemicals, where it would emerge ready for paste up or film make-up.

HISTORY

1950s and 60s

Initial phototypesetting machines

Phototypesetting machines projected characters onto film for offset printing. In 1949, the Photon Corporation in Cambridge, Mass. developed equipment based on the Lumitype of Rene Higonnet and Louis Moyroud. The Lumitype-Photon was first used to set a complete published book in 1953, and for newspaper work in 1954. Mergenthaler produced the Linofilm using a different design and Monotype produced Monophoto. Other companies followed with products that included Alphatype and Varityper.

The major advancement presented by the phototypesetting machines over the Linotype machine "hot type" machines was the elimination of metal type, an intermediate step no longer required once offset printing became the norm. This "cold type" technology could also be used in office environments where "hot metal" machines (the Mergenthaler Linotype, the Harris Intertype and the Monotype) could not. The use of phototypesetting grew rapidly in the 1960s when software was developed to convert marked up copy, usually typed on paper tape, to the codes that controlled the phototypesetters.

To provide much greater speeds, the Photon Corporation produced the ZIP 200 machine for the MEDLARS project of the National Library of Medicine and Mergenthaler produced the Linotron. The ZIP 200 could produce text at 600 characters per second using high speed flashes behind plates with images of the characters to be printed. Each character had a separate xenon flash constantly ready to fire. A separate system of optics positioned the image on the page.

Use of CRT screens for phototypesetting

An enormous advance was made by the mid-1960s with the development of equipment that projected the characters onto CRT screens. Alphanumeric Corporation (later Autologic) produced the APS series. Rudolf Hell developed the Digiset machine in Germany. The RCAGraphic Systems Division manufactured this in the U.S. as the Videocomp, later marketed by Information International Inc.. Software for operator-controlled hyphenation was a major component of electronic typesetting. Early work on this topic produced paper tape to control hot metal machines. C. J. Duncan, at the University of Durham in England, was a pioneer. The earliest applications of computer controlled phototypesetting machines produced the output of the Russian translation programmes of Gilbert King at the IBM Research Laboratories, and built-up mathematical formulas and other material in the Cooperative Computing Laboratory of Michael Barnett at MIT.

There are extensive accounts of the early applications, the equipment and the PAGE I algorithmic typesetting language for the Videocomp, that introduced elaborate formatting

In Europe, the company of Berthold had no experience in developing hot-metal typesetting equipment, but being one of the largest German type foundries, they applied themselves to the transference. Berthold successfully developed its Diatype (1960), Diatronic (1967), and ADS (1977) machines, which led the European high-end typesetting market for decades.

1970s

Expansion of technology to small users

Compugraphic produced phototypesetting machines in the 1970s that made it economically feasible for small publications to set their own type with professional quality. One model, the Compugraphic Compuwriter, used a filmstrip wrapped around a drum that rotated at several hundred revolutions per minute. The filmstrip contained two fonts (a Roman and a bold or a Roman and an italic) in one point size. To get different sized fonts, the typesetter loaded a different font strip or used a 2x magnifying lens built into the machine, which doubled the size of font. The CompuWriter II automated the lens switch and let the operator use multiple settings. Other manufacturers of photo compositing machines included Alphatype, Varityper, Mergenthaler, Autologic, Berthold, Dymo, Harris (formerly Linotype's competitor "Intertype"), Monotype, Star/Photon, Graphic Systems Inc., Hell AG, MGD Graphic Systems, and American Type Founders.

Released in 1975, the Compuwriter IV held two filmstrips, each holding four fonts. (Usually a Roman, italic, bold, and bold italic font). It also had a lens turret which had eight lenses giving different point sizes from the font, generally 8 or 12 sizes, depending on the model. Low-end models offered sizes from 6 to 36 point, while the high-end models went to 72 point. The Compugraphic EditWriter series took the Compuwriter IV configuration and added floppy disk storage on an 8-inch, 320K disk. This allowed the typesetter to make changes and corrections without rekeying. A CRT screen let the user view typesetting codes and text.

Because early generations of phototypesetters couldn't change text size and font easily, many composing rooms and print shops had special machines designed to set display type or headlines. One such model was the PhotoTypositor, manufactured by Visual Graphics Corporation, which let the user position each letter visually and thus retain complete control over kerning. Compugraphic's model 7200 used the "strobe-through-a-filmstrip-through-a-lens" technology to expose letters and characters onto a thin strip of phototypesetting paper that was then developed by a photo-processor.

Some later phototypesetters utilized a CRT to project the image of letters onto the photographic paper. This created a sharper image, added some flexibility in manipulating the type, and created the ability to offer a continuous range of point sizes by eliminating film media and lenses. The Compugraphic MCS (Modular Composition System) with the 8400 typesetter is an example of a CRT phototypesetter. This machine loaded digital fonts into memory from an 8-inch floppy. Additionally, the 8400 was able to set type in point sizes between 5 and 120 point in 1/2-point increments. It was extremely fast and was one of the first output systems (the other was also a Compugraphic machine, the 8600) that was able to create camera-ready output with a maximum width of 12 inches.

As phototypesetting machines matured as a technology in the 1970s, more efficient methods were found for creating and subsequently editing text intended for the printed page. Previously, "hot metal" typesetting equipment had incorporated a built in keyboard, such that the machine operator would create both the original text and the medium (lead type slugs) that would create the printed page. Subsequent editing of this copy required that the entire process be repeated. The operator would re-keyboard some or all of the original text, incorporating the corrections and new material into the original draft.

CRT based editing terminals, which could work compatibly with a variety of phototypesetting machines, were a major technical innovation in this regard. Keyboarding the original text on a CRT screen, with easy-to-use editing commands, was faster than keyboarding on a Linotype machine. Storing the text magnetically for easy retrieval and subsequent editing also saved time.

An early developer of CRT-based editing terminals for photocomposition machines was Omnitext of Ann Arbor, Michigan. These CRT phototypesetting terminals were sold under the Singer brand name during the 1970s.

Problems with early phototypesetters

Early machines had no text storage capability; some machines only displayed 32 characters in uppercase on a small LED screen and spellchecking was not available. Proofing typeset galleys was an important step after developing the photo paper. Corrections could be made by typesetting a word or line of type and by waxing the back of the galleys, and corrections could be cut out with an X-Acto knife and pasted on top of any mistakes.

Since most early phototypesetting machines could only create one column of type, long galleys of type were pasted onto layout boards in order to create a full page of text for magazines and newsletters. Paste-up artists played an important role in creating production art. Later phototypesetters had multiple column features that allowed the typesetter to save paste-up time.

Early electronic typesetting programmes were designed to drive phototypesetters, most notably the Graphic Systems CAT phototypesetter that troff was designed to provide input for. Though such programmes still exist, their output is no longer targeted at any specific form of hardware. Some companies, such as TeleTypesetting Co. created software and hardware interfaces between personal computers like the Apple II and IBM PS/2 and phototypesetting machines which provided computers equipped with it the capability to connect to phototypesetting machines. With the start of desktop publishing software, Trout Computing in California introduced VepSet, which allowed Xerox Ventura Publisherto be used as a front end and wrote a Compugraphic MCS disk with typesetting codes to reproduce the page layout.

FLEXOGRAPHY

Flexography (often abbreviated to flexo) is a form of printing process which utilizes a flexible relief plate. It is essentially a modern version of letterpress which can be used for printing on almost any type of substrate, including plastic, metallic films, cellophane, and paper. It is widely used for printing on the non-porous substrates required for various types of food packaging (it is also well suited for printing large areas of solid colour).

HISTORY

In 1890, the first such patented press was built in Liverpool, England by Bibby, Baron and Sons. The water-based ink smeared easily, leading the device to be known as "Bibby's Folly". In the early 1900s, other European presses using rubber printing plates and aniline oil-based ink were developed. This led to the process being called "aniline printing". By the 1920s, most presses were made in Germany, where the process was called "gummidruck," or rubber printing. In modern-day Germany, they continue to call the process "gummidruck."

During the early part of the 20th century, the technique was used extensively in food packaging in the United States. However, in the 1940s, theFood and Drug Administration classified aniline dyes as unsuitable for food packaging. Printing sales plummeted. Individual firms tried using new names for the process, such as "Lustro Printing" and "Transglo Printing," but met with limited success. Even after the Food and Drug Administration approved the aniline process in 1949 using new, safe inks, sales continued to decline as some food manufacturers still refused to consider aniline printing. Worried about the image of the industry, packaging representatives decided the process needed to be renamed.

In 1951 Franklin Moss, then the president of the Mosstype Corporation, conducted a poll among the readers of his journal *The Mosstyper* to submit new names for the printing process. Over 200 names were submitted, and a subcommittee of the Packaging Institute's Printed Packaging Committee narrowed the selection to three possibilities: "permatone process", "rotopake process", and "flexographic process". Postal ballots from readers of *The Mosstyper* overwhelmingly chose the last of these, and "flexographic process" was chosen.

Evolution

Originally, flexographic printing was rudimentary in quality. Labels requiring high quality have generally been printed using the offset process until recently. Since 1990, great advances have been made to the quality of flexographic printing presses, printing plates and printing inks.

The greatest advances in flexographic printing have been in the area of photopolymer printing plates, including improvements to the plate material and the method of plate creation.

Digital direct to plate systems have been a good improvement in the industry recently. Companies like Asahi Photoproducts, AV Flexologic, Dupont, MacDermid, Kodak and Eskohave pioneered the latest technologies, with advances in fast washout and the latest screening technology.

Laser-etched ceramic anilox rolls also play a part in the improvement of print quality. Full-colour picture printing is now possible, and some of the finer presses available today, in combination with a skilled operator, allow quality that rivals the lithographic process. One ongoing improvement has been the increasing ability to reproduce highlight tonal values, thereby providing a workaround for the very high dot gain associated with flexographic printing.

PROCESS OVERVIEW

Platemaking

The first method of plate development uses light-sensitive polymer. A film negative is placed over the plate, which is exposed to ultra-violet light. The polymer hardens where light passes through the film. The remaining polymer has the consistency of chewed gum. It is washed away in a tank of either water or solvent. Brushes scrub the plate to facilitate the "washout" process. The process can differ depending on whether solid sheets of photopolymer or liquid photopolymer are used, but the principle is still the same. The plate to be washed out is fixed in the orbital washout unit on a sticky base plate. The plate is washed out in a mixture of water and 1 per cent dishwasher soap, at a temperature of approximately 40°C. The unit is equipped with a dual membrane filter. With this the environmental burdening is kept to an absolute minimum. The membrane unit separates photopolymer from the washout water. After addition of absorb gelatine for example, the photopolymer residue can be disposed of as standard solid waste together with household refuse. The recycled water is re-used without adding any detergent.

The second method used a computer-guided laser to etch the image onto the printing plate. Such a direct laser engraving process is called digital platemaking. Companies such as AV Flexologic, Esko, Polymount and Screen from The Netherlands are market leaders in manufacturing this type of equipment.

The third method is to go through a molding process. The first step is to create a metal plate out of the negative of our initial image through an exposition process (followed by an acid bath). In the early days the metal used was zinc, leading to the name 'zincos'. Later magnesium was used.This metal plate in relief is then used in the second step to create the mold that could be in bakelite board or even glass or plastic, through a first molding process. Once cooled, this master mold will press the rubber or plastic compound (under both controlled temperature and pressure) through a second molding process to create the printing plate.

Mounting

For every colour to be printed, a plate is made and eventually put on a cylinder which is placed in the printing press. To make a complete picture, regardless of printing on flexible film or corrugated paper, the image transferred from each plate has to register exactly with the images transferred from the other colours. To ensure an accurate picture is made, mounting marks are made on the flexographic plates. These mounting marks can be microdots (down to 0.3 mm) and/or crosses. Special machinery is made for mounting these plates on the printing cylinders to maintain registration.

Printing

A flexographic print is made by creating a positive mirrored master of the required image as a 3D relief in a rubber or polymer material. Flexographic plates can be created with analog and digital platemaking processes. The image areas are raised above the non- image areas on the rubber or polymer plate. The ink is transferred from the ink roll which is partially immersed in the ink tank. Then it transfers to the anilox or ceramic roll (or meter roll) whose texture holds a specific amount of ink since it is covered with thousands of small wells or cups that enable it to meter ink to the printing plate in a uniform thickness evenly and quickly (the number of cells per linear inch can vary according to the type of print job and the quality required). To avoid getting a final product with a smudgy or lumpy look, it must be ensured that the amount of ink on the printing plate is not excessive. This is achieved by using a scraper, called a doctor blade. The doctor blade removes excess ink from the anilox roller before inking the printing plate. The substrate is finally sandwiched between the plate and the impression cylinder to transfer the image. The sheet is then fed through a dryer, which allows the inks to dry before the surface is touched again. If a UV-curing ink is used, the sheet does not have to be dried, but the ink is cured by UV rays instead.

Basic parts of the press

- *Unwind and infeed section* – The roll of stock must be held under control so the web can unwind as needed.
- *Printing section* – Single colour station including the fountain, anilox, plate and impression rolls.
- *Drying station* – High velocity heated air, specially formulated inks and an after-dryer can be used.
- *Outfeed and rewind section* – Similar to the unwind segment, keeps web tension controlled.

OPERATION

Operational overview

Fountain roller

The fountain roller transfers the ink that is located in the ink pan to the second roller, which is the anilox roller. In Modern Flexo printing this is called a Meter or "metering" roller.

Anilox roller

This is what makes flexography unique. The anilox roller meters the predetermined ink that is transferred for uniform thickness. It has engraved cells that carry a certain capacity of inks that can only be seen with a microscope. These rollers are responsible to transfer the inks to the flexible-plates that are already mounted on the Plate Cylinders.

Doctor Blade (optional)

The doctor blade scrapes the anilox roll to insure that the predetermined ink amount delivered is only what is contained within the engraved cells. Doctor blades have predominantly been made of steel but advanced doctor blades are now made of polymer materials. With several different types of beveled edges.

Plate cylinder

The plate cylinder holds the printing plate, which is soft flexible rubber-like material. Tape, magnets, tension straps and/or ratchets hold the printing plate against the cylinder.

Impression Cylinder (optional)

The impression cylinder applies pressure to the plate cylinder, where the image is transferred to the substrate. This impression cylinder or " print Anvil" is NOT optional. The Plate Cylinder NEEDS something to apply pressure(Impression) to.

Flexographic printing inks

The nature and demands of the printing process and the application of the printed product determine the fundamental properties required of flexographic inks. Measuring the physical properties of inks and understanding how these are affected by the choice of ingredients is a large part of ink technology. Formulation of inks requires a detailed knowledge of the physical and chemical properties of the raw materials composing the inks, and how these ingredients affect or react with each other as well as with the environment. Flexographic printing inks are primarily formulated to remain compatible with the wide variety of substrates used in the process. Each formulation component individually fulfills a special function and the proportion and composition will vary according to the substrate.

There are five types of inks that can be used in flexography: solvent-based inks, water-based inks, electron beam (EB) curing inks, ultraviolet (UV) curing inks and two-part chemically-curing inks (usually based on polyurethane isocyanate reactions), although these are uncommon at the moment. Water based flexo inks with particle sizes below 5 μm may cause problems when deinking recycled paper.

Ink controls

The ink is controlled in the flexographic printing process by the inking unit. The inking unit can be either of fountain roll system or doctor blade system. The fountain roll system is a simple old system yet if there is too much or too little ink this system would likely not control in a good way. The doctor blade inside the anilox/ceramic roller uses cell geometry and distribution. These blades insure that the cells are filled with enough ink.

PRESSES

Stack press

Colour stations stack up vertically, which makes it easy to access. This press is able to print on both sides of the substrate.

Central Impression press

All colour stations are located in a circle around the impression cylinder. This press can only print on one side. Advantage: excellent registry

In-line press

Colour stations are placed horizontally. This press prints on both sides, via a turnbar. Advantages: Can print on heavier substrates, such as corrugated boards.

APPLICATIONS

Flexo has an advantage over lithography in that it can use a wider range of inks, water based rather than oil based inks, and is good at printing on a variety of different materials like plastic, foil, acetate film, brown paper, and other materials used in packaging. Typical products printed using flexography include brown corrugated boxes, flexible packaging including retail and shopping bags, food and hygiene bags and sacks, milk and beverage cartons, flexible plastics, self-adhesive labels, disposable cups and containers, envelopes and wallpaper. In recent years there has also been a move towards laminates, where two or more materials are bonded together to produce new material with different properties than either of the originals. A number of newspapers now eschew the more common offset lithography process in favour of flexo. Flexographic inks, like those used in gravure and unlike those used in lithography, generally have a low viscosity. This enables faster drying and, as a result, faster production, which results in lower costs.

Printing press speeds of up to 600 meters per minute (2000 feet per minute) are achievable now with modern technology high-end printers. Flexo printing is widely used in theconverting industry for printing plastic materials for packaging and other end uses. For maximum efficiency, the flexo presses produce large rolls of material that are then slit down to their finished size on slitting machines.

Terms

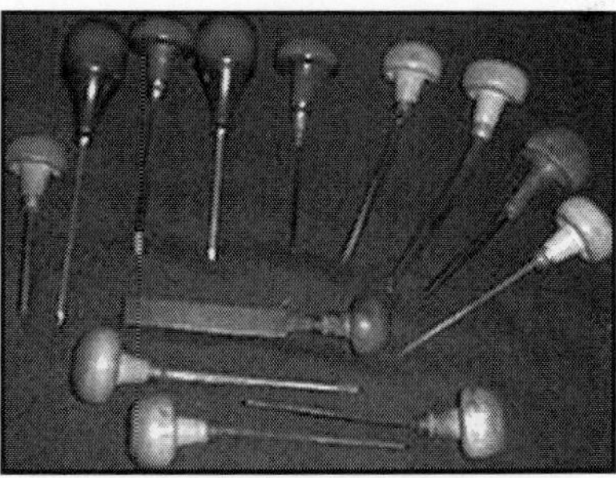

Fig. An assortment of hand engraving tools

Other terms often used for printed engravings are copper engraving, copper-plate engraving or *line engraving*. Steel engraving is the same technique, on steel or steel-faced plates, and was mostly used for banknotes, illustrations for books, magazines and reproductive prints, letterheads and similar uses from about 1790 to the early 20th century, when the technique became less popular, except for banknotes and other forms of security printing. Especially in the past, "engraving" was often used very loosely to cover several printmaking techniques, so that many so-called engravings were in fact produced by totally different techniques, such as etching ormezzotint. "Hand engraving" is a term sometimes used for engraving objects other than printing plates, to inscribe or decorate jewellery, firearms, trophies, knives and other fine metal goods. Traditional engravings in printmaking are also "hand engraved", using just the same techniques to make the lines in the plate.

Process

Fig. At an engravers workshop: Miniature engraving on a *Louis George*watch movement: Smallest engraving of the royal Prussian eagle on a watch movement. It takes about 100 passes to create the figure.

Each graver is different and has its own use. Engravers use a hardened steel tool called a burin, or graver, to cut the design into the surface, most traditionally a copper plate. However, modern hand engraving artists use burins or gravers to cut a variety of metals such as silver, nickel, steel, brass, gold, titanium, and more, in applications from weaponry to jewellery to motorcycles to found objects. Modern professional engravers can engrave with a resolution of up to 40 lines per mm in high grade work creating game scenes and scrollwork. Dies used in mass production of molded parts are sometimes hand engraved to add special touches or certain information such as part numbers.

In addition to hand engraving, there are engraving machines that require less human finesse and are not directly controlled by hand. They are usually used for lettering, using a pantographic system. There are versions for the insides of rings and also the outsides of larger pieces. Such machines are commonly used for inscriptions on rings, lockets and presentation pieces.

Tools and gravers or burins

Gravers come in a variety of shapes and sizes that yield different line types. The burin produces a unique and recognizable quality of line that is characterized by its steady, deliberate appearance and clean edges. The angle tint tool has a slightly curved tip that is commonly used in printmaking.

Florentine liners are flat-bottomed tools with multiple lines incised into them, used to do fill work on larger areas or to create uniform shade lines that are fast to execute. Ring gravers are made with particular shapes that are used by jewelry engravers in order to cut inscriptions inside rings. Flat gravers are used for fill work on letters, as well as "wriggle" cuts on most musical instrument engraving work, remove background, or create bright cuts.

Knife gravers are for line engraving and very deep cuts. Round gravers, and flat gravers with a radius, are commonly used on silver to create bright cuts (also called bright-cut engraving), as well as other hard-to-cut metals such as nickel and steel. Square or V-point gravers are typically square or elongated diamond-shaped and used for cutting straight lines. V-point can be anywhere from 60 to 130 degrees, depending on purpose and effect. These gravers have very small cutting points. Other tools such as mezzotint rockers, roulets and burnishers are used for texturing effects. Burnishing tools can also be used for certain stone setting techniques.

Musical instrument engraving on American-made brass instruments flourished in the 1920s and utilizes a specialized engraving technique where a flat graver is "walked" across the surface of the instrument to make zig-zag lines and patterns. The method for "walking" the graver may also be referred to as "wriggle" or "wiggle" cuts. This technique is necessary due to the thinness of metal used to make musical instruments versus firearms or jewelry. Wriggle cuts are commonly found on silver Western jewelry and other Western metal work.

Tool geometry

Tool geometry is extremely important for accuracy in hand engraving. When sharpened for most applications, a graver has a "face", which is the top of the graver, and a "heel", which is the bottom of the graver; not all tools or application require a heel.

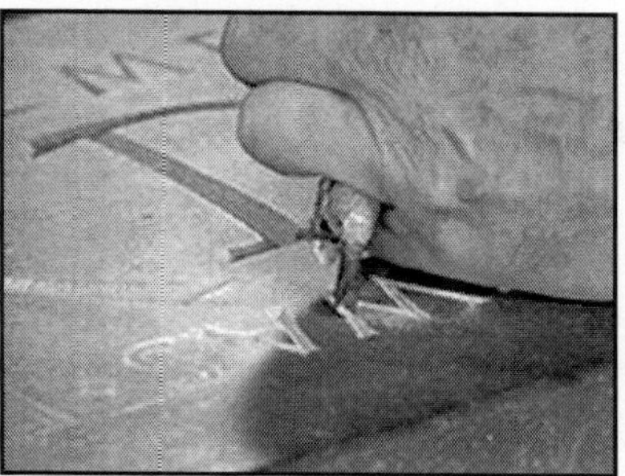

Fig. Stone engraving

These two surfaces meet to form a point that cuts the metal. The geometry and length of the heel helps to guide the graver smoothly as it cuts the surface of the metal. When the tool's point breaks or chips, even on a microscopic level, the graver can become hard to control and produces unexpected results. Modern innovations have brought about new types of carbide that resist chipping and breakage, which hold a very sharp point longer between resharpening than traditional metal tools.

Tool sharpening

Sharpening a graver or burin requires either a sharpening stone or wheel. Harder carbide and steel gravers require diamond-grade sharpening wheels; these gravers can be polished to a mirror finish using a ceramic or cast iron lap, which is essential in creating bright cuts. Several low-speed, reversible sharpening system made specifically for hand engravers are available that reduce sharpening time. Fixtures that secure the tool in place at certain angles and geometries are also available to take the guesswork from sharpening to produce accurate points. Very few master engravers exist today who rely solely on "feel" and muscle memory to sharpen tools. These master engravers typically worked for many years as an apprentice, most often learning techniques decades before modern machinery was available for hand engravers. These engravers typically trained in such countries as Italy and Belgium, where hand engraving has a rich and long heritage of masters.

Artwork design

Design or artwork is generally prepared in advance, although some professional and highly experienced hand engravers are able to draw out minimal outlines either on paper or directly on the metal surface just prior to engraving. The work to be engraved may be lightly scribed on the surface with a sharp point, laser marked, drawn with a fine permanent marker (removable with acetone) or pencil, transferred using various chemicals in conjunction with inkjet or laser printouts, or stippled. Engraving artists may rely on hand drawing skills, copyright-free designs and images, computer-generated artwork, or common design elements when creating artwork.

Handpieces

Originally, handpieces varied little in design as the common use was to push with the handle placed firmly in the center of the palm. With modern pneumatic engraving systems, handpieces are designed and created in a variety of shapes and power ranges. Handpieces are made using various methods and materials. Knobs may be handmade from wood, molded and engineered from plastic, or machine-made from brass, steel, or other metals. The most widely known hand engraving tool maker, GRS Tools in Kansas is an American-owned and operated company that manufacture handpieces as well as many other tools for various applications in metal engraving.

Cutting the surface

The actual engraving is traditionally done by a combination of pressure and manipulating the workpiece. The traditional "hand push" process is still practiced today, but modern technology has brought various mechanically assisted engraving systems. Most pneumatic engraving systems require an air source that drives air through a hose into a handpiece, which resembles a traditional engraving handle in many cases, that powers a mechanism (usually a piston). The air is actuated by either a foot control (like a gas pedal or sewing machine) or newer palm/ hand control. This mechanism replaces either the "hand push" effort or the effects of a hammer. The internal mechanisms move at speeds up to 15,000 strokes per minute, thereby greatly reducing the effort needed in traditional hand engraving. These types of pneumatic systems are used for power assistance only and do not guide or control the engraving artist. One of the major benefits of using a pneumatic system for hand engraving is the reduction of fatigue and decrease in time spent working.

Hand engraving artists today employ a combination of hand push, pneumatic, rotary, or hammer and chisel methods. Hand push is still commonly used by modern hand engraving artists who create "bulino" style work, which is highly detailed and delicate, fine work; a great majority, if not all, traditional printmakers today rely solely upon hand push methods. Pneumatic systems greatly reduce the effort required for removing large amounts of metal, such as in deep relief engraving or Western bright cut techniques.

Finishing

Finishing the work is often necessary when working in metal that may rust or where a coloured finish is desirable, such as a firearm. A variety of spray lacquers and finishing techniques exist to seal and protect the work from exposure to the elements and time. Finishing also may include lightly sanding the surface to remove small chips of metal called "burs" that are very sharp and unsightly. Some engravers prefer high contrast to the work or design, using black paints or inks to darken removed (and lower) areas of exposed metal. The excess paint or ink is wiped away and allowed to dry before lacquering or sealing, which may or may not be desired by the artist.

Modern hand engraving

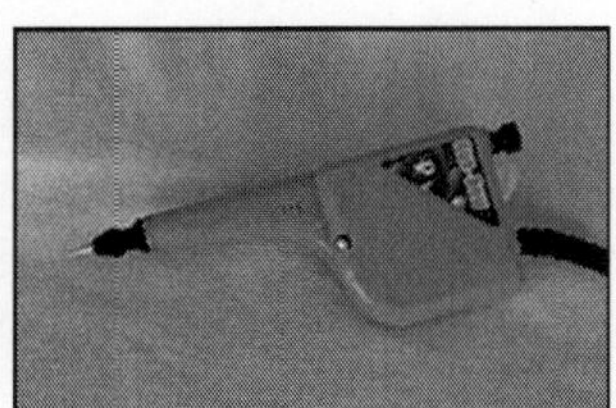

Fig. Hand Engraving Tool Example

Because of the high level of microscopic detail that can be achieved by a master engraver, counterfeiting of engraved designs is well-nigh impossible, and modern banknotes are almost always engraved, as are plates for printing money, checks, bonds and other security-sensitive papers. The engraving is so fine that a normal printer cannot recreate the detail of hand engraved images, nor can it be scanned. In the U.S. Bureau of Engraving and Printing, more than one hand engraver will work on the same plate, making it nearly impossible for one person to duplicate all the engraving on a particular banknote or document.

The modern discipline of hand engraving, as it is called in a metalworking context, survives largely in a few specialized fields. The highest levels of the art are found on firearms and other metal weaponry, jewellery, and musical instruments.

In most commercial markets today, hand engraving has been replaced with milling using CNC engraving or milling machines. Still, there are certain applications where use of hand engraving tools cannot be replaced.

Machine engraving

In some instances, images or designs can be transferred to metal surfaces via mechanical process. One such process is roll stamping or roller-die engraving. In this process, a hardened image die is pressed against the destination surface using extreme pressure to impart the image. In the 1800s pistol cylinders were often decorated via this process to impart a continuous scene around its surface.

Computer-aided machine engraving

Engraving machines such as the K500 (packaging) or K6 (publication) by Hell Gravure Systems use a diamond stylus to cut cells. Each cell creates one printing dot later in the process. A K6 can have up to 18 engraving heads each cutting 8.000 cells per second to an accuracy of.1 μm and below. They are fully computer-controlled and the whole process of cylinder-making is fully automated.

It is now common place for retail stores (mostly jewellery, silverware or award stores) to have a small computer controlled engrave on site. This enables them to personalise the products they sell. Retail engraving machines tend to be focused around ease of use for the operator and the ability to do a wide variety of items including flat metal plates, jewelry of different shapes and sizes, as well as cylindrical items such as mugs and tankards. They will typically be equipped with a computer dedicated to graphic design that will enable the operator to easily design a text or picture graphic which the software will translate into digital signals telling the engraver machine what to do. Unlike industrial engravers, retail machines are smaller and only use one diamond head. This is interchangeable so the operator can use differently shaped diamonds for different finishing effects. They will typically be able to do a variety of metals and plastics. Glass and crystal engraving is possible, but the brittle nature of the material makes the process more time consuming.

Retail engravers mainly use two different processes. The first and most common 'Diamond Drag' pushes the diamond cutter through the surface of the material and then pulls to create scratches. These direction and depth are controlled by the computer input. The second is 'Spindle Cutter'. This is similar to Diamond Drag, but the engraving head is shaped in a flat V shape, with a small diamond and the base. The machine uses an electronic spindle to quickly rotate the head as it pushes it into the material, then pulls it along whilst it continues to spin. This creates a much bolder impression than diamond drag. It is used mainly for brass plaques and pet tags. With state-of-the-art machinery it is easy to have a simple, single item complete in under ten minutes. The engraving process with diamonds is state-of-the-art since the 1960s. Today laser engraving machines are in development but still mechanical cutting has proven its strength in economical terms and quality. More than 4,000 engravers make approx. 8 Mio printing cylinders worldwide per year.

A renaissance in hand-engraving

During the mid-1900s, a renaissance in hand-engraving began to take place. With the inventions of pneumatic hand-engraving systems that aided hand-engravers, the art and techniques of hand-engraving became more accessible. In the years past, hand-engraving was an extremely secretive art where masters would carefully and rarely choose apprentices to pass on the trade. Even into the 1970s, many engravers were reluctant to share trade secrets and kept methods closely guarded.

Music engraving

The first music printed from engraved plates dates from 1446 and most printed music was produced through engraving from roughly 1700–1860. From 1860–1990 most printed music was produced through a combination of engraved master plates reproduced through offset lithography.

In music printing, engraving is an intaglio technique. The first comprehensive account is given by Mme Delusse in her article "Gravure en lettres, en géographie et en musique" in Diderot's Encyclopaedia. The technique involved a five-pointed raster to score staff lines, various punches in the shapes of notes and standard musical symbols, and various burins and scorers for lines and slurs. For correction, the plate was held on a bench by callipers, hit with a dot punch on the opposite side, and burnished to remove any signs of the defective work. The process involved intensive pre-planning of the layout, and many manuscript scores with engraver's planning marks survive from the 18th and 19th centuries.

By 1837 pewter had replaced copper as a medium, and Berthiaud gives an account with an entire chapter devoted to music (*Novel manuel complet de l'imprimeur en taille douce*, 1837). Printing from such plates required a separate inking to be carried out cold, and the printing press used less pressure. Generally, four pages of music were engraved on a single plate. Because music engraving houses trained engravers through years of apprenticeship, very little is known about the practice. Fewer than one dozen sets of tools survive in libraries and museums. By 1900 music engravers were established in several hundred cities in the world, but the art of storing plates was usually concentrated with publishers. Extensive bombing of Leipzig in 1944, the home of most German engraving and printing firms, destroyed roughly half the world's engraved music plates.

APPLICATIONS TODAY

Examples of contemporary uses for engraving include:

- Creating text on the inside of engagement- and wedding rings to include text such as the name of the partner.
- Representing the logo of the manufacturing company and country of production on items such as eating utensils, such as forks,knives, and spoons.

Another application of modern engraving is found in the printing industry. There, every day thousands of pages are mechanically engraved onto rotogravure cylinders, typically a steel base with a copper layer of about 0.1 mm in which the image is transferred. After engraving the image is protected with an approximately 6 μm chrome layer. Using this process the image will survive for over a million copies in high speed printing presses. Engraving machines such as GUN BOW (one of the leading engraving brands) are the best examples of hand engraving tools, although this type of machine is typically not used for fine hand engraving.

CREATING TONE

In traditional engraving, which is a purely linear medium, the impression of half-tones was created by making many very thin parallel lines, a technique called hatching. When two sets of parallel-line *hatchings* intersected each other for higher density, the resulting pattern was known as *cross-hatching*. Patterns of dots were also used in a technique called stippling, first used around 1505 by Giulio Campagnola. Claude Mellan was one of many 17th-century engravers with a very well-developed technique of using parallel lines of varying thickness (known as the "swelling line") to give subtle effects of tone. One famous example is his *Sudarium of Saint Veronica* (1649), an engraving of the face of Jesus made from a single spiraling line that starts at the tip of Jesus's nose.

BIBLICAL REFERENCES

The earliest allusion to engraving in the Bible may be the reference to Judah's seal ring (Ge 38:18), followed by (Ex 39.30). Engraving was commonly done with pointed tools of iron or even with diamond points. (Jer 17:1).

Each of the two onyx stones on the shoulder-pieces of the high priest's ephod was engraved with the names of six different tribes oflsrael, and each of the 12 precious stones that adorned his breastpiece was engraved with the name of one of the tribes. The holy sign of dedication, the shining gold plate on the high priest's turban, was engraved with the words: "Holiness belongs to Adonai." Bezalel, along with Oholiab, was qualified to do this specialized engraving work as well as to train others.

THERMOGRAPHIC PRINTING

Thermographic printing refers to two types of printing, both of which rely on heat to create the letters or images on a sheet of paper.

The simplest type is where the paper has been coated with a material that changes colour on heating. This is called thermal printing and was used in older model fax machines and is used in most shop till receipt printers. This is called direct thermal.

More complex is thermal transfer printing that melts print off a ribbon and onto the sheet of paper.

THERMOGRAPHY AS RAISED PRINT PROCESS

Thermography is also the name of a post print process that is achieved today using traditional printing methods coupled with thermography machines. Thermography machines consist of three sections with a through conveyor.

The first section applies thermographic/embossing powder, made from plastic resins, to the substrate (normally paper). The areas selected for raised printing are printed with slow-drying inks that do not contain dryers or hardeners so that they remain wet during the application of powder. This ink is dried and hardened later during the heating process. The second section of the process is a vacuum system that removes excess powder from uninked areas of the substrate.

The third section of the process conveys the product through a radiant oven where it is exposed to temperatures of 900 to 1300 degrees Fahrenheit. The heating process takes on the order of 2.5 to 3 seconds. The substrate (usually paper) has a peak in IR absorption at the wavelength used. Through conduction from the paper, the powder temperature rapidly increases and starts melting. When the process is correctly adjusted, the center of the largest filmed areas reach sufficient quality level as the product exits the heater. The melted ink then solidifies as the product cools.

This process is sometimes produced using manual powdering. The substrate with the wet ink is dipped into the powdered polymer. The sheet is then tilted back and forth, rolling the powder across the image. The excess powder is then removed by raising the substrate to a vertical position and lightly tapping the back side. The powdered sheet is then fed into a radiant heating system (as above) at a speed that achieves a good-quality melted film. In the case of craft applications, the powder is melted using a heatgun that blows hot air.

It is commonly used on wedding invitations, letterheads, business cards, greetings cards, gift wrap, packaging and can also be used to print braille text. It is sometimes used indiploma printing as an attractive alternative to the more expensive engraving option.

WOODBLOCK PRINTING

Fig. Young monks printing Buddhist scriptures using the rubbing technique,Sera Monastery in Tibet

Woodblock printing is a technique for printing text, images or patterns used widely throughout East Asia and originating in China in antiquity as a method of printing on textiles and later paper. As a method of printing on cloth, the earliest surviving examples fromChina date to before 220, and woodblock printing remained the most common East Asian method of printing books and other texts, as well as images, until the 19th century. *Ukiyo-e* is the best known type of Japanese woodblock art print. Most European uses of the technique for printing images on paper are covered by the art term woodcut, except for the block-books produced mainly in the 15th century.

SEALS AND STAMPS

Prior to the invention of woodblock printing, seals and stamps were used for making impressions. The oldest of these seals come from Mesopotamia and Egypt. The use of round "cylinder seals" for rolling an impress onto clay tablets goes back to early Mesopotamian civilization before 3000 BC, where they are the most common works of art to survive, and feature complex and beautiful images. A few much larger brick (*e.g.* 13×13 cm) stamps for marking clay bricks survive from Akkad from around 2270 BC. There are also Roman lead pipe inscriptions of some length that were stamped, and amulet MS 5236 may be a unique surviving gold foil sheet stamped with an amulet text in the 6th century BC. However none of these used ink, which is necessary for printing (on a proper definition), but stamped marks into relatively soft materials. In both China and Egypt, the use of small stamps for seals preceded the use of larger blocks. In Europe and India, the printing of cloth certainly preceded the printing of paper or papyrus; this was probably also the case in China. The process is essentially the same—in Europe special presentation impressions of prints were often printed on silk until at least the 17th century.

TECHNIQUE

The wood block is carefully prepared as a relief pattern, which means the areas to show 'white' are cut away with a knife, chisel, or sandpaper leaving the characters or image to show in 'black' at the original surface level. The block was cut along the grain of the wood. It is necessary only to ink the block and bring it into firm and even contact with the paper or cloth to achieve an acceptable print. The content would of course print "in reverse" or mirror-image, a further complication when text was involved. The art of carving the woodcut is technically known as *xylography*, though the term is rarely used in English. For colour printing, multiple blocks are used, each for one colour, although overprinting two colours may produce further colours on the print. Multiple colours can be printed by keying the paper to a frame around the woodblocks. There are three methods of printing to consider:

Stamping

Used for many fabrics, and most early European woodcuts (1400–40). These items were printed by putting paper or fabric on a table or a flat surface with the block on top, and pressing, or hammering, the back of the block.

Rubbing

Apparently the most common for Far Eastern printing. Used for European woodcuts and block-books later in the 15th century, and very widely for cloth.

The block is placed face side up on a table, with the paper or fabric on top. The back of the paper or fabric is rubbed with a "hard pad, a flat piece of wood, a burnisher, or a leather frotton".

Printing in a press

"Presses" only seem to have been used in Asia in relatively recent times. Simple weighted presses may have been used in Europe, but firm evidence is lacking. Later, printing-presses were used (from about 1480). A deceased Abbess of Mechelen in Flanders in 1465 had "unum instrumentum ad imprintendum scripturas et ymagines... cum 14 aliis lapideis printis" ("an instrument for printing texts and pictures... with 14 stones for printing") which is probably too early to be a Gutenberg-type printing press in that location.

In addition, *jia xie* is a method for dyeing textiles (usually silk) using wood blocks invented in the 5th-6th centuries in China. An upper and a lower block is made, with carved out compartments opening to the back, fitted with plugs. The cloth, usually folded a number of times, is inserted and clamped between the two blocks. By unplugging the different compartments and filling them with dyes of different colours, a multi-coloured pattern can be printed over quite a large area of folded cloth. The method is not strictly printing however, as the pattern is not caused by pressure against the block.

HISTORY OF WOODBLOCK PRINTING

Origins in Asia

The earliest woodblock printed fragments to survive are from China and are of silk printed with flowers in three colours from the Han Dynasty (before AD 220). It is clear that woodblock printing developed in Asia several centuries before Europe. The Chinese were the first to use the process to print solid text, and equally that, much later, in Europe the printing of images on cloth developed into the printing of images on paper (woodcuts). It is also now established that the use in Europe of the same process to print substantial amounts of text together with images in block-books only came after the development of movable type in the 1450s.

In China, an alternative to woodblock printing was a system of reprography since the Han Dynasty using carved stone steles to reproduce pages of text. The three necessary components for woodblock printing are the wood block, which carries the design cut in relief; dye or ink, which had been widely used in the ancient world; and either cloth or paper, which was first developed in China, around the 3rd century BC or 2nd century BC. Woodblock printing onpapyrus seems never to have been practised, although it would be possible.

A few specimen of wood block printing, possibly called *tarsh* in Arabic, have been excavated from a 10th-century context in Arabic Egypt. They were mostly used for prayers and amulets. The technique may be spread from China or an independent invention, but had very little impact and virtually disappeared at the end of the 14th century. In India the main importance of the technique has always been as a method of printing textiles, which has been a large industry since at least the 10th century. Large quantities of printed Indian silk and cotton were exported to Europe throughout the Modern Period.

Because Chinese has a character set running into the thousands, woodblock printing suits it better than movable type to the extent that characters only need to be created as they occur in the text. Although the Chinese had invented a form of movable type with baked clay in the 11th century, and metal movable type was invented in Korea in the 13th century, woodblocks continued to be preferred owing to the formidable challenges of typesetting Chinese text with its 40,000 or more characters. Also, the objective of printing in the East may have been more focused on standardization of ritual text (such as the Buddhist canon Tripitaka, requiring 80,000 woodblocks), and the purity of validated woodblocks could be maintained for centuries. When there was a need for the reproduction of a text, the original block could simply be brought out again, while moveable type necessitated error-prone composition of distinct "editions".

In China, Korea, and Japan, the state involved itself in printing at a relatively early stage; initially only the government had the resources to finance the carving of the blocks for long works. The difference between East Asian woodblock printing and the Western printing press had major implications for the development of book culture and book markets in East Asia and Europe.

Early printed books in China and Korea

Woodblock printing in China is strongly associated with Buddhism, which encouraged the spread of charms and sutras. In the Tang Dynasty, a Chinese writer named Fenzhi first mentioned in his book "Yuan Xian San Ji" that the woodblock was used to print Buddhist scriptures during the Zhenguan years (AD 627~649).

An early example of woodblock printing on paper was discovered in 1974 in an excavation in Xi'an (the capital of Tang-Dynasty China, then called Chang'an), Shaanxi, China, whereby individual sheets of paper were pressed into wooden blocks with the text and illustrations carved into them. It is a *dharani* sutra printed on hemp paper and dated to 650 to 670 AD, during the Tang Dynasty (618–907). Another printed document dating to the early half of the Chinese Tang Dynasty has also been found, the *Saddharma pundarika*sutra printed from 690 to 699.

The oldest existing print done with wood-blocks is the Mugujeonggwang great Dharani sutra that is dated between AD 704 and 751. It was found at Bulguksa, South Korea in 1966. Its Buddhisttext was printed on a 8 cm × 630 cm (3.1 in × 248.0 in) mulberry paper scroll in the early Korean Kingdom of Unified Silla. Another version of the Dharani sutra, printed in Japan around AD

770, is also frequently cited as an example of early printing. One million copies of the sutra, along with other prayers, were ordered to be produced by Empress Shôtoku. As each copy was then stored in a tiny wooden pagoda, the copies are together known as the *Hyakumantô Darani*.

The world's earliest dated (AD 868) printed book is a Chinese scroll about sixteen feet long and containing the text of the Diamond Sutra. It was found in 1907 by the archaeologist Sir Marc Aurel Stein in Mogao Caves in Dunhuang, and is now in the British Museum. The book displays a great maturity of design and layout and speaks of a considerable ancestry for woodblock printing. The colophon, at the inner end, reads: *Reverently [caused to be] made for universal free distribution by Wang Jie on behalf of his two parents on the 13th of the 4th moon of the 9th year of Xiantong [i.e. 11 May, AD 868].*

In late 10th century China the complete Buddhist canon Tripitaka of 130,000 pages was printed with blocks, which took between 1080 and 1102, and many other very long works were printed. Early books were on scrolls, but other book formats were developed. First came the *Jingzhe zhuang* or "sutra binding", a scroll folded concertina-wise, which avoided the need to unroll half a scroll to see a passage in the middle. About AD 1000 "butterfly binding" was developed; two pages were printed on a sheet, which was then folded inwards. The sheets were then pasted together at the fold to make a codex with alternate openings of printed and blank pairs of pages. In the 14th century the folding was reversed outwards to give continuous printed pages, each backed by a blank hidden page. Later the bindings were sewn rather than pasted. Only relatively small volumes were bound up, and several of these would be enclosed in a cover called a *tao*, with wooden boards at front and back, and loops and pegs to close up the book when not in use. For example one complete Tripitaka had over 6,400 *juan* in 595 *tao*.

Japanese woodblock prints

The earliest known woodblock printing dates from 764-770, when an Empress commissioned one million small wooden pagodascontaining short printed scrolls—typically 6 cm × 45 cm (2.4 in × 17.7 in)—to be distributed to temples. Apart from the production ofBuddhist texts, which became widespread from the 11th century in Japan, the process was only adopted in Japan for secular books surprisingly late, and a Chinese-Japanese dictionary of 1590 is the earliest known example.

Though the Jesuits operated a movable type printing-press in Nagasaki, printing equipment which Toyotomi Hideyoshi's army stole from Korea in 1593 had far greater influence on the development of the medium. Four years later, Tokugawa Ieyasu, even before becoming shogun, effected the creation of the first native movable type, using wooden type-pieces rather than metal. He oversaw the creation of 100,000 type-pieces, which were used to print a number of political and historical texts. An edition of the Confucian *Analects* was printed in 1598, using a Korean moveable type printing press, at the order of Emperor Go-Yôzei. This document is the oldest work of Japanese moveable type printing extant today. Despite the appeal of moveable type, however, it was soon decided that the running script style of Japanese writings would be better reproduced using woodblocks, and so woodblocks were once more adopted; by 1640 they were once again being used for nearly all purposes.

It quickly gained popularity among artists of ukiyo-e, and was used to produce small, cheap, art prints as well as books. Japan began to see something of literary mass production. The content of these books varied widely, including travel guides, advice manuals, *kibyôshi* (satirical novels), *sharebon* (books on urban culture), art books, and play scripts for the *jôruri* (puppet) theatre. Often, within a certain genre, such as the *jôruri* theatre scripts, a particular style of writing would come to be the standard for that genre; in other words, one person's personal calligraphic style was adopted as the standard style for printing plays.

Colour woodblock printing

The earliest woodblock printing known is in colour—Chinese silk from the Han Dynasty printed in three colours.

On paper, European woodcut prints with coloured blocks were invented in Germany in 1508 and are known as chiaroscuro woodcuts.

Colour is very common in Asian woodblock printing on paper; in China the first known example is a Diamond sutra of 1341, printed in black and red at the Zifu Temple in modern day Hubei province. The earliest dated book printed in more than 2 colours is Chengshi moyuan, a book on ink-cakes printed in 1606 and the technique reached its height in books on art published in the first half of the 17th century. Notable examples are the Hu Zhengyan's *Treatise on the Paintings and Writings of the Ten Bamboo Studio* of 1633, and the*Mustard Seed Garden Painting Manual* published in 1679 and 1701.

In Japan, a multi-colour technique, called nishiki-e ("brocade pictures"), spread more widely, and was used for prints, from the 1760s on. Japanese woodcut became a major artistic form, although at the time it was accorded a much lower status than painting.

In both Europe and Japan, book illustrations were normally printed in black ink only, and colour reserved for individual artistic prints. In China, the reverse was true, and colour printing was used mainly in books on art and erotica.

Diffusion in Eurasia

The technique is found through East and Central Asia, and in the Byzantine world for cloth, and by AD 1000 examples of woodblock printing on paper appear in Islamic Egypt. Printing onto cloth had spread much earlier, and was common in Europe by 1300. "In the 13th century the Chinese technique of blockprinting was transmitted to Europe," soon after paper became available in Europe. The print inwoodcut, later joined by engraving, quickly became an important cultural tradition for popular religious works, as well as playing cardsand other uses.

Many early Chinese examples, such as the Diamond Sutra (above) contain images, mostly Buddhist, that are often elaborate. Later, some notable artists designed woodblock images for books, but the separate artistic print did not develop in China as it did in Europe and Japan. Apart from devotional images, mainly Buddhist, few "single-leaf" Chinese prints were made until the 19th century.

15th-century Europe

Block-books, where both text and images are cut on a single block for a whole page, appeared in Europe in the mid-15th century. As they were almost always undated and without statement of printer or place of printing, determining their dates of printing has been an extremely difficult task. Allan H. Stevenson, by comparing the watermarks in the paper used in blockbooks with watermarks in dated documents, concluded that the "heyday" of blockbooks was the 1460s, but that at least one dated from about 1451. Block books printed in the 1470s were often of cheaper quality, as a cheaper alternative to books printed by printing press. Block books continued to be printed sporadically up through the end of the 15th century.

The most famous block-books are the Speculum Humanae Salvationis and the Ars moriendi, though in this the images and text are on different pages, but all block-cut. The Biblia pauperum, a Biblical picture-book, was the next most common title, and the great majority of block-books were popular devotional works. All block-books are fairly short at less than fifty pages. While in Europe movable metal type soon became cheap enough to replace woodblock printing for the reproduction of text, woodcuts remained a major way to reproduce images in illustrated works of early modern European printing.

Most block-books before about 1480 were printed on only one side of the paper — if they were printed by rubbing it would be difficult to print on both sides without damaging the first one to be printed. Many were printed with two pages per sheet, producing a book with opening of two printed pages, followed by openings with two blank pages (as earlier in China). The blank pages were then glued together to produce a book looking like a type-printed one. Where both sides of a sheet have been printed, it is presumed a printing-press was used.

The method was also used extensively for printing playing cards.

Further development in East Asia

In East Asia, woodblock printing proved to be more enduring than in

Europe, continuing well into the 19th century as the major form of printing texts, especially in China, even after the introduction of the European printing press. In countries using Arabic, Turkish and similar scripts, works, especially the Qur'an were sometimes printed by lithography in the 19th century, as the links between the characters require compromises when movable type is used which were considered inappropriate for sacred texts.

Nianhua were a form of coloured woodblock prints in China, depicting images for decoration during the Chinese New Year.

Type of wood used by the Chinese

Dr. Henry, in his "Notes on the Economic Botany of China," refers to your wish to obtain specimens of the woods used in China for printing blocks.

The name which the neighbouring city of Wuchang enjoys for the excellence of its printing work has led me to enquire into the woods used there, and I am sending you specimens of them by parcel post.

The wood which is considered the best is the Veng li mu, which has been identified as the Pyrus betulcefolia, Bunge., and which grows in this Province. Slabs of this wood 1 ft. x 6 ins. x 1 ^ in. cost 150 cash, or about 5½.d.

A cheaper wood generally used for printing proclamations is the tu chung mu. Eucommia ulmoides, Oliv., has been determined to be the tu chung mu. The tu chung here used is a native of this Province. A wood used in Kiangsu is the yin hsing mu, which is one of the names of the Salisburia adiantifolia.

Boxwood, huang yang mu, is obtained from Szechuen, but only in small pieces, which are mainly used for cutting the stamps used for private seals on letters and documents. In the third volume of the Japanese work, the "So Mokn Sei Fu," a drawing is given of the huang yang, together with a quotation from the Chinese Materia Medica, which speaks of the tree as growing an inch a year, except in these years which have an intercalary moon, when it grows backwards. From this it would appear to be a slow growing tree.

MATERIALS OTHER THAN PAPER

Block printing has also been extensively used for decorative purposes such as fabrics, leathers and wallpaper. This is easiest with repetitive patterns composed of one or a small number of motifs that are small to medium in size (due to the difficulty of carving and handling larger blocks). For a multi-colour pattern, each colour element is carved as a separate block and individually inked and applied. Block printing was the standard method of producing wallpaper until the early 20th century, and is still used by a few traditionalist firms. It also remains in use for making cloth, mostly in small artisanal settings, for example in India. William Morris used woodblock printing and on the Victoria and Albert museum web site you can see the process he went through to create such works.

3

Development of Printing Press

INTRODUCTION

Origin and development of printing Press is an important part of the general history of civilization. Printing has been the principal vehicle for the conveying of ideas during the past 500 years to fully understand political, constitutional, ecclesiastical and economic events, and sociological, philosophical and literary movements one must take into account the influence which the printing press has exerted on them.

In the Mid-15th Century, things begin to change with the advent of the printing press. In 1452, Gutenberg conceives of the idea for movable type. In his workshop, he brings together the technologies of paper, oil-based ink and the wine–press to print books. Prior to the advent of the printing press, books were made of vellum because of its durability. Vellum is extremely durable.

In San Simeon, there are lampshades that William Randolph Hearst had made from 15th century Gregorian prayer books and the vellum is still in excellent condition. For books that took more than a year to produce, paper was too flimsy. However, for print books, vellum was too costly to produce.

- The development of oil-based inks. These had been around since the 10th century, but smeared on the vellum used to make books. The religious manuscripts used an egg-based tempera. This was unsuitable for printing with type.
- Gutenberg's contribution to printing was the development of a a punch and mold system which allowed the mass production of the movable type used to reproduce a page of text. These letters would be put together in a type tray which was then used to print a page of text. If a letter broke down, it could be replaced. When the printing of the copies of one page was finished, the type could be reused for the next page or the next book.

These technological improvements stretch across five centuries. They do not cluster around Gutenberg's time. However, it is also said that mechanical printing device for making copies of identical text on multiple sheets of paper.

Movable type, which allowed individual characters to be arranged to form words, was invented in China by Bi Sheng between 1041 to 1048.

The use of movable type to mass produce printed works was popularized by a German goldsmith and eventual printer, Johannes Gutenberg, in the 1440s. While there are several local claims for the invention of the printing press in other parts of Europe, including Laurens Janszoon Coster in the Netherlands and Panfilo Castaldi in Italy, Gutenberg is credited by most scholars with its initial invention.

EARLY PRINTING

BLOCK PRINTING

The original method of printing was block printing, pressing sheets of paper onto individually carved wooden blocks. Block printing is believed to have originated in Asia. Recently, an excavation of a Korean pagoda unearthed a Buddhist sutra which predates the dates to AD 750–751, and is now considered the oldest discovered printed work in the world.

Before this discovery, it was believed that the earliest known printed text was the *Diamond Sutra*, printed in China in mid-9th century. The technique was also known in Europe, where it was mostly used to print Bibles. Because of the difficulties inherent in carving massive quantities of minute text for every block, and given the levels of illiteracy at the time, texts such as the "Pauper's Bibles" emphasized illustrations and used words sparsely. As a new block had to be carved for each page, printing different books was an incredibly time consuming project.

MOVABLE TYPE

Movable type allowed for much more flexible processes than hand copying or block printing. It was invented in 1041 by Bi Sheng in China. Sheng used clay type, which broke easily, but Wang Zhen later carved more durable type from wood. Eventually, invention of movable type metal printing press came about in 1234 during the Goryeo Dynasty of Korea by Chwe Yun-Ui. Examples of this metal type are on display in the Asian Reading Room of the Library of Congress in Washington, D.C.

The oldest extant movable metal print book is the Jikji, printed in Korea in 1377. Since there are thousands of Chinese characters, the benefit of the technique was not as large as with alphabetic based languages, which typically are made up of fewer than 50 characters. Still, movable type spurred scholarly pursuits in Song China and facilitated more creative modes of printing.

Nevertheless, movable type was not extensively used in China until the European-style printing press was introduced in relatively recent times.Johann Gutenberg is credited with inventing the first printing press. Gutenberg is also credited with the first use of a soy-based ink. He printed on both vellum and paper, the latter having been introduced in Europe somewhat earlier from China by way of the Arabs, who had a paper mill in operation in Baghdad as early as 794.Before inventing the printing press in the 1440s, Gutenberg had worked as a goldsmith.

The skills and knowledge of metals that he learned as a craftsman were crucial to the later invention of the press. Gutenberg made his type from an alloy of lead, tin, and antimony, which was critical for producing durable type that produced high-quality prints.

THE ART OF BOOK PRINTING

For years, book printing was considered a true art form. Typesetting, or the placement of the characters on the page, including the use of ligatures, was passed down from master to apprentice. In Germany, the art of typesetting was termed the "black art". It has largely been replaced by computer typesetting programmes, which make it possible to get similar results with less human involvement. Some few practitioners continue to print books the way Gutenberg did. For example, there is a yearly convention of traditional book printers in Mainz, Germany.

PRINTING IN THE INDUSTRIAL AGE

The Gutenberg press was much more efficient than manual copying, and as testament to its effectiveness, it was essentially unchanged from the time of its invention until the Industrial Revolution, some three hundred years later. The "old style" press was constructed of wood and could produce 240 impressions per hour of simple work using a well experienced two-man crew.

The invention of the steam powered press, credited to Friedrich Koenig and Andreas Friedrich Bauer in 1812, made it possible to print over a thousand copies of a page per hour. Koenig and Bauer sold two of their first models to *The Times* in London in 1814, capable of 1,100 impressions per hour. The first edition so printed was on November 28, 1814. Koenig and Bauer went on to perfect the early model so that it could print on both sides of a sheet at once.

This began to make newspapers available to a mass audience and from the 1820s changed the nature of book production, forcing a greater standardization in titles and other metadata. Koenig and Bauer's press was improved by Applegath and Cooper. Later on in the middle of the 19th century the rotary press allowed millions of copies of a page in a single day. Mass production of printed works flourished after the transition to rolled paper, as continuous feed allowed the presses to run at a much faster pace. Also, in the middle of the 19th century, there was a separate development of jobbing presses, small presses capable of printing small–format pieces such as billheads, letterheads, business cards, and envelopes.

Jobbing presses were capable of quick set-up and quick production. Job printing emerged as a reasonably cost-effective duplicating solution for commerce at this time. Movable type has been credited as the single most important invention of the millennium.

Later inventions in this field include the following:

- Lithography
- Offset printing
- Desktop publishing
- Electronic publishing
- Computer printer
- Composing stick

IMPACT OF PRINTING

In Europe, books were copied mainly in monasteries, or in commercial scriptoria, where scribes wrote them out by hand. Books were therefore a scarce resource. While it might take someone a year or more to hand copy a Bible, with the Gutenberg press it was possible to create several hundred copies a year, with two or three people who could read and a few people to support the effort.

Each sheet still had to be fed manually, which limited the reproduction speed; and the type had to be set manually for each new page, which limited the number of different pages created per day. Books produced in this period, between the first work of Johann Gutenberg and the year 1500, are collectively referred to as incunabula.

The rise of printed works was not immediately popular. Not only did the papal court contemplate making printing presses an industry requiring a license from the Catholic Church but as early as the 15th century some nobles refused to have printed books in their libraries, thinking that to do so would sully their valuable hand copied manuscripts. Similar resistance was later encountered in much of the Islamic world, where calligraphic traditions were extremely important, and also in the Far East. Despite this resistance, Gutenberg's printing press spread rapidly, and within thirty years of its invention in 1453, towns and cities across Europe had functional printing presses. Johann Heynlin, for example, introduced the first press to Paris in 1470.

The city of Tübingen saw its first printed work, a commentary by Paul Scriptoris, in 1498. It has been suggested that this rapid expansion shows not only a higher level of industry than expected, but also a significantly higher level of literacy than has often been estimated. The first printing press in a Muslim territory opened in Andalusia in the 1480s. This printing press was run by a family of Jewish merchants who printed texts with the Hebrew script. After the reconquista in the 1490s, the press was moved from Granada to Istanbul.

EFFECTS OF PRINTING ON CULTURE

The discovery and establishment of the printing of books with movable type marks a paradigm shift in the way information was transferred in Europe. The impact of printing is comparable to the development of language, and the invention of the alphabet, as far as its effects on the society. It is, however, important to note that there has been much recent doubt about the dominance of print. Handwritten manuscripts continued to be produced, and the influence of the printed word on oral communication meant that no one form of communication could dominate.

They also led to the establishment of a community of scientists who could easily communicate their discoveries, bringing on the scientific revolution. Also, although early texts were printed in Latin, books were soon produced in common European vernacular, leading to the decline of the Latin language. Because of the printing press, authorship became more meaningful.

It was suddenly important who had said or written what, and what the precise formulation and time of composition was. This allowed the exact citing of references, producing the rule, "One Author, one work, one piece of information".

Before, the author was less important, since a copy of Aristotle made in Paris might not be identical to one made in Bologna. For many works prior to the printing press, the name of the author was entirely lost. Because the printing process ensured that the same information fell on the same pages, page numbering, tables of contents, and indices became common. The process of reading was also changed, gradually changing from oral readings to silent, private reading. This gradually raised the literacy level as well, revolutionizing education.

It can also be argued that printing changed the way Europeans thought. With the older illuminated manuscripts, the emphasis was on the images and the beauty of the page. Early printed works emphasized principally the text and the line of argument. In the sciences, the introduction of the printing press marked a move from the medieval language of metaphors to the adoption of the scientific method. In general, knowledge came closer to the hands of the people, since printed books could be sold for a fraction of the cost of illuminated manuscripts.

There were also more copies of each book available, so that more people could discuss them. Within 50-60 years, the entire library of "classical" knowledge had been printed on the new presses. The spread of works also led to the creation of copies by other parties than the original author, leading to the formulation of copyright laws. Furthermore, as the books spread into the hands of the people, Latin was gradually replaced by the national languages.

This development was one of the keys to the creation of modern nations. Some theorists, such as McLuhan, Eisenstein, Kittler, and Giesecke, see an "alphabetic monopoly" as having developed from printing, removing the role of the image from society. Other authors stress that printed works themselves are a visual medium. But in another sense the advent of the printing press did not bring about a great shift in the social organization of learning in Europe.

The first books to show up in print shops were bibles and religious tracts. The next books to attract publishers were the "humanist" texts brought back from Byzantium by the Crusades, and other texts of antiquity but there was little or no printing of new ideas.

Many people went into the printing business and went right back out again. The reason was that the distribution of books was poorly organized. The market was there, and the potential for filling the demand, but the transport and control and "advertising" mechanisms were not in place.

In addition, there was still a low literacy rate in Europe. Most people did not know how to read at all. But non-literates were still affected by the book trade because the elites, who controlled society, were affected by books. And people who could not read still had access to book culture because there were traveling raconteurs who stood in the market and read from books as a means of making a living as entertainers.

The situation was improved by the introduction of the Frankfort Book Faire. Cities in Europe held yearly fairs, featuring whatever kinds of things the city and surrounding area was good at producing. Frankfort was an early center for printing and so it sponsored a book fair which drew publishers, booksellers, collectors, scholars, who could find what they needed for their livelihoods. This helped coordinate supply and demand.

The fair also produced a catalog of all the works shown at the fair-an early Books in Print. None of this is to say that new book printing posed much of a challenge to the power and prestige of the church. Early print books were conservative in content, and were filled with medieval images and ideas.

However, the creation of the Printing Press is observed as the formal beginnings of mass media. Often referred to as the bridging of "The Great Divide," its creation in 1440 by Johannes Gutenberg opened up the possibilities of a public sphere in a way that never before existed. With increasingly fasted creation and distribution of ideas and information, the public not only had an increase in material, but also an incentive to become literate, and the public sphere owes its existence to a literate population.

Jurgen Habermas, leading scholor on the emergence of the public sphere explains that the development of the press allows the public to become more active and critical, to more easily express its acceptance or rejection of policies and laws.

This process came about in three main stages:

1. *Stage* 1: The press first supported the needs of large merchants and traders, protecting their economic interests.
2. *Stage* 2: Later, the press became responsible for informing the public

of policies and laws, and was used by the public authority to communicate with the general population.

3. *Stage* 3: Finally, the press became a voice that allows the public to communicate its concerns with the state. This development allows for discourse between parties. The initial forms for this communication were newspapers, gazettes, and pamphlets which resulted in social interaction, connections, the formation of opinions, and reflection.

Following the progression of the above stages, the first newspapers were more closely related to today's catalogues, than to contemporary newspapers. They were used to advertise products, and simple announcements. The continuing decades would see the emergence of local news, and then national and world news. The emergence of magazines as a part of the public sphere grew to target several audiences. General audiences were targeted for news regarding entertainment, special interests, news, and shopping. Specialized audiences were reached through journals, serving a particular, targeted audience who shared a specific field of interest, occupation, or political affiliation.

In the era of the printing press, before the invention of more advanced media via radio and television, idea were processed in a linear fashion. Of utmost importance was the standardization of the written word. Therefore, uniformity was dictated by the creation of dictionaries, thesauri, and grammar books which popularized standard spelling, punctuation, and abbreviations.

THE IMPACT OF PRINT TECHNOLOGY IN THE PUBLIC SPHERE

Print technology increasingly plays a central role in the mediation of social networks. Any socially grounded theory of the public sphere will have to take into account these social network structures and the communications systems that bind them.

Habermas discusses how the "public sphere" emerged in bourgeois society in the 18th century. He sees the public sphere as a kind of mediator between society and state, between public and private interests, through which the public can categorize its opinion.

Therefore, the public sphere is a forum in which people are "unrestricted" in what they say and are guaranteed freedom of expression in all of its forms. The new public sphere permitted people to shape public opinion. The public could make their private concerns known through several means, but print became extremely imperative.

During the periods of the American and French revolutions, Habermas observed that people were fast to gather and grab newspapers as political tools. Upon allocation, the more private publications showed an unbelievably loud voice of the public in response to the state publications. Karl Bucher describes the situation that unfolded as an outcome of the changing press, "Newspapers changed from mere institutions for the publication of news into bearers and leaders of public opinion—weapons of party politics. This transformed the newspaper business.

A new element emerged between the gathering and publication of news: the editorial staff. But for the newspaper publisher it meant that he changed from vendor recent news to a dealer in public opinion." The state of newspapers described by Bucher seems ideal, because it is a forum that is open to and certainly created by the joint voices of the public. Yet, this state of journalism was brief.

"Although the liberal model of the public sphere is still instructive today with respect to the normative claim that information be accessible to the public, it cannot be applied to the actual conditions of an industrially advanced mass democracy organized in the form of the social welfare state."

Habermas continues with, "Because of the diffusion of press and propaganda," the public sphere lost its voice. Groups of people have had to alter their voice and their stances in order to obtain any voice at all in the media. If their plan doesn't please the political authorities then it's just not fit to print.

THE IMPACT OF DEVELOPMENTS IN PRINT TECHNOLOGY ON JOURNALISM

Today, magazines, in their secular context tend to report on current events, trends, issues, and prominent people in society and around the world. However, the progression up to this point is complicated and full of its own trends. After the invention of the printing press, the first newspapers followed in the years 1605–1690.

A half century later, the public demand rose, and their prominence in the public sphere has not lost its weight. The beginning of the 1700's was paired with an increased interest in the arts, as a higher class grew in America. Benjamin Franklin and Andrew Bradford were the editors and creators of the first prominent magazines in their areas of the country.

Although most of the population was occupied with work and could not give their attention to the emerging science, medical, and agricultural magazines being published, their popularity exploded in what is known as the Golden Age of Magazines, when it became profitable to write. 10 cent magazines of the 1890's emerged, well illustrated, coloured, and supported by a rise in advertising.

The less educated middle class became a targeted audience, as the idea of self-improvement raged, and national events gave way to Muckraking. McClure's magazine from 1903–1912 employed writers Ida Tarbell and Lincoln Steffins, among others, and magazines became the national media voice of the time. The magazine became the weapon of political struggle as corruption was reported for the public, and investigative journalism began. As the Muckrakers completed their purpose, and the American public felt that the issues were addressed politically through Progressivism and the election of Wilson, magazines went back to publishing personal interest stories, fiction, and romance. However, the Muckrickers had set the stage for a continuing tradition of radicalism in the public sphere, and made an easy transition to new forms of journalism. Magazines became the carriers of mass popular culture, although today's special interest journals have taken on the radical nature of radical journalism, while popular magazines today are the carriers of mass popular culture.

PRINTING AND PUBLISHING LANDMARKS

- c 594 The Chinese began to practice printing from a negative relief. Their method of rubbing off impressions from a wood block spread along the caravan routes to the West. From China also came the invention of paper which was to provide the ideal surface for printing.
- c 1400 The technique of printing with wooden blocks arrived in Europe from the Far East
- c 1450 Johann Gutenberg adapted the screw printing press from the wine presses which had been used in the Rhine Valley since the days of the Roman Empire. He used a recently perfected oil-based ink and devised a mould of metal prism matrices, punch-stamped typeface moulds and invented a functional metal alloy to mould the type. The printed word enabled information and knowledge, which was previously restricted to ecclesiastical establishments, to be widely disseminated and the first mass media 'explosion' soon, hit Europe. By 1500 more than 9 million printed books were in circulation. What is perhaps Gutenberg's greatest claim to fame is the fact that, after an early experimental period of which nothing is known, he soon reached a state of technical efficiency not materially surpassed until the beginning of the 19th century. Punch cutting, matrix fitting, type casting, composing and printing remained, in principle, for more than three centuries as they were in Gutenberg's time. Improvements to the printing press were insignificant and until the end of the 18th century Gutenberg's original design was still much the same and regarded as the 'common' press. One thing to remember is that Gutenberg gets credit for an invention that is thought to have been developed simultaneously in Holland and in Prague. The other inventions brought together by Gutenberg in his pursuit of a printing press were:
  - The adaptation for printing, of the wine or olive oil, screw-type press that had been in use for hundreds of years, throughout Europe and Asia.
  - The adaptation of block-print technology–known in Europe since the return of Marco Polo from Asia at the end of the 13th century.

- The development of mass production paper-making techniques. Paper was brought from China to Italy in the 12th C. but was thought too flimsy for books.

- c 1460 Printer's ink invented only fifteen years after the first use of oil paints for pictures. It had to be able to stick onto a metal surface and it was based on heat–bodied linseed oil, kept for a year to allow the mucilage to settle. Resin may then have been added. The black pigment would have made from the soot collected from burning pitch and then roasted it several times the get rid of the tarry oils. Many printers were still making their own ink as late as 1850.
- 1500s Printing provided the first mass medium vehicle for advertising and in the 1500s printed handbills began to replace the town criers.
- 1600s The screw press was improved for the first time since Gutenberg's day with the introduction of springs to aid the platen to lift rapidly. It was then able to print a maximum of 250 impressions an hour. Newspapers began to appear. They developed from newsletters and printed pamphlets. The relationship between advertising and newspapers enabled both to flourish from the early 17th century. The printed medium changed advertising from announcements to persuasion.
- 1799 Printing by lithography was invented by an Austrian printer Alois Senefelder. He found that he could print from the flat, smooth, surface of fine-grained limestone. The process works on the principle that oil and water do not mix. Waxed illustrations are transferred onto the stone block. When ink is added to the surface of the stone the wax areas retain it and it can be washed off elsewhere. In the 19th century lithography became the preferred method for reproducing quality illustrations for books and magazines in both colour and monochrome. Early this century it was found that the reproduction was even better if the ink was transferred to the paper via a rubber 'blanket' instead directly from the stone. This became called offsetting and, after further technical refinements, it is the principle that is used in the modern offset presses of today.
- 1803 Machine made paper begins to replace hand-made paper. The first practical paper machine was invented by Nicholas Louis Robert at the Essonnes Mill, France, but the patent was taken to England where the first efficient machines were set up. Paper was mainly produced from linen and cotton rags. Esparto grass was also used.
- 1804 The third Earl of Stanhope replaced the wooden screw press, virtually unchanged since Gutenberg's time, with an iron framed lever press. The press used by Andrew Bent, now at the TMAG, to publish his Hobart Town Gazette and Van Diemen's Land Advertiser in the early 1820s is Stanhope's improved model of 1807.

- 1805 Lord Stanhope also introduced stereotyping, which made the saving of pages of type for reprinting a commercial proposition. Pages of type for future reprints were preserved using plaster or metal matrices from which a stereotype could be cast, instead of having to reset the text.
- 1814 Frederich Koenig's steam printing machine with rollers was adopted by The Times, London, in 1820, and raised the output of a printing press from 300 to 1100 copies an hour.
- 1822 The letter founding machine, invented by Dr William Church and a forerunner to the linotype machine, raised the number of letters that could be cast daily from 3 000/7 000 to 12 000/20 000.
- 1827 The New Press of Applegath and Cowper enabled The Times to produce 5 000 copies an hour from a single machine. Prior to this rows of Stanhope presses had been used.
- 1829 The stereotyping process improved. Clumsy plaster and metal matrices were replaced by papier mache ones, reducing labour, weight and bulk in storage.1831-French engineer Gaveaux designed a two-cylinder version of the New Press which handled the paper better and further increased production.
- 1840 American Richard March Hoe developed a revolving perfecting press which could turn out 20 000 impressions an hour.
- 1840 The manufacture of paper from wood pulp was accomplished this year and within a decade production had spread everywhere. The outward appearance and 'feel' of paper was altered and it became much cheaper to produce, which was particularly advantageous to newspaper production.
- 1846 Hoe developed the first version of a rotary press. He found a way to fit the type around the cylinder which was inked by automated rollers while four smaller rollers brought the sheets of paper in contact with it. This raised the number of impressions that could be taken from 22 000 to 24 000 an hour.
- 1853 Claude Genoux and Nicholas Serriere improved the system for making page moulds on papier mache flongs, as they came to be called. A flong prepared from flat type could be curved to permit moulding of the cylindrical type needed for a rotary press. Flongs were used until recent times when the introduction of offset presses and computer technology revolutionised the printing process.
- 1854 James Gordon Bennett in his New York Herald developed a method using a metal plate impression of the type rather than the type itself.
- 1859 Photo-lithography. A French lithographer, Firmin Gillot, developed a new method for etching metal plates. In 1872 his son invented zincography, which combined photography with etching so

that the resulting picture could be sized up and down as required. But it was limited to uniform black on white. By 1880 a method of producing intermediate tones was devised by a system of dots of different sizes. By the end of the century photo-lithography had become a new branch of the journalistic profession. Photo-lithographic 'block' making in zinc was performed until photo-composition in the 1970s.

- 1863 William Bullock perfected a method of feeding paper into a machine continuously instead of by sheets. He also incorporated Bennett's metal plate system and the use of stereotypes, shaped to fit the rollers, instead of hand set set type, came into general use.
- 1885 Linotype and Monotype machines were developed. Between 1815 and 1871 seventy attempts had been made to create a machine capable of setting type and adjusting the spacing of words. A machine that did this work, the Linotype was developed by Ottmar Mergenthaler in America who was inspired by a punch-cutting machine invented in Milwaukee, USA, by Linn Boyd Benton. Mergenthaler's invention had a keyboard which set not type but matrices of letters which formed the mould of a line. Molten lead alloy was used to set the line of type and the name 'linotype' evolved from this procedure. Afterwards the linotype slugs could be melted for re-use. The Monotype machine, invented about the same time by Tolbert Lanston, was similar to Mergenthaler's machine but it cast hot metal type letter by letter instead of by line. Linotypes were a major advance and they also solved the problem of being able to automatically justify lines and mechanically distribute type. Before this development a proficient compositor could only set 40-50 lines of type an hour. As with all major technological advances, linotype machines met strong resistance in Britain from compositors who saw their introduction as a threat to their jobs. Linotypes came on the market in America in 1892 and a few years later in Britain.
- 1889 Hippolyte Marinoni at the Paris Exposition demonstrated a rotary press which turned a roll of paper back on its path, enabling successive sheets of large and small size to be printed on both sides and then cut and folded into piles of completed newspapers, the whole operation performed at great speed.
- 1890 By now there was a wide choice of fast rotary presses to choose from. Each had its own specialised technology. The great advances in newspaper production technology were over until the development of web offset printing and photo-composition in the 1970s.
- 1900–1970s Manufacturers added speed and quality to the production capacity of their presses. After 1900 electricity replaced steam and

provided a new easily conducted energy, which enabled a variety of electrical devices and innovations to be installed. 1920s Automatic devices were developed for making stereotypes.Improved folding mechanisms for presses with stuffing devices for carrying extra supplements appeared.

- 1960s early—Web offset presses were used for the first time for small newspaper runs.

4

Role of Women in the Print Media

INTRODUCTION

The project on the.Status of Women Journalists in the Print Media. was initiated by the National Commission for Women to look into issues affecting the role of women working in the print media. As part of a broader study on working women in India, it was executed by the Press Institute of India (PII), through empirical data that was collected from almost all the States and Union Territories of the country. The objective of the research was to examine the problems and issues confronting women working in the media, to gauge the extent of direct and indirect discrimination in the workplace and to identify contemporary issues that need to be addressed.

METHODOLOGY

The research was coordinated by me with the support of media representatives from various regions—Linda Chhakchhuak from Shillong, Rajashri Dasgupta from Calcutta, Sushmita Malaviya from Bhopal, R. Akhileshwari from Hyderabad and Surekha Sule from Mumbai—who together formed a National Study Group.

The National Study Group assisted with the design and implementation of the 20-page questionnaire. Usha Rai, Deputy Director, Press Institute of India, guided and steered the group. A brain storming session with a focus group of women journalists in Delhi preceded the study, to ensure that the questionnaire was suitable and that critical aspects were addressed. The questionnaire was then pilot tested to iron out discrepancies and ambiguities. Experiences from the field surveys are outlined later in the report.

SAMPLING AND RESPONSE RATE

A total of 410 women working in the print media responded. Although there are no definite figures on the number of questionnaires distributed, estimates put the sample size at approximately 3500. This means the response rate was approximately 11.5 per cent. This was one of the most disappointing aspects of the study. There was total non-cooperation in filling in the questionnaire, especially by journalists from the English language national media. Some of them had even attended the brain storming session at the NCW. They kept reassuring us that they would complete the questionnaire, but never got down to it. Some respondents said the questionnaire was too long and would require too much time to fill up.

Most of the data collected was through personal interaction, which though time—consuming, gave many great quotes and observations that women were hesitant to put on paper.

A hundred and ninety respondents from the regional press and 220 from the English press were surveyed. Ten were above 50 years while the rest were between 20 and 40. An overwhelming number were employed on contract. 239, while only 60 were on wage board scales. Forty were freelancers and a few were casual employees.

ORGANISATIONS COVERED

Andhra Pradesh:

- Vipula Chatura (Magazine, Eenadu)
- Eenadu Daily (News Today Pvt. Ltd.)
- Andhra Jyothi
- News Today
- Vasundhra Publications. Eenadu
- Newstime (Now shut down)
- The Times of India
- The Hindu

Bihar:

- Hindusthan
- Rajparivar (monthly)
- The Hindustan Times
- Indian Express
- The Times of India
- Sarvottam Nari Kalyan Samiti
- Dainik Jagran
- Haribhoomi
- Prabhat Khabar
- UNI

Chhattisgarh:

- The Hindustan Times
- The Hitavada
- Nav Bharat
- Jansatta
- Haribhumi

- Sandhya Danik Jagran
- Desh Bandhu
- Dainik Bhaskar

Delhi:

- Indian Express
- Women.s Feature Service
- Deutsche Presse-Agentur, dpa
- Business Standard

Gujarat:

- The Asian Age
- Gujarat Samachar
- Indian Express
- The Times of India
- Stree Sandesh
- Navchetan
- Financial Express

Jammu and Kashmir:

- Kashmir Times
- Daily Sandesh

Jharkhand:

- Prabhat Khabar
- Ranchi Express
- Janhul
- The Times of India
- The Hindustan Times

Karnataka:

- Deccan Herald
- Vijaya Karnataka
- Udayavani
- Karmaveera (weekly)

Kerala:

- Kairali News
- Malyalam Daily
- Matrubhumi
- Malyalam Manorama
- Deepika
- Deshabhimani
- Indian Express
- Hindu

Madhyapradesh:

- Dainik Bhaskar
- Nai Duniya

- Desh Bandhu
- Nav Bharat
- Free Press
- Central Chronicle
- The Hindustan Times
- The Times of India

Maharashtra:

- The Dayview. A Gavakari Group Publication.
- Indian Express
- Lokmat (Daily Lokmat/Lokmat Times)
- The Economic Times
- Navakal
- Dainik Lokmat
- Kesari (Daily Kesari)
- Maharashtra Times
- Loksatta
- Pundhari (Daily Pundhari)
- Tarun Bharat
- Navbharat Times
- The Times of India
- Magna Publishing (magazine)
- The Hitavada
- The Hindu Businessman Line
- Business Standard
- One India One People (magazine)
- The Economic Times
- Mid Day

North-east:

- GL Publications
- Shillong Times
- The Assam Tribune
- ABP Limited
- The Telegraph
- The Sentinel
- The Imphal Free Press
- Aji (Ramdhenu Publications Pvt. Ltd.)
- Asomiya Pratidin
- Non-gsain Hima
- ORISSA:
- Sambad
- Dhariti
- New India Express

Punjab:
- Danik Jagran
- Hind Samachar (Magazine section)
- Naritva (Magazine)
- Jag Bani (Hind Samachar group newspaper)
- The Pioneer
- The Hindustan Times
- Indian Express
- The Times of India
- *Rajasthan*:
- Hindustan Dainik (Hindustan Times.Hindi)
- Rajasthan Patrika
- The Hindustan Times
- Dainik Bhaskar
- Indian Express
- Deccan Herald
- Vanijya Setu (weekly)
- *Tamil Nadu*:
- Businessline (Hindu group)
- Ananada Vikatam
- Indian Express
- Kumudam Snehidhi
- Dinamani (IE)
- Vikatam

Uttaranchal:
- Dainik Jagran
- UNI
- Himachal Times

Uttarpradesh:
- The Hindustan Times
- Swatantra Bharat
- Dainik Jagran
- Rashtra Bhasha Sandesh
- Kranti Navyug
- The Times of India
- PTI
- Northern India Patrika
- Lucknow Times (Times of India)
- Jansatta

West-bengal:
- The Statesman
- Business Standard

- United News of India
- The Telegraph
- Aajkaal
- The Times of India
- Ananda Bazar (Anand Bazar Patrika)
- The Asian Age
- The Hindustan Times
- Bartman
- PTI
- Pratidin
- Satjug
- Jan Sansar (fortnightly)
- Akbar-E-Mashriq
- Khoj Ekhan (magazine)
- Aajkaal (newspaper)
- Business India Magazine

The Survey

The primary input of the study was issues and concerns that emerged from a.Brain Storming Session. of women journalists from the print media. The questionnaire included 11 parameters, 86 sets of indices, 27 variables and was in three languages. English, Hindi and Urdu.

The survey took into account a wide range of issues: from recruitment and job segregation to promotions and work conditions; training and development to childcare and maternity facilities; sexual harassment, union involvement, superannuation and freelancing. The maze of data under so many different heads with further sub-divisions into specific indices, initially seemed easy to read but proved arduous to analyse.

Consequently, all the information was tabulated into more comprehensive nuggets of pie charts and bar charts and also aggregated, both state-wise and at the national level. The size of the respondent sample (410) and the fact that we had to depend on questionnaires filled and did not necessarily have a representative cross section of journalists, places some limitations on the data.

However, the results are important indicators of the views and perceptions of women journalists, especially since their impact on various issues in the newsroom is steadily increasing as their numbers expand. Even where the numbers are low, as in the regional press, and discrimination between male and female employees is a reality, the study shows that women journalists still infuse their careers with a hopeful and positive attitude. Many of them are committed to contributing to the industry, often against all odds and far beyond the expectations of managements and co-workers. In fact women report that, too many times, their goals are stifled long before they even have a chance to flourish. Despite this the growing number of women entering the media profession and continuing to pursue careers, demonstrates their determination to keep voices of women alive.

As Preeti Misra from Hindustan Times in Jharkhand says.Though women are well represented in the media their voices are largely unheard. They are supposed to report on the predicaments of society at large but when it comes to themselves, they are seldom heard. From a historical perspective, women journalists clearly have made great advances in the last two decades their share of jobs in all media has increased, they are not restricted to fashion, cookery, art and culture but are also reporting from the battlefields, stock market and the Parliament's press gallery.

In fact women journalists are radically changing the media and giving it a broader base by mainstreaming health, environment, social concerns and women's issues. Sudha Menon of the Hindu Businessline says that though she has experienced a fair deal of fulfillment and professional dignity., her counterparts in other organisations have not been so privileged. Women journalists are often overworked, underpaid and have very little access to equal employment.

In fact a large number of organisations often deny women promotions on the flimsy excuse that they cannot do night duty. Childcare, flexi-hours, a more sensitive approach to the limitations she faces when she is in the child-rearing phase can do wonders for both the organisation and women employees.. In many cases they have built their careers on the premise that they have to be.twice as good as their male counterparts just to get their foot in the door.

Others report that the stress of working hard to keep up standards, and to forestall any negative expectations, can be debilitating. Alka Kshirsagar from Pune had a similar concern. Women journalists have to work twice as hard as male colleagues and have to constantly battle suggestions or perceptions that we are using sexuality to get ahead in our careers. We are more vulnerable than male colleagues to gossip, to promotion prospects; and age too is a factor for discrimination.. In the same vein Rashme Sehgal from Delhi said.After spending so many years in journalism, I.ve found that no matter how many awards I win, and how productive I am, my talents will be recognised only to a certain extent. In addition, news organisations prefer hiring younger girls. It's frustrating because once one has acquired the skills and experience, one is too old or over qualified.

Most of the senior journalists believe they have given their best effort to an industry that simply doesn't quite know how to utilize their talents, or refuses to allow them to be as outspoken or proactive as their male colleagues. The survey team frequently met women journalists who were working far below their capacities, who may have started off strong but wind up stalling in their careers.

Senior Delhi-based journalist Vichitra Sharma said:.I no longer look forward to career advancement as a reporter or network correspondent, something that satisfied me in my thirties. One needs to grow in one's profession, but if the institution doesn't give the opportunities needed to satisfy your growth, then you have to look elsewhere.. Observers may conclude that women journalists are still adopting a.victim stance., refusing to acknowledge the many gains they have made because that might mean having to admit there is an even playing field for all journalists.

The fact is that there are also those who have developed a tangible strategy for negotiating their careers. They say they are determined to concentrate on their goals, to not walk into every setting expecting to be harassed or discriminated against, and to stay focussed on career advancement. Latika Shyam shares her philosophy on taking advantage of the opportunities that one finds: You are what you make of yourself. Take responsibility and be answerable first and foremost to yourself.

The industry is more prepared for women moving all the way to the top than it has been ever before. Take advantage of it and go after what you want to do. On the lack of advancement among women journalists, a stronger comment came from a veteran:.Some just believe they are entitled to better opportunities than the rest of the staff and they become disenchanted when they do not move fast enough. Major concerns that emerged from the study were job insecurity because journalists were employed like daily wage labour, signing a muster at the end of the month to get a pittance of ₹ 1500 to ₹ 3000 as wages; contract system of employment; neglect of maternity and child-care provisions and sexual harassment.

Other issues raised by respondents were:

- More women are employed in the media now since they are available at lower salaries on the contract system. In such circumstances gender fair reporting and practices are more difficult to promote..
- After initial resistance, even women journalists start justifying organisational insensitivity. They are instrumental in perpetuating lack of recognition of women's special needs and functions in society. childbirth, childcare, confinement, security after night duty etc. Many believe the myth that women journalists have limitations within organisations since they cannot do night shifts..
- Regular dilemma is childcare vs. profession. Effect of work on marital relations differ between male journalists and women journalists..
- Longer maternity leave is important since confinement and childcare are very demanding on health and emotions. This would usually be required once or twice in all working life so no big deal..
- Women's most productive years are also their reproductive years..
- Women journalists are conscientious, diligent and people relate more

easily to us. However, male bosses do not give credit for professionalism instead they speak of women exploiting their gender..

- As a profession, very satisfying and stimulating but work environment needs to be egalitarian and encouraging. At present enthusiasm often watered down by unresponsive organisations that are not sensitive to gender specific requirements which are often viewed as liabilities transport, maternity leave, childcare facilities, rest rooms etc.
- There is no transparency in policy matters entitlements, rights and promotion criteria.

An astounding 20.5 per cent of respondents said that women were discriminated against for promotion. 45.5 per cent felt it was because of their sex, some felt it was because of age and a large proportion refused to comment. 21.2 per cent. In fact 8.4 per cent were forced to leave a media organisation due to promotion discrimination.

Evidence also emerged that having children has an impact on women's work in the media: 29.2 per cent of all respondents were sure that having children affects promotion and 37.8 per cent felt that this was because of the perception that having children affects women's ability to put in late hours. Though most of the respondents had not deferred marriage or pregnancy due to job insecurity, only 56.7 per cent of those with children had availed of maternity leave and a further 10.6 per cent had availed of unpaid or part maternity leave.

Reasons for this varied from no such provision, job insecurity and even, not given despite requesting. An astonishing 17.5 per cent were not aware of any such facility in their organisation and of those without children, 54.2 per cent said that they would avail of maternity benefits in the future if such a provision existed. During personal interaction sexual harassment emerged as a major concern of most respondents.

But when asked whether they had to put up with sexist remarks/ gestures or if they had been sexually harassed in any way at their workplace or in association with their work, 22.7 per cent said they had, 8 per cent said they were.not sure. and many others had either denied or refused to comment.

An interesting finding is that, of those who had experienced sexual harassment, 31.5 per cent said it had.seriously. undermined their confidence and affected their work, 24 per cent said it had.mildly. but an alarming 41.3 per cent said it had had.no affect.. These findings show sexual harassment is part of work culture in media organisations in India but women either do not know how or for a wide variety of reasons, choose not to do anything about it. Only 15.2 per cent of women who experienced sexual harassment had made a formal complaint. In regards to working conditions, the overwhelming majority of women (76.2 per cent) believe their working conditions are similar to their male colleagues. 10.8 per cent said they were better, while 3 per cent said they were worse.

However, the level of awareness of basic working conditions is very low on some key issues:

- 31 per cent were not aware if any equal employment policy existed in their organisation.
- 29 per cent did not know if women were targeted for filling vacancies in their organisations.
- 19.5 per cent did not know whether formal appeal procedures or mechanisms for handling grievances existed in their organisation while 50.7 per cent were sure of no such facility.
- 10 per cent are not aware of any formal training programme in their organisation while 42.3 said that no such facility was provided.
- 87.6 per cent are not aware of any superannuation scheme or believe that it does not apply to them.

Job segregation was an issue of significance for many of the respondents. 24.7 per cent feel that they do not have access to all areas of work and that lifestyle, arts, gender, fashion and education are traditional areas reserved for women. But 87.3 per cent believe that women have capability in all areas of journalism.

The changes that women want in their workplace include:

- Positions advertised and proper selection and interview procedures introduced;
- Provision of training about equal employment opportunity and gender issues for their male colleagues;
- Transparency in terms and conditions of contract system of employment;
- Childcare facilities;
- Maternity leave;
- Insurance;
- An elected (not nominated) body for redressal of grievances.

Interestingly, childcare at work place and insurance cover emerged as the most required facilities. 54.4 per cent thought that there had been no development (permanent part-time, flexibility of working hours, special leave, childcare facilities, study leave etc.) at their workplace in the interest of women generally.

Only 29.4 per cent of the respondents felt that their employers were responsible for changes that had taken place. Most of these were perceived to have been brought about in response to individual demands. Notwithstanding this, women journalists say they are making the most of what career opportunities they find, while conceding that they may not have the opportunity to reach the kind of high profile beats that male journalists attain.

Often, this is because they are.left out of the loop for various reasons. not available for night shifts as a consequence of which not assigned important beats that often results in being buttonholed into accepting a lesser deal. Or they say that while they might be very successful as assistant editors, a shot at the top job may not come their way because they are not considered.management material.

Just what are the barriers to opportunities for women journalists:

- Newspapers are high pressure environments where male gender, talent and hustle are incontrovertible tickets to success..
- Women are sometimes hampered because they refuse to assimilate into the work culture. We need to be more aggressive to promote our work.
- Women journalists face daunting stereotypes about their abilities.

The survey has demonstrated that comments from women journalists portray resilience bred from years of experience. They have learnt that hard work, a supportive management, and a positive attitude can be keys to success, but they have also learned that within the newsroom, resentment, exclusion and hostility are flip sides of those coins. By and large, women journalists have a positive perspective and believe that advancement opportunities in the industry have improved over the last few years.

IMAGES OF WOMEN IN PRINT MEDIA

Communication is the powerful means of bringing about social changes. The revolution in the media of communication has helped to accelerated the pace of social change during these few decades. Radio, television, newspapers and other mass media have not only made this world ‘shrunk’ but also have revolutionized the values. Attitudes, interests and social milieu. Mass communication has opened many challenges and creative doors which lead to the path of glamorous world. Journalism is one of the important stars of creativity in the universe of mass communication. Journalism means the communications or information regarding the events of the day through written words, sounds or pictures. Journalism is a mirror or the society. The journalist acts as a spokesman of mankind.

He must therefore, provide a truthful, comprehensive and intelligent account of the events is a context that gives meaning. The journalist should act as an effective medium for two way communication between readers and different organizations of the society. A journalist observes the events, transmits facts about the events and act as an interpreter of theses events. He/She also explains the significances of the facts and offers opinions on contemporary issues. In modern times, journalism has become an exciting and interesting profession in the field of communication. These is no doubt that it is a noble profession aiming at the service of the people by the denomination of new. It is a very dynamic profession, which moves with times. Very often it becomes the initiating factor for many new development and achievement.

WOMEN AS JOURNALISTS—THE CHALLENGING PROFESSION

The general assumption according to societal trend seems to be that it is difficult for women to reach unto managerial position due to their socalled inherent inability and the traditional upbringing at home. There is no reason why women cannot choose journalism as career. Just as there is no reason why women cannot choose any discipline or area as career. Women are not handicapped by birth nor have they been found intellectually unfit. They are however, burdened with certain disadvantages as a result or the responsibilities. These get further accentuated when confronted by male prejudice in professions that have been traditionally male dominated, like journalism. Just as there is no reason why women cannot choose any discipline or area as career. One of the journalist named 'Charlie Hands' reported that revolution is bound to come when more women then ever in newspaper work, reporting, sub-editing, news editing and even do editing.

Further, he added that all the advantages are with women. Firstly, do not drink. Secondly, they are more with touch with the realities of life, women are better judges, they have more taste, and they are more human... their outlook is really wider than that of men. Women journalists have proved a every bit as resourceful and enterprising in their work as their male colleagues, and they have gone places winning laurels on the way by way of awards, fellowships abroad and prestigious assignments.

FUTURE SCOPE FOR WOMEN IN JOURNALISM PROFESSION

Women are crucial part in this profession. There was a belief that male members would overpower this profession. But, with the passage of time, the thoughts of the people have changed and this profession gave space for women journalists. L. K. Advani, the Deputy Prime Minister, state in National Conference on Women and Media, that women are coming into media and journalism in larger numbers.

There is immense potential for the combination of media and voluntary sector as a force for bringing about the empowerment of women. He added that this would bring women's power and media power together as a formidable weapon. Thus, knowing women's role in media, specifically in journalism, it provided that the future is bright for women in this field. But, time and again women have to prove their worth in every sphere of life, so, in this profession. She has to constantly excel in every field of journalism. There are many qualities that women ingrain in them from birth, and many she accepts from the environment. Hence, given the chance and congenial environment, women have flourishing future in thi.s field.

RATIONAL OF THE STUDY

The present study will focus on the scope of entry of women in journalism, which would prepare the present female youth for this novel and challenging profession. The study will also focus on understanding the sociology and professional status of women journalist and may provide guide lines to the employers to workout the structure, which provides conducive atmosphere to the women journalists to carry out their responsibilities.

POPULATION AND SAMPLE OF THE STUDY

The population of the study comprised of journalists from English and Gujarati press, local cable and broadcast network in Baroda. A formal list of journalists was taken from the office of the Deputy director, Information Bureau. An informed survey was conducted to identify the journalists from the English and Gujarati press, local cable network and from All India Radio Station in the city of Baroda in the year 2003. Thus twenty journalists were identified and they comprised the sample for the study.

DATA COLLECTION

Data was collected through an interview schedule. Journalists were contacted on phone to take prior appointment for interview. Thereafter they were contacted personally to conduct an in-depth interview.

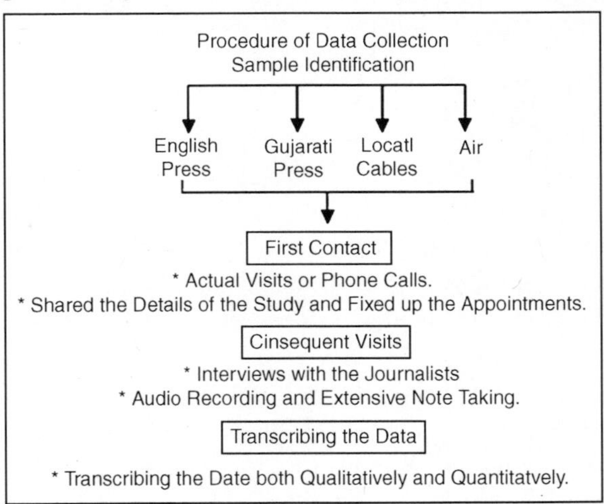

DISCUSSION

Regarding the scope of women in journalism, journalist unanimously felt that women have tremendous scope in this field. This may be due to the fact that in this brave new world, large number of women are entering the field of journalism.

A number of older hands are nearing the top of the editorial ladder and a handful have achieved what would have been unthinkable just a couple of decades age. Such periodic changes and other developing trends in the press will continue to influence the experience of and prospects for women in journalism.

Therefore, it was reported that:

- Women can join as reporters and can become chief editors"
- The opportunities for women are there in journalism, but they have to grab the opportunities."

Journalists under the study, strongly felt that English Press does not discriminate between journalists on the basis of gender and there is no gender based division of labour, which is a very progressive trend.

Contrary to this, male journalists from vernacular press reported that population of female journalists is very this in these press due to unconducive work environment for females and the images of women in these press organizations are stereotypical. This is a very serious problem faced by the women of developing countries, irrespective of the extent of development, face discrimination of the ground of sex in varying degrees in the matter of employment opportunities, working conditions and career growth.

This shows that there are barriers and limitations for women in the vernacular press. Women journalists who entered this profession in 60's and 70's had to work and fight hard to escape from the professional ghettos into which stray women in the media were then customarily herded.

A number of them managed to get into the coveted reporting stream, slowly making their way from flower shows to fires and eventually, event battle fronts of various kinds. They also forced newspaper establishments to contend with issues like maternity leave.

Now, at the turn of the century and millennium, women journalists seems to be everywhere streaming in and out of newspaper and magazine offices, bustling around in news rooms, and milling about wherever news of various sorts is being made. This trend shows women journalists do not have to undergo the same struggle as their counterparts in earlier years of entry.

Work environment, thinking of the people, awareness about various jobs has increased tremendously since the last two decades, which makes this profession worth for women to work. There is no doubt now, that women are in this profession to stay, and what is more, to make their mark.

On enquiry about whether men were more suitable for jobs in print media than female, mixed feelings and reactions were expressed. The reactions ranged from traditional to modern, to feminist thinking about women's suitability for journalism.

Some of the male as well as female journalists expressed that:

- Men are generally more suitable because women find it difficult to keep up with that long hours, odd hours and visit cretin places".
- Family do not allow women to go out at odd hours, during crisis.
- This is true during crisis. Women themselves do not like to go to various sensitive areas. Editors and senior reporters are responsible for them and therefore they do not allow women to cover controversial and sensitive issues".
- Thinking of journalist have changed towards women, but society has not changed.
- At times yes, especially at the time of riots, it is easier for males to move around.

From such reactions, one can conclude that men journalists are still considered superior and suitable. It confirms that women journalists were burdened with certain disadvantages are result of the responsibilities assigned to them and the social restrictions placed on them. One of the most damaging jobs.

The bosses invariably male, in their bias tend to give "softer" assignments to women that is the mofussil page if a subeditor, since it does not require a night shift. If given night duty, then her "safety" is the responsibility of males who have recruited her. They are made to realise that being women they cannot or should not handle crisis or emergencies.

On the other hand, there were men and women journalists, with modern views:

- Gender does not make difference. Sometimes men are also not able to handle the situations like riots".
- No today it is not so. Women journalists are equally creative, talented and hard working".

Such reactions show that there is no reason for unsuitability of women in journalism. It confirms that journalists have realised the competencies existing in female journalists. Gender does not confirm the suitability of person in the profession of journalism, but there are various other factors, which can be considered—like sincerity, dedication, confidence and personality of a person. There was one female journalist who revealed that, "The hazards of hard professional work are all man made, man borne, and man created. It is just the commitment and determination in individual which matters'.

In fact, one of the male journalists was also having the same views. "It is the male only who do not give her opportunity. In fact, women like to take challenges". There are very few respondents who had modern and feminist thoughts. It is surprising to know that journalists themselves are biased and are still blaming the society and societal roles which they have to follow. Such diverse views shows that a proper way thinking has to be generated amongst the literate masses towards women. Gender biases needs to be dissolved and a socialization pattern has to be favouring girls growth and development. Only then, as suggested, find our country a developed country, with equal rights to all human beings irrespective of gender.

Majority of the respondents irrespective of their sex, agreed that young women in print media are committed to their job. Respondents reported that women are serious, clear with their goals, determined, dedicated, interested and more ethical in their profession. However, a couple of male journalists had unfavourable responses.

They expressed that they might otherwise agree that women are more sincere workers, but with marriage and children, women are not able to do justice to journalism profession because of long job hours and irregular time schedules. Hence males in this profession are better options, women would not be able to do justice to this job.

According to Kapoor, A. in practice, though there are very few mothers working as full time correspondents in this field of journalism, many have not only done double duty, but also carved a niche for themselves in this profession. This includes name like Mrinal Pande, Coomi Kapoor, Usha Rai, Pamela Philipose and Rasheeda Bhagat, women who were among the first to bread the male bastion and work their way up, despite these prejudices.

When asked about the difference between men and women regarding their perception of news, majority of the male journalists expressed that women are more sensitive and emotional especially when it comes to women's issues. However, one journalist expressed absolutely different response. According to him, "In print media journalists are not looked as male and female. They are in the profession and unbiased.

The emotions and sentiments are put aside and they talk on the issue". Female respondents unanimously reported that the gender does not come in the way of their profession. The treatment to the news differs, but only on the basis of individuals and not gender wise. "Women think more critically", "do not take decisions in haste", are some of the other added responses of women journalists. Thus, the expression about women journalists regarding their approach to deal with the news and views, seemed to be free of gender bias. Males as. well as females more or less held the same view in this regard. Jha Rama also expressed that "women in the print media as professionals will have the same news sense as a male colleague would have with a bit of an extra. They would see the human angle in the story a little more quickly and would avoid doing a dry analysis".

"Women's issues do not find a place in print media", when told to the female respondents, almost ninety per cent of them expressed that it was true earlier. Over the years, it has improved. Today media is vigilant and women's issues are given weightage by giving adequate coverage. A couple of journalists expressed that women's issues are covered in print media, but they are mainly on atrocities on women and not on women's achievement in different areas. Researches stressed that "Women issues" are written about, but one of the things that has gone wrong is that these are written with such stringency and militancy that he reader does not read them. And as a result of this, the newspaper carry fewer and fewer articles on women. She suggested that. "They have to be written in much more human, much less militant way".

However, some studies refused to categorize women's issues as male and female concerns and responded, "Frankly I think if these issues are to be taken up, it is not for women journalists only, why shouldn't male journalists write about these? These issues are important to society as whole and, I am against the stereotoype of women writing on women's issues.

Thus, it is implied that coverage of women's issues, in print media is not adequate and not without its set of cultural biases. And even after the strides that women journalists in India have made, much remains to be achieved. These cultural biases in media in general will take time to completely vanish.

Meanwhile certain suggestions can be made which can go a ling way in eliminating gender biases and help bring in a certain buoyancy where women will have their due place without having to offer any justification to occupy. A very interesting finding emerged when the question regarding imbalance of the projection of women's atrocities' and women's achievements, in print was asked to the respondent. High majority of the males expressed that we do cover the women's achievement along with news on women's atrocities. But "we have to write according to the demands of the society, moreover we have to sell the newspaper so some sensational news is must". One of the male respondents conveyed that our society is not so bold to boast loudly about women's achievements.

In addition to the same, Anklesaria, also expressed, that newspaper project stories of atrocities on women like rape, etc. and never bother to project women achievers. The reasons she recounts are that. "There are so very few women actually committed to women's issues. And then so little is written about them. And if as a journalist, you cover only women's issues, it sometimes turns against you.

You are slotted and never given any other beat". Thus to conclude, on the part of journalists, "Self-Restraint" is a must, particularly on women's issues. Other wise there is a danger of sensationalizing reports on atrocities on women. Atrocities are atrocious enough. What is needed is a cool, objective, factual hard look at these, so that the subversion of women's interests that goes in the male dominated press does not occur.

When asked whether women's supplements in newspapers and magazines were women development oriented. Irrespective of the gender, respondents agreed that magazines do have scope for women's development, but unfortunately women are more or less interested with stereotypical areas, interested and want to stick to cooking, interior decoration and family care etc. The journalists expressed that average female reader would like to read about these stereotypical areas and very few would like to thrive for the articles which reflect the growth and development of women in the areas like education, career, etc. Thus, journalists have to cater to the demands of the majority of the readers.

Respondents were asked the possible ways of improving the image of women in print media. Majority of the male respondents expressed that this task can be fulfilled only when women themselves try hard for it. Women should change the stereotypical images in all spheres and thus the change will be reflected in media. Whereas the female journalists opined that women should build positive image in the society by becoming more aware about the surrounding, by raising voices against all odds, by encouraging other women for upliftment, by demanding women's development in all spheres and by becoming more inspired and motivate.

GLAMOROUS. INDUSTRY FAILS TO LOOK AFTER ITS OWN

Like in the rest of the country, in Madhya Pradesh, Chhattisgarh, Bihar and Jharkhand though the number of women in the media is steadily increasing, it continues to remain a male dominated field, one in which women have to struggle to create their own identity. In these four states, journalism itself has yet to establish professional norms.

The status of women journalists in the region is fraught with daily struggle. They are constantly battling discrimination at the workplace in terms of salary, promotions, amenities, benefits, areas of work allotted to them and sexual harassment. In Madhya Pradesh and Chhattisgarh the concept of women journalists with permanent jobs still does not exist.

While the.lucky. ones are those on contracts with a measure of job security for two to three years, most women work without appointment letters or designations and are hired and fired on the whims of the management. The method of payment for both men and women is a bit like that for daily wage labour on muster rolls.

They are verbally asked to begin work on a hazy work profile and at the end of the month sign a muster roll. Should there be any reason for either party to terminate the.understanding. the final settlement is made on a voucher. In some cases the journalists sign for a lump sum amount, payment for several months, on a voucher.

Most young journalists begin their careers in these states on ₹ 1500 as against the starting wage of ₹ 7000 to ₹ 8000 in the Delhi newspapers. If a journalist has to be axed, it is most often a woman who is asked to leave. The management.s reason for easing out women could range from the whimsical.can you justify what you have been doing for the last few months, to demoralising her by saying her work is not up to the mark without qualifying it or the edition is not doing well and we have to downsize. Along with gender specific problems the women journalists face, they also face area specific problems. Working conditions in urban areas differ to those in the rural areas and each has its own set of problems. While in Bihar, the All-Bihar Women Journalists. Forum has been formed and is quite active in helping women journalists with their work-related problems, in Madhya Pradesh and Chhattisgarh the union movement is weak. Despite the fact that women journalists in the region do not have the scope and facilities of those working in the bigger metropolitan cities they have still contributed to broadening press coverage, including reporting on a much neglected field—social issues.

They have played a major role in highlighting development issues and introducing human interest in the media. Despite this, the number of women in decision-making capacities is almost negligible. Work began by contacting editors of regional local newspapers. The response was mixed. Some cooperated and allowed us to meet journalists while others were not so helpful. After the initial visits to Chhattisgarh, Bihar and Jharkhand, few people were assigned specific responsibility.

For Chhattisgarh. Sapna Giri, for Bihar. Nivedita Jha, for Jharkhand. Vasavi, and for Indore. Archana Pillai. This effort was necessary because journalists in this region did not have easy access to the Internet. The experiences in filling in the questionnaires too have been mixed. In Rajya ki Nai Dunia, Bhopal there was just one woman reporter who readily filled the questionnaire and was open to an interview too. However, in Dainik Bhaskar, Bhopal, which has a good number of women journalists, many of them stalled filling the questionnaires on the pretext of a heavy workload.

In another local daily, Central Chronicle, women journalists refused to fill the questionnaire saying the management would not allow them and might take action against them if they did so. There was some tangible pressure on the employees, therefore, we did not insist. In their sister organisation, Nava-Bharat, reporters and sub-editors filled the questionnaires without hesitation.

In Deshbandhu, the lone woman sub-editor said she would not be able to fill questionnaires because of work pressure. In few small newspapers like Swadesh and Dainik Nai Dunia, no women journalists were employed. When people working there were asked why there were no women, they said the payment was not lucrative and the management found it easier to employ men who could do multiple jobs—report, work on the desk, do night shifts. They said many women refused to go out into the field and work nights, forcing the management to give preference to men. Some journalists who had left newspapers and had moved into the electronic media were curious to know if the questionnaires would translate into action that would benefit women journalists. Few journalists hinted that they had tough professional lives but did not reveal their stories for fear of losing their jobs.

In Bhopal most journalists claimed they did not have the time to fill the long questionnaire and agreed only after many requests. In Chhattisgarh, journalists were directly contacted in their offices and homes. They were very cooperative and every journalist spoke of her struggle to stay afloat in the profession. All of them wanted an improvement in their working conditions. Even responding to the questionnaire seemed to remove some of their frustrations and they wanted a follow up to the survey.

For Bihar and Jharkhand, Nivedita Jha and Vasavi followed up the questionnaires with personal interviews. Since Nivedita Jha has been actively involved in the All-Bihar Women Journalists. Forum she was able to co-ordinate the filling of questionnaires even at the district level. The survey included journalists from the electronic media, some of who had moved from the print to the electronic media.

It has not been possible to get a proper estimate of the actual number of women journalists because many of them, both in Hindi and English newspapers, and either refused to fill the forms or did not have the time to do so. Many of them were afraid of the management's reaction, were insecure and in some cases they were just indifferent. In Madhya Pradesh, 16 women responded. eight each from the Hindi and English language media.

Most of them are in their early twenties. Two were between 40 to 44 and there was none below the age of 20. Two were freelancers. None had permanent full-time jobs. All were on contracts and many were on the voucher system which meant they are not entitled to provident fund, gratuity and other benefits. There was not a single woman journalist in a senior position the highest being a sub-editor. Though most of them are post-graduates and had field experience, the average monthly salary is below ₹ 10,000. In Chhattisgarh too the 12 respondents, nine from the Hindi and three from the English language media, were all post-graduates, most of them below 35 years but none was earning over ₹ 10,000 a month. The highest position they had was that of a sub-editor and none of them was a permanent full-time employee. All are on contracts or worse still, as in Madhya Pradesh, on the voucher system.

In Bihar, of the 18 respondents, 11 were from the Hindi and seven from the English language media. Here too most of the women were on contracts. Five, however, were permanent full time employees and five were freelancers. As in MP and Chattisgarh most of them were below 35 years and their average monthly salary below ₹ 10,000.

Five, however, were earning up to ₹ 15,000 a month and one more than that. One was a bureau chief and eight are sub-editors. Most of them were post-graduates and some were graduates and almost all of them have been through a course in journalism. There were nine respondents from Jharkhand, four from the Hindi and five from the English language media. Most of them were below 35 years.

Three were freelancers, four on contracts and there was only one permanent full-time employee. Most of them worked for newspapers, one worked for a magazine, and none of them was in the senior echelons. Most of them were post-graduates and their average monthly salary was between ₹. 10,000 and ₹. 15,000. Most of them had done courses in journalism or served as apprentice journalists.

POORLY PAID, INSECURE IN NORTH EAST

Of the 35 questionnaires handed out, which was about the total number of women working in the print media in the North East—22 women responded. There were six respondents from the regional press and 16 from the English media. The age group of the 22 women who responded was between 20 to 40. Only three were above 40.

The major area of concern that emerged out of the survey was job security, low pay and lack of prospects:

- Only 35 per cent worked as permanent full time employees. The rest worked as permanent part timers or on contract basis.
- None of the respondents were in senior positions, the highest being a senior reporter and sub editor
- 72 per cent of them got salaries ranging between ₹.1500-₹.5000. Of this 7 per cent received salaries below ₹.1500.
- 40 per cent said that they had never been promoted, while 31 per cent said that they had been promoted once.
- There was no mechanism for addressing grievances or making appeals and even where there was such a mechanism it was inadequate.
- Only 27 per cent were members of some superannuation scheme.

NORTH-EAST, A WORLD APART

The number of women in the field of journalism in the states of north-east. Arunachal Pradesh, Assam, Manipur, Meghalaya, Mizoram, Nagaland and Tripura is minuscule. Not more than 35 women scribes work in the region, a majority of them at the desk. This is not surprising as journalism in general is still at a nascent stage in most parts of the region, barring Assam where its premier English daily, The Assam Tribune, is more than a century old.

The survey showed that most of the newspapers of the region are in the tiny scale (1000-10,000) and small sector and organised in an ad hoc manner. The bigger newspaper houses are based mainly in Assam. There are four of them and they do not have anything substantially better to offer to the journalists in general, leave alone women journalists.

Barring one House implementing the Bachawat Award, none of the others are implementing the wage board recommendations. Even among those media houses.partially. implementing the wage board recommendations, the management have a structure which divides journalists into two categories: one section of the few who are shown on the official records as permanent staff getting all the recommended benefits of the wage board and the other section of workers who are not shown on the official employees rolls, but are maintained separately as some kind of semi-permanent-temporary workers, not given the wage board recommended salaries, though they may have worked in the same media house for several years. Metropolitan newspapers (some call them.national newspapers.), such as The Telegraph, The Times of India, The Hindustan Times, The Asian Age etc which have their headquarters outside the region either in Delhi, Kolkata or Mumbai, have a multiple (based on the place of recruitment) employment policy.

The northeast editions of these newspapers recruit journalists locally in the states on a yearly contract with a consolidated take-home pay. In some other cases the journalist works without a contract of any kind as a stringer for a small, consolidated monthly payment, which keeps the journalists on tenterhooks.

In many cases there is no system of getting reimbursements for telephone bills, transport used for reporting etc. These newspapers maintain their regional bureau offices at Guwahati where they have built up good infrastructure. However, the outstation reporters and correspondents, functioning from the other states of the region, work on a measly consolidated payment from which they are supposed to meet their living expenses as well as work related expenses such as use of phone, e-mailing, transport, stationery etc.

This is an important reason for the big struggle for most journalists. In some cases, if the journalists had a.good relationship with the.manager. (who is usually a senior journalist) at the bureau headquarters, the payment of the phone bills, transport and other expenses could be negotiated. But these are not available to the journalist worker as a matter of job expenses.

There are examples of the management not clearing the bills of their correspondents for covering important happenings, which they had been assigned to cover. One of them had been asked to cover the last Lok Sabha elections in Garo Hills, Meghalaya. The expenses incurred during the field trip including hotel bills, travel, hiring vehicles etc are yet to be reimbursed and the correspondent has given up in disgust. This is not to speak of the amount of money already spent on telephoning the head office for clearing these bills. But all the reports filed from the location were published prominently by the daily. The wage board recommendations, as far as these newspapers are concerned, are applicable only to workers recruited at the head office of the newspaper wherever that may be, whether Delhi, Kolkata or elsewhere. This has led to a clear differentiation between staffers on the one hand and contract workers and stringers, based in the region. Moreover, the contracts signed with a local manager of the edition, and these contracts remain confidential so that none of the journalists knows what the other person is being paid. The.secret. contract system is used to play up one journalist against the other and this was experienced in many of the newspapers houses of the region.

During the survey journalists said that this was highly discriminatory, promoting sycophancy, creating an unhealthy working atmosphere and heightening job insecurity. Journalists interviewed said this chaotic and unfair system of employment is at the root of the lackadaisical journalistic culture. The survey showed that journalism was a low option as a long-term career. The pay packet is extraordinarily small.

It ranges largely between ₹.1500-₹. 3000 even for those who had worked for more than two years. Another journalist, from the same organisation, who had worked for 15 years as a permanent staffer was receiving a salary ranging between ₹.10,000 to ₹.15,000. The survey showed that there was no upward mobility both in terms of promotion and pay scales. As for special facilities for women journalists in terms of maternity leave etc, they are non-existent in most cases. Journalists are underpaid and most of the time work on undignified terms and conditions.

They can be fired at the whim and fancy of the proprietor. In some of the better newspaper houses journalists work on a one year contract basis.temporary permanent, while in most others they are not even issued proper appointment letters outlining their job, pay scale etc. Chayamoni Bhuyan illustrates the problem of journalists in general. In her mid-twenties Chayamoni, worked for a Guwahati-based Assamese daily, claimed to be the highest circulated daily. She had been working there for about three years when she was chosen along with nine other journalists of the country to cover the September 11 anniversary functions in the USA under a United States Information Service programme. She found to her dismay when she returned home that she was out of job. She was refused her salary for the month when she was on tour on the ground that she was absent from work.

It did not make any difference to the management that she had filed more than a dozen stories from the various locations they had visited all of which were carried prominently in her newspaper. The newspaper management did not even think it necessary to reimburse the amount she had spent getting her stories faxed from the various locations in the US to her newspaper. Moreover, when she stood up for her rights she was given the cold shoulder by the management and had to quit.

There was no mechanism for any kind of redressal or compensation. She did not have any appointment letter but had been working in good faith that all these would be provided sooner or later. She had joined a new daily, launched around that time, where it was clear that a proper salary could not be expected for a long time to come. But despite all the drawbacks in working conditions and lack of recognition, she is not prepared to leave the profession, which she has grown to love and respect.

All the women journalists interviewed were graduates or post-graduates, with several of them holding diplomas or professional degrees in journalism and mass communication. However, despite holding high degrees and having experience in the media their pay scales were not commensurate with their qualifications. While most of the journalists said that there was no gender discrimination at the work place, there was a general feeling that the existing general male bias in the larger society was all-pervasive.

These are manifested in various ways such as the kind of beats women are traditionally assigned to cover. Some newspaper houses have an unwritten policy not to employ women reporters as they bring.lot of trouble. in the sense that they do not want to do night shifts, need to be dropped home at night, need special rest rooms, and so on. Most of the women interviewed did not consider their gender a handicap, but definitely felt that the general view that women were handicapped because of their gender hampered their aspirations But of far more concern was the lack of training, exposure and hope for better employment opportunities which continued to be a major drawback for them as well as for their male colleagues. Experience during the survey All the journalists were very happy that such a survey was being undertaken. They hoped that it would help better their professional lives. However, almost all of them found the questionnaire.inadequate. or.confusing. and some of them said that the.questions did not apply to them.. The paucity of funds hampered travel as transport is costly in the north eastern states. Added to this is the time consuming nature of hill travel as all transport is by road. Several times appointments fixed were put off as the interviewees had to rush off to cover a spot story.

About fifty questionnaires were distributed but few were returned. It is also to be noted since the questionnaire did not correspond to their prevailing situation; the interviewer took the liberty of doing the survey through question and answer sessions with the journalists.

JOURNALISM IN THE NORTH-EAST REGION

It is important to remember that the growth of journalism in the region has taken off at a somewhat different tangent from the way the news business has grown in other parts of the country or even the world. Because of its peculiar history and experience, the region is one of the high-intensity conflict zones not only within the country but globally.

There are more than 300 different tribes and communities inhabiting the region scattered across state and international boundaries. Scores of tribal and ethnic armies fighting for homelands based on the theory of self-determination, preserving their identity etc. against each other and with the Government in a tangled web of discords. All these have made the region a zone of strife where journalism has been spawned in the fires of activism for these various causes. One of the many questions, which were raised during the survey, was how the style of reporting and the intense focus on sensational scoops in such a scenario could be contributing to the strife in the region. The journalist reporting in the region has a tough task of maintaining some semblance of journalistic ethics and objectivity amidst this cacophony of conflicting causes and still manage to write the.news as it happens.

Therefore besides the need for general training, special capacity building for conflict reporting is an urgent requirement here. The total readership has grown by leaps and bounds over the years. So has the number of newspapers hitting the stands. But this has not meant better working conditions for the journalists.

Another aspect of the growth of the newspaper industry in the region is that while there is a market boom, with four metropolitan newspapers often referred to as.national newspapers. setting up north-east or Guwahati Editions, the northeast editions of these newspapers sold in the seven states are 50 to 100 per cent costlier than the other editions sold in other parts of the country. Paradoxically there is no reflection of this prosperity in the working conditions of the journalists in these newspapers, nor is there wider information flow as is to be expected. In fact, the finding of this survey is that these media houses have looked upon the north-east region purely from the market point of view, casting aside their social responsibility *i.e.* disseminating information. The information generated from north-east correspondents is published only in these north-east editions, leading to a situation where the northeast is effectively blacked out in their.national. editions.

The alienation of the people of the region, and the ignorance of the rest of the nation about the region, has only been compounded by this market-based media policy. A study could be made on the advertisement policy of these newspapers which garner advertisements for all-India publications from the north-east governments under the garb of being.nationally circulated newspapers. at exorbitant rates. This.unfair. trade practice is slowly strangling the local newspaper houses which are finding it difficult to compete with the slick production and unabashed market strategy of these.north-east editions.. At another tangent reflecting the diversity of culture and languages in the region, there is a proliferation of tiny scale newspapers all over the region to serve the reading needs of these diverse populations. These newspapers are usually far from economically viable but have a powerful role to play in society.

PRESS IN THE SOUTH

In the regional language journalism in the four southern states of Andhra Pradesh, Karnataka, Tamil Nadu and Kerala, only Kannada has two women journalist-editors who reached the top from the ranks, one each for a daily and a magazine. There is also a woman assistant editor in a Kannada daily. In Tamil, a.working journalist. is the editor of a Tamil magazine while there are none in the Telugu and Malayalam press.

Although there are women at senior positions (exactly one in Telugu and one in Malayalam) in other languages, there are no women editors. Reporting remains a male preserve although youngsters are breaching it in all the four languages. Women might be reporting and interviewing people for articles, but it is only occasionally and out of personal interest.

They are basically appointed to the desk and are full time sub editors. While there are no women journalists outside the metropolitan cities or state capitals, in Kannada one finds women as district correspondents. In Telugu although there are newspapers that publish editions from the district headquarters, women are absent in editorial areas. Telugu and Kannada journalism have at least a 30-year history of recruiting women journalists even if they have been very few.

While Kannada women journalists did election surveys, in Andhra women journalists as far back as the mid-70s were doing the night shift. The mainstream Malayalam press had an unwritten law on not recruiting women while the ideological dailies did employ a few, all of them on the desk. Even today the Tamil press has the least number of women in comparison to the other languages in the south. The language dailies have followed the English press in recruiting women for their features desk as most have a daily a supplement. The opportunities in.soft writing. have opened up the newspapers to women since they are believed to be good in writing features. This also involves reporting, mostly on non-political issues. While this is true of the Telugu, Kannada and Malayalam press, the strong presence of magazines in Tamil has prevented the Tamil dailies from providing space for feature pages and colour supplements and thus opportunities for women in newspapers are very few.

In total contrast to the situation in the regional press, English language press is literally teeming with women especially in Bangalore, Chennai and Hyderabad where papers like Times of India, Deccan Herald (of Bangalore), The Hindu, The New Indian Express and Deccan Chronicle (of Hyderabad) have a strong presence. In Trivandrum, the Malayalam press dominates and the circulation of English papers is comparatively small.

In Bangalore and Hyderabad the English newspapers employ women in large numbers and they occupy important positions such as editor, chief reporter, chief sub editor. Generally women are concentrated in features and Sunday magazine sections. Occasionally women are reporters on the crime beat but rarely do they do politics and legislature reporting.

There are half dozen women correspondents of outstation English papers in all the capital cities in the south and they invariably cover politics too. They have been appointed because of their seniority and at times because they work for news magazines which requires feature writing too and so the preference for women.

WOMEN IN ENGLISH PRESS

Women in the English language press do not have the same problems as their sisters in the language press. They are better paid, and even if on contract, have better facilities at workplace, have toilets and washrooms, get transport back home after night shift, get maternity leave and various perks and privileges. (Andhra Jyoti, a Telugu daily of Andhra, has a common toilet for men and women while Malayalam Manorama had to find space to build toilets for women when they began to recruit women a few years ago). There are several women at mid-level and senior level in The Hindu. women who worked themselves up from the ranks to the position of deputy editors, special correspondents, chief sub editors and so on. The Indian Express has had a long tradition of employing women as reporters many of whom have risen to the position of chief reporter. So also in Deccan Herald of Bangalore where women have been assistant editors, chief reporters, foreign correspondent, special correspondent, chief sub editor.

Deccan Chronicle has a woman editor while Times of India has a woman bureau chief in Bangalore. Nirmala Laxman, Associate Editor of The Hindu, said there had been a 25-30 per cent increase in women's intake in the organisation but she believes there has to be a concerted effort to recruit women. Quite a few women believe there are no discrimination and no glass ceiling in major English language papers. However, there is a tendency to push women into feature writing and even non-serious writing such as reporting parties and social events. The feature desks in The Hindu and Deccan Chronicle and Deccan Herald are all-women affairs. Some women believe this ghettoisation. of women, and keeping them out of.mainstream news papering does no good for their future in journalism.

Ammu Joseph for instance points out that an acknowledged tendency among girls is to focus on serious issues but with more jobs in non-serious journalism, the girls tend to be herded into celebrity and lifestyle journalism. Like the women's columns or women's clubs of earlier times, women tend to get bogged down in their features sections. Sudha Ramachandran, former Assistant Editor of Deccan Herald, who is perhaps the only woman who writes on a regular basis from home for DH even after quitting it, believes that women should get into the mainstream of the paper..Let them stop sitting in the supplements; politics is the core of the newspaper; they should do more politics, she says.

Also she says women should insist on a level playing field because whenever women play wimpy they damage other women's cause. Women journalists in English newspapers believe that they are at a disadvantage compared to men because they do not politick or network. They are not glass-mates nor do they have.bar-room bonding.. So they lose out in terms of promotions and prized assignments. Even when in senior positions, women lose out in power struggles because they do not or cannot use their power as they are not used to it. Another reason why women in senior and decision making positions admit they do not use their power is because the system does not enable or empower women. Being emotional too they get easily upset and so prefer to avoid any kind of confrontation as it impacts upon their performance. This kind of being loners, keeping away from others concerns also makes women indifferent to standing by their colleagues or friends during times of crisis like sexual or personal harassment.

They prefer not to get embroiled because they are fearful of the consequences. In two instances of sexual harassment in Deccan Chronicle of Hyderabad, women colleagues of the women harassed did not support them. Nor did the women colleagues stand by a senior woman in Praja Vani, a Kannada daily from Bangalore when she was personally harassed for more than a year forcing her to resign. If there is a network or a group or greater camaraderie then they could develop enough mental strength to fight for a cause. Another solution could be to get more and more women on a newspaper's rolls so that there would be strength in numbers.

WAGES AND CONTRACT SYSTEM

Women might have been well off in the English lagnuage press in terms of salaries and other perks compared to the regional language press but with the contract system becoming a norm now, women seem to be getting short-changed. They do not know how to read a contract, or how to negotiate.

They have no idea of the benefits they can get or perks they should demand. They tend to accept what is offered and end up getting less than their male colleagues who are junior to them or do not get normal benefits like leave, reimbursements, Provident Fund and so on. In the regional press, especially in Telugu newspapers, no pay scales are prevalent, neither for women nor men. They are paid consolidated amounts, even in vouchers in some cases. In the case of leading newspaper groups like Eenadu, differential scales are given for employees working in different magazines.

Only a handful of senior people get the Wage Board pay scales. Gradually all the newspapers are opting for the contract system for new recruits. In Andhra Jyoti, a Telugu daily, that changed hands and was revived a year ago after closure for a few years, every person negotiates salary personally. Almost all the 12/14 women took what was offered to them. At least half of them work for less than what they were earning earlier or less than their male colleagues who are junior to them in the profession. The situation seems better in other languages in the south but the contract system is seen as a bane in the English newspapers.

The Hindu seems to be the only organisation that continues to recruit people on Wage Board scales.

Women are not clear about the implications of the contract system, what to ask and what to expect as they are being pressurised to move to the contract system. In fact, a senior woman journalist wondered if the substantial number of women in senior positions in English newspapers was due to the fact that the managements got them cheap!

MARRIAGE, MATERNITY AND DOMESTIC RESPONSIBILITIES

The biggest burden on women in journalism is their domestic responsibilities as wife, mother and daughter-in-law. The brightest and most successful journalists have left a bright career to settle down in matrimony or have moved to less demanding jobs when children arrive. For women, almost invariably, the home comes first. A T Jayanti editor of Deccan Chronicle, believes that as home is always a woman.s responsibility it naturally affects her work.

.I have no problem with any girl until she marries. she says. For most of them, home comes first whatever the concessions given, says Jayanti. Most girls, even in the middle class, urban, educated families, fettered by conventions and customs of society, find it difficult to break out of constraints imposed on them. Women editors both in English and language press have admitted to being extra considerate and going the extra mile to retain women on their rolls especially the brighter ones but often they fail because the girls are hesitant to break out of the mould into which they have been cast. The biggest problem they believe is that the girls have no clear picture of what they want, of what their dreams are for themselves or where their future lies. So they get pressurised by their parents to opt for marriage or by in-laws and husbands to quit the newspapers and opt for routine jobs where they will have regular timings, no pressures of deadlines and no great expectations of them. Women across the four states said they were successful when backed by cooperative husbands or kind mothers-in-law.

Others depended on their mothers to help them out when office pressures increased. Vasantalakshmi, features editor of Andhra Jyoti, says that before marriage girls take great interest in their work, even moving house near the office or ask parents or brothers to pick them up after late shift. However, once they marry and have children, they shift to other departments or drop out of the profession because of the responsibility they feel for their children. They feel guilty and this affects their self-esteem. If women can afford it financially, they prefer to opt out of the profession. Some do want to return after the children grow up but there are not many opportunities.

Quite a few women especially in the English language press have put off having children in favour of their careers. Most women who took a break to bring up children or even those who stayed home for a few months to have children believe they lost out on growth and promotions. Some women even lose their jobs as maternity leave is not available to them. Quite a few women especially in the English language press put off marriage and children either to stabilise professionally or because of the demands of the job. Some organisations go out of the way to be considerate to women with young children but mostly women are on their own where children are concerned. Young mothers would like child care facilities in their workplace so that they can concentrate on their work instead of worrying about leaving the kid with an unreliable maid or a crèche. Some suggested that organisations should consider having child care facilities not just for women employees but also for men as it would go a long way in building an enabling atmosphere for new and young mothers and fathers.

PROMOTIONS

Promotions are rare in both the English language and the regional press and no newspaper organisation has any transparent system of assessing performance. The result is that promotions are arbitrary and capricious, giving rise to frustration. There are instances of women not having been promoted even in 10-15 years or being promoted only once in a career of 20 years. There is no policy of promotion in any organisation. While The Hindu promotes everyone across the line every few years, its financial daily has introduced a system of performance assessment wherein two best stories of the day are rated.

While this is expected to give instant recognition and reward to the staffers and encourage them, some believe that it does not take into consideration that stories depend on the kind of beat one is given. Also this system ignores the performance of the desk. In organisations where women are in good numbers they say there is equal opportunity in writing and reporting assignments but not in promotions. In fact while a woman journalist said discrimination against women was an.archaic. thing, K H Savitri, editor of the Kannada magazine Karmaveera said it will take at least 20 years for the regional press to match the facilities and opportunities for women in the English language press. Nirmala Lakshman of The Hindu believes there is hope for women in journalism..But the biggest hope for us is the younger generation of men who are more gender-sensitive.

BUTTERFLIES NO MORE

The pursuit of equality is not just some grand feminist design. It is a matter of human rights, as much in the media as in the other spheres of life journalists routinely report on. With women increasingly joining the media, it has been a long way that women journalists as a group have travelled in the profession. Certainly a long way since the day the patriarch of West Bengal's most well-known media group commented in mock-horror when he spotted the first batch of women in the news room:.What are these butterflies doing here?. The study of how these women in the media perceive their position was conducted in four states: West Bengal, Uttar Pradesh, Uttaranchal and Orissa among women journalists from both English and regional media. It revealed, sometimes, glaringly different perspectives between the two, whether in terms of the attitude among journalists and the management or in opportunities and facilities available to the staffers.

NO NIGHT DUTY PLEASE, THEY ARE LADIES

Media houses like the Bartaman in Kolkata would still like to believe that women journalists are like butterflies. fragile, to be protected. Women are not given duty after 7 pm, as a result of which even experienced journalists are denied responsible decision-making positions and challenging assignments, and also forced to forego promotions.

Though they agree on the one hand, that the management's concern for their safety has led to a friendly work atmosphere, on the other, its paternal preoccupation with their security has shackled their progress as professionals. In sharp contrast, it was way back in 1981 when Aajkal's founder editor, Gour Kishore Ghosh was the first, in both the English and Bengali media, to actively encourage women to take up night shifts. He was far sighted enough to realise that if they avoided it, it would be the basis of discrimination against them in the organisation.

He provided for a healthy atmosphere, say women staffers appreciatively, by assuring them that misbehaviour. by male colleagues would not be tolerated in the workplace. The largest Bengali daily, Ananda Bazar Patrika, was to follow suit and go even one step further to facilitate women journalists in their professions by providing for car lifts for both the evening and night shifts.

MIXED RESPONSE FROM THE MANAGEMENT

But many regional media houses like Amar Ujjala in Dehradun, the second largest Hindi daily, don't even employ a woman journalist in the organisation..They are difficult to get, commented the editor. Yet he showed great interest when informed about the study, quizzed the interviewer about the trends emerging among Hindi journalists and immediately published a short report in his newspaper.

Other media managements in UP and in Orissa are said to be keen to promote women journalists. A senior editor of a Hindi newspaper in Lucknow enthusiastically asked his women staffers to cooperate with the study and confided.They are very backward, they need greater exposure to women' issues.. While there was some truth in his observation, it was, nevertheless, patronising to imply that male employees are abreast of the situation and do not need to develop awareness of the issues. However, the scenario was quite different among women journalists of Dharitri, a new Oriya newspaper. They spoke glowingly of the editor who encourages them to overcome hurdles and opt for reporting. While actively promoting equal opportunities in the media house, the management combines it with commercial interest. It is perhaps the only one in the country to celebrate March 8 as International Women' Day in a swanky city hotel sponsored by the beauty industry.

GENDER IS NOT AN ISSUE

If media managements are grappling—willy-nilly—to keep up with the times, some women journalists themselves would not like to perceive the issue through a gender lens. A few refused to participate in the study and objected to the prefix.women. journalists voicing the apprehension it would go against them professionally, which implied that the prefix has a negative nuance.

One journalist in Kolkata withdrew her response to the interview when it came to the section on sexual harassment, outraged that such a question should even be asked of journalists who belong to a.respectable and educated profession. It does not happen among people like us, she maintained..To even accept that such an incident could happen is to spit on one' own face. On the other hand, while enthusiastically participating in the study, Sunita Araon, resident editor of Hindustan Times, Lucknow correctly cautioned.Don' make gender an issue to shirk work or bargain for special favours.

This goes against us. There is of course need and scope to improve the mechanics of the system.. However, the hostility shown by many journalists in being classified shows a level of confidence and coming-of-age in the profession. Yet it could also imply a tacit acceptance of the prevalent false notion. that being professional and assertive is a male thing. By denying one' gender, argue some, is to be defensive about an essential part of one' identity and follow norms and culture set by men so as to be part of the baradiri or brotherhood. It could be a coincidence that those who questioned the separate study on the group were senior journalists from the English language media, as also those who were given the questionnaire in the four states but withheld participation in the study, despite numerous reminders and counter-promises. Even the occasional curtness encountered while conducting the study was by colleagues from the English language media.

THE QUESTIONNAIRE ITSELF WAS A LEARNING PROCESS

To the majority of the interviewees, answering the questionnaire itself. though all complained of the cumbersome length!. was a process of learning, debating and becoming aware of issues they had not registered earlier or given much importance. Whether it was on matters of appointment, job assignment or office atmosphere, many said they had to confront questions closely related to their professional life for the first time, before they could commit an answer. For example, when a senior journalist in Uttar Pradesh maintained that facilities for both men and women journalists were the.same, little did the interviewer realise that she meant it literally when she was directed to the.common toilet for both men and women staffers.

Only when she refused to use the toilet and was led to an abandoned rooftop did the journalist understand the incongruity of the situation she had unwittingly accepted for years! When some women journalists lamented they had never tried reporting or were limited to a few.feminine beats, they came to realise that in most instances it was not their lack of competence but the absence of opportunity, editor' lack of trust in their ability or bias in the department that allows male reporters to unquestioningly bag plum assignments.

Though the majority of the English language journalists expressed no aversion or discomfort with the study on.women. journalists, in general it was the journalists of the regional press who were more enthusiastic and less cynical about the study. First, they showed more curiosity about other media houses in the country and progress by women journalists and were keen to discuss the recent trends in journalism. Second, the journalists in the regional media seemed to work harder than their English-language counterparts.

This is perhaps because they have to make do with fewer office facilities, job opportunities in the market and their relatively less.polished. academic background. Personal conversations revealed the struggle against bias many had to undergo both in the family and the work place to earn grudging acceptance of their livelihood.

NETWORKING IS POWER

The interviews in Orissa, for example, were easier facilitated because of the banding together of women journalists into an organisation, however fledgling, which is part of the newly formed Network of Women in Media, India. Low budget but safe accommodation in a new city and facilitating networking and interviews all within a span of one-and-a-half days were possible perhaps, due to the network' guidance and help.

Though some have questioned the need for a segregated professional body, many have felt the need for a support group and a special space to share and exchange. When informed of the initiative during the interviews, journalists especially in Uttar Pradesh and Uttaranchal showed keen interest and in Kolkata a few even joined the Bengal Network (part of NWMI). But it was also only in Kolkata that a few journalists who could not get over their obsession with politics probed whether the study or the network had any.party connections..

POOR PAY, POOR QUALITY

The good news is that compared to the English media, there is a phenomenal rise in the circulation of regional language print media in the country. The bad news is this does not translate into higher quality of news content in the pages. The strides made by the Hindi press are, says editor of Amar Ujjala, because of the multiple editions of a newspaper with the front page dealing with local news in contrast to English newspapers whose claim to being.national. make them obsessed with Delhi for the lead. Media observers in Lucknow say that the phenomenon of hiring contract workers in the multiple editions of Hindi newspapers has adversely affected the quality of journalism. The sense of insecurity among journalists due to lack of labour laws and poor pay sometimes as low as ₹ 1,000.2000 a month has led to the best brains seeking other professions..As a result we now have poorly educated journalists who can' even write a straight sentence in Hindi, said a senior editor of Dainik Jagaran, the largest selling Hindi daily.

She could be talking of other regions too. The media managements in the states surveyed are today increasingly expecting journalists especially in the districts to procure advertisements for the organisation along with news, thereby compromising their professional ethics as it becomes a quid pro quo relationship with the firms obliging. As a result, editors complain, on the one hand, about spurious news with no means to cross check.

People in the area on the other hand, accuse the mushrooming journalists, which newspapers are increasingly depending on, of becoming centres of power, using the press card as a tool to threaten and spread fear if they do not comply. This phenomenon of.stringers. is largely restricted to the men as women are unable to find a foothold in the toughness that the job requires.

BREAKING BOUNDARIES

The media has thrown up many women who are making progress by leaps and bounds. Whether it is Sunita Aron, resident editor in UP or Jaskiran Chopra heading the UNI bureau of the newly-formed Uttaranchal state, or Gouri Chatterjee, editor of the most popular feature section of The Telegraph, they have impacted the media and their respective organisations with their consummate capabilities and astute insights. Still others are inching forward, working capably in the most difficult situations. Archana whizzes around in her two-wheeler wherever there is news in the making and does not allow the absence of safety and transport in Bhubaneswar to deter her. Suman of Ghaziabad has never missed an event in volatile Ayodhya, however high the political tempers on the mandir/nmasjid issue. Then there are those who have penetrated the male bastions like Madhumita Bose, the first business reporter in Kolkata, Elora Sen who heads a Sports desk, Mitali Ghosh covers cricket in the fields and Seema edits a Hindi weekly Science page. Today these women journalists are breaking grounds in their demanding profession, and breaking free at last from being fossilised butterflies.

WE DEDICATED THE WOMEN'S PAGE TO RAPE

Data collection for the study was amazingly revealing, interesting but also exasperating when response rates to the formatted questionnaires were not exactly gratifying. In travelled to Chandigarh, Jullundur, Amritsar and Jammu where I met some interesting women journalists. But most revealing was the meeting with Mr Hari Jaisingh, former editor of Tribune, who more than underlined the attitude to women not only in media organisations but also in Indian society. We don't discriminate here work conditions for women are more than fair. We provide ntransport at night and even have an all women team in the magazine section.

I sent Ruchika (a young reporter) to cover the Gujarat earthquake for 12 days and Aditi (another young reporter) for 17 days to cover elections and this despite both being better looking than Barkha Dutt! Maternity leave in my view, upsets the balance of work schedules and creates the practical problem of leave. Do you know this is the only Chandigarh paper with a weekly women's page?

You can understand my commitment to women's issues by the fact that last week we dedicated that page to rape. As a policy we do not publish revealing pictures or offensive language. In fact we even edit Khushwant Singh. Looking for broad-based inputs, interviews were conducted with Urdu, Punjabi, Hindi and English writers of different seniority. In Jullundur, Vandana Walia Bali of Punjab Kesri nspoke about being denied seniority after maternity leave and about the moral dilemma of leaving a new-born child to pursue her career that was the toughest period of my life when In was filled with self-doubt, guilt, hate and cried all the time.

Three young journalists from Hindustan Times, Indian Express and Dainik Jagran spoke about the sexual harassment by seniors within their organisations and their extreme vulnerability since.no one wants women as colleagues in the first place.. All complaints are countered by.we told you so. This is no place for women.. All of them had followed a sister, brother, father or husband into the profession. In Amritsar the small Indian Express office was very basic and even lacked a separate washroom.

The group I met were from Indian Express and Hindustan Times with a well thought out list of requirements which were similar to those demanded by most, irrespective of small town papers or of metros. They believed that training is required not only for value addition but also for self-esteem; that contract system plays havoc with ability to hold organisations accountable for work conditions and facilities. They faced various vexing problems at their workplace. Colleagues and subordinate staff view blue films and porn sites on their computers, which are left to embarrass them on start up.

Another irritating ploy was to carry on loud embarrassing personal and private conversations on the telephone. Male bosses indulged in blatant professional cheating (plagarising stories) for projecting themselves at the cost of the careers of the young journalists.

What they wanted to know was how to address such problems and whom to approach for advocacy and redressal. In Chandigarh, senior columnist Rita Sharma made some very revealing observations. According to her, when she joined the profession 20 years ago, sexual harassment was not an issue since the feudal mindset of men here made them protective but at the same time they did not acknowledge women as professionals.

They insisted that her husband was her ghostwriter. But now with increasing numbers and growing visibility of women, things are different. Women journalists are almost like trophies to be displayed my daughter-in-law is a journalist so it puts greater pressure on young journalists who despite adverse conditions, cannot quit.

At the level of sources, from personal experience she noticed that after the Shivani Bhatnagar episode, people were scared to meet a woman journalist alone. Rita has been instrumental in highlighting women's concerns in her capacity as Chairperson of the Women Journalists Committee of the Chandigarh Press Club..Our young women too need to be more aware, she says, while narrating an incident where she told a group of young women journalists that they could benefit from becoming members of the Press Club. They retorted. But we don't believe in clubbing!. Echoing her observations is Donna Suri. Here you cannot appeal to what is the law or what is ethically right. It is the grand patriarchal view that is more easily acceptable. Her reference is to an episode that took place while she was with the Tribune. The editor announced withdrawal of transport facilities for her.

She confronted him with.how would you feel if your daughter had to travel alone at odd hours? Transport was restored Donna Suri moved to India from USA after she married her.brown man in a funny hat. Since then, for the last 22 years, she has been part of the journalism scene in Chandigarh. Back then this place was full of kakas and beebas and the environment was very stuffy.. In 1982 she was the first woman to join the Tribune where she was allocated a small, isolated room.almost as if I was in purdah.. She quickly removed all illusions by wandering into newsrooms and shaking hands with everyone. The response was.

Foreigners are like this. Very nice! She has adjusted well Donna has lived through some trying times. She spoke about a certain editor who would often extract money and sexual favours for approving bylines. Prem Bhatia's (the boss) attitude to such people was every good journalist is a bit of a crook. Donna did not consider reporting against the sexual-favours seeker since she was quite sure that she would be victimised. In another instance, on joining a new organisation, her remuneration commiserate to her experience, happened to be more than that of several male assistant editors.

They were up in arms because she was a woman. The editor requested her to voluntarily take a pay cut. Donna refused and also walked out because. I didn't want to work in an environment where the editor couldn't stand up to his staff.

Though very confident about the abilities of young women journalists who she says are include to opportunities, constantly seeking stimulation, committed to themselves and do push for more professionally; she warns against continued desk work where zombification is rapid. She insists that in her experience, the best strategy for women is to believe in themselves and that the best line of defence is always your own. Ironically, in Jammu, while the Daily Excelsior, an English daily, has a policy against employing women journalists, an Urdu daily has been headed by Begum Imrana Samnani for the last 30 years..Initially I was a rarity and the attitude to my presence in press-conferences and other media happenings was negative. But my attitude was–I am here to stay so you have got to accept me.

Data collection was particularly frustrating in the nation's capital. Journalists were contacted on e-mail, by personal interaction, individually, collectively at the Indian Women's Press Corps and also through friends of friends. But the response was very poor—indifferent and apathetic. It was also poignant that a PII (Press Institute of India) peon on an errand to deliver n35 sets of responses in hard copy was mugged. The incident resulted in the loss of data, his precious ₹ 75/- and a lot of legwork for PII staff who lodged an FIR, but to no avail.

In all the dialogue and discussions with women journalists, one common strain was the concern about the threat to stability in their private lives that the profession seemingly poses. In almost all cases, conversation veered to domestic life and wherever there was no problem, women didn't see it as a normal situation but one for which they had to be grateful to the spouse/mother-in-law/parents. Having it all, according to most, is fiction. Women can either have successful, satisfying careers with either broken relationships or guilt-ridden motherhood or dysfunctional families. But most of the time they opt for satisfying family lives and compromise on their careers.

WOMEN JOURNALIST: NO BIG DEAL

The women journalists survey personally has been an enriching experience. I enjoyed meeting fellow journalists in so many cities and states and speaking diverse languages. But for this survey, I would never have visited various media houses. The memories of these meetings range from very many happy ones to some unpleasant ones.

In was allotted four states. Maharashtra, Goa, Gujarat and Rajasthan. Maharashtra is relatively more progressive with women journalists being represented even in the Marathi newspapers of smaller towns. In Gujarat, however, metro cities like Baroda and Ahmedabad too do not have women journalists except two women proprietor journalists and three women journalists in Ahmedabad. In contrast, Rajasthan, almost similar to Gujarat in its sociocultural traditions, has a sizeable number of women journalists in Hindi newspapers in Jaipur.

In Jodhpur and Udaipur there were one and three respectively. In Maharashtra, the metro cities, Mumbai, Pune, Nagpur, as well as smaller cities like Kolhapur, Nashik, Aurangabad and Solapur have at least half a dozen women writing in Marathi. By and large, in metro cities like Mumbai, Pune, Nagpur, Jaipur, Baroda, Ahmedabad and Panaji women journalists are well represented in the English media.

Places like Mumbai and the Pune Indian Express in particular, have more women than men and they often joke with their women bosses to.Get a male for a change. Women journalists in the English press, by and large, come from a progressive atmosphere middle or higher class families and society and work among people from similar sociocultural background. Hence they do not have to face conservative, traditional outlook towards women.

Again these women have empowered themselves intrinsically they appear strong willed and are women of substance. Most of them seem to have developed a defence shield around themselves with a stern, no non-sense personality. a barrier difficult to break. The same is true about women in Marathi media in Mumbai and to some extent in Pune, Nashik and Nagpur. Even the women in Jaipur's Hindi media are strong women. The female Hindi journalist from Jodhpur is an epitome of courage. In contrast, women in vernacular media in smaller cities like Sangli, Kolhapur, Solapur, Aurangabad, Jaipur, Udaipur are pretty vulnerable and do not seem to be taken seriously.

Table. Response of Women Journalists

Centre WJ	Respondents	Vernacular	% Age of Vernacular to Total No.	Total No. of WJ Contacted of Respondents	% Age of Respondents to Total No. of Contacted
Mumbai	40	18	45	200	20
Pune	18	2	11	61	30
Nashik	2	1	50	14	14
Nagpur	15	5	33	37	41
Aurangabad	1	1	100	7	14
Kolhapur	0	0	0	5	0
Solapur	2	2	100	4	50
Satara	1	1	100	1	100
Sangli	5	5	100	5	100
Ahmedabad	27	6	22	33	82
Vadodara	4	0	0	12	33
Jaipur	28	20	71	37	76
Jodhpur	1	1	100	1	100
Udaipur	3	3	100	4	75
Total	**147**	**65**	**44**	**421**	**35**

While some take their work as a mere job and accept they have limitations as women, others are ambitious but are not given opportunities to prove their calibre. The condition of these women in the vernacular media is largely due to the socio-cultural background of their colleagues and the local people with whom they have to interact.

The condition and image of women journalists is a reflection of society. While metros have an open environment and people are used to seeing women in all walks of life, in smaller cities like Kolhapur women remain within the confines of their homes and people are not used to seeing women in offices or in public life.

5

Development of Newspaper Printing

INTRODUCTION

Since newspapers began as a journal, or record of current events, the profession involved in the making of newpapers began to be called journalism. Much emphasis has been placed upon the value of the journalist to be accurate and fair in the historical record. In the yellow journalism era of the 19th century, many newspapers in the United States relied on sensational stories that were meant to anger or excite, rather than to inform.

The more restrained style of reporting that relies on fact checking and accuracy regained popularity around World War II. Criticism of journalism is varied and sometimes vehement. Charges of sensationalism have diminished to a degree. But credibility is questioned because of anonymous sources; errors in facts, spelling, and grammar; real or perceived bias; and scandals involving plagiarism and fabrication.

Newspapers have often been owned by so-called press barons, either as a rich man's toy, or used as a political tool. Even though the opinions of the owners are often relegated to the editorial section, and the opinions of the readers are in the opned and letters to the editors sections of the paper, newspapers have been used for political purposes by insinuating some kind of bias outside of the editorial section and into straight news.

For example, the New York Times is often criticized for a leftist slant to its stories, whereas the Wall Street Journal has a history of emphasizing the position of the right. Some ways newspapers have tried to improve their credibility are: appointing ombudsmen, developing ethics policies and training, using more stringent corrections policies, communicating their processes and rationale with readers, and asking sources to review articles after publication.

HISTORY OF NEWSPAPER

A newspaper is a publication containing news and information and advertising, usually printed on low-cost paper called newsprint. It may be general or special interest, most often published daily or weekly. The first printed newspaper was published in 1605, and the form has thrived even in the face of competition from technologies such as radio and television. Recent developments on the Internet are posing major threats to its business model, however.

Paid circulation is declining in most countries, and advertising revenue, which makes up the bulk of a newspaper's income, is shifting from print to online; some commentators, nevertheless, point out that historically new media such as radio and television did not entirely supplant existing media. General-interest newspapers are usually journals of current news. Those can include political events, crime, business, culture, sports, and opinions.

Many also include weather news and forecasts. Newspapers use photographs to illustrate stories; use editorial cartoonists, usually to illustrate writing that is opinion, rather than news; and also often include comic strips and other entertainment, such as crosswords and horoscopes. A daily newspaper is issued every day, often with the exception of Sundays and some national holidays.

Saturday, and where they exist Sunday, editions of daily newspapers tend to be larger, include more specialized sections, and cost more. Weekly newspapers are also common and tend to be smaller and less prestigious than daily papers. However, those Sunday newspapers that do not have weekday editions are not considered to be weekly newspapers, and are generally equivalent in size and prestige to daily newspapers. Most nations have at least one newspaper that circulates throughout the whole country: a national newspaper, as contrasted with a local newspaper serving a city or region.

In the United States and Canada, there are few truly national newspapers, with the notable exceptions *The Wall Street Journal* and *USA Today* in the US and *The Globe and Mail* and *The National Post* in Canada. Large metropolitan newspapers with expanded distribution networks such as *The New York Times* and *The Washington Post* can fill the role of *de facto* national newspapers. In the United Kingdom, there are numerous national newspapers, including *The Times, The Daily Telegraph, The Guardian, The Observer, The Daily Mail, The Sun, The Daily Mirror, The Daily Express* and *The Independent.*

As English has become the international language of business and technology, newspapers formerly in non-English languages have been publishing an English–language edition. In places as varied as Jerusalem and Mumbai, newspapers are printed to a local and international English-speaking public. The advent of the Internet has also allowed the non-English newspapers to put out a scaled-down English version to give their newspaper a global outreach.

There has also, been an emerging class of international newspapers. Some, such as *The Stageman International Weelky, Christian Science Monitor* and *The International Herald Tribune*, have always had that focus, while others are repackaged national newspapers or "international editions" of national–scale or large metropolitan newspapers. Often these international editions are scaled down to remove articles that might not interest the wider range of readers.

Most modern newspapers are in one of three sizes:

1. *Broadsheets*: 600mm by 380mm, generally associated with more intellectual newspapers, although a trend towards 'compact' newspapers is changing this.
2. *Tabloids*: Half the size of broadsheets at 380mm by 300mm and often perceived as sensationalist in contrast to broadsheets.
3. *Berliner or Midi*: 470mm by 315mm used by European papers such as *Le Monde* in France, *La Stampa* in Italy or, from 12 September 2005, *The Guardian* in the United Kingdom.

Newspapers are usually printed on inexpensive, off-white paper known as newsprint. Since the 1980s, the newspaper industry has largely moved away from lower-quality letterpress printing to higher–quality, four-colour process, offset printing. In addition, desktop computers, word processing software, graphics software, digital cameras and digital prepress and typesetting technologies have revolutionized the newspaper production process.

These technologies have enabled newspapers to publish colour photographs and graphics, as well as innovative layouts and better design. To help their titles stand out on newsstands, some newspapers are printed on coloured newsprint. For example, the *Financial Times* is printed on a distinctive salmon pink paper, the Italian sports newspaper *La Gazzetta dello Sport* is printed on pink paper, while *L'Équipe* is printed on yellow paper. Both the latter promoted major cycling races and their newsprint colours were reflected in the colours of the jerseys used to denote the race leader; thus, the leader in the Giro d'Italia wears a pink jersey, while the Tour de France leader wears a yellow jersey, or maillot jaune.

The First Western Communication Revolution:

- 1452: Metal plates used in Printing
- 1545: Garamond designs his typeface
- 1609: First regularly printed newspaper appears in Germany
- 1631: French newspaper runs classified ads
- 1639: First printing press in the Colonies
- 1650: Leipzig has a daily newspaper
- 1689: Newspapers printed as unfolded broadsides

Printers in the West began to grow and expand their already evolving influence only 250 years after the invention of the printing press. A majority of communications growth occurred in Europe, it's roots being in the Far and Middle East. But initially, Europe is given the title of the founding country of journalism.

In Germany over 150 years after Gutenberg, a regularly printed newspaper appeared for the first time. While only 22 years after that, another form of mass communication was born on the pages of a French newspaper—that of Advertising. This started with the placement of classified ads. It took many years for main stream advertising as we know it to find the magnitude of prominence which it enjoys nowadays.

The fast growth of the newspaper industry showed how much people wanted information and news. Despite the fact that printing was expanding at such a fast-paced rate, colonial printing began much more slowly. There was a lack of desire for information. Yet in 1639, the first printing press came to the colonies and within only 100 years span of time, the colonies thrived on newspapers much as Europe did.

The Heyday of Print:

- 1704: Newspaper in Boston prints advertising
- 1710: German Engraver Le Blon develops three-colour printing
- 1714: Henry Mill receives English patent for typewriter
- 1790: Hydraulic press invented in England
- 1814: Steam powered rotary press prints The Times in England
- 1819: Napier builds a rotary press
- 1833: Penny for Papers begins mass market
- 1841: The advertising agency is born
- 1846: Double cylinder Rotary Press prints 8,000 sheets per minute
- 1848: Forerunner of the AP founded in NYC

Communications finally had reached a place where it could truly flourish; that time period was known as the Renaissance. A typical Renaissance man was expected to be well versed both with earlier and present day material. Due to this drive for knowledge, censorship of all kinds became prominent. In England, the efforts towards censorship was not widely approved of, this the power of the print grew more and more influencial in the lives of people.

In America, the concept of a free press was born out of trial and of fire. Many people, such as Peter Zenger are remembered even today for their genuine efforts in advancing and promoting freedom of the press in a society where such freedoms were new and had never been seen. Zenger was put to stand of trial for printing comments in his New York newspaper that the governer of the time took exception to.

Andew Hamilton defended Zenger with success, and the idea of a free press was not only a case in justice, but accepted by the common man and the arrisocrat alike. The importance of Benjamin Franklin cannot be neglected when discussing the history of journalism. Franklin was American's first true Renaissance man. He first made an impact with his ideas of communication in Boston, then later in Philadelphia. He was a printer at some points during his lifetime, and he used his wit to rile authorities.

He later published Poor Richard's Almanac for the benefit of colonial life. He stirred up national sentiment amongst the colonies. In the early part of the eighteenth century, the business of newspapers became porpularized all over the country. First emerging in the northeast and later moving on towards the south, newspapers started by reporting information and later became a source for commentary within society. It was this part of journalism which caused much discontent amongst England, the controlling country over the Colonies at the time.

During the final quarter of the eighteenth century, this desire for freedom resulted in the American Revolution. Newspapers also became home for one of the most celebrated American traditions of all time: the political cartoon. The first political cartoon was used as an artistic comemntary on Franklin's "Join or Die" cajoling colonists to join the efforts against the French in 1754, as war with them was looming overhead.

Modern Mass Media:

- 1851: Cable laid across the English Channel
- 1855: Printing telegraph invented in the US
- 1865: Atlantic cableties Europe and US for instant communication
- 1878: Full page newspaper ads
- 1886: The linotype machine is invented to set type

NEWSPAPERS: A BRIEF HISTORY

For centuries, civilizations have used print media to spread news and information to the masses. The Roman *Acta Diurna*, appearing around 59 B.C, is the earliest recorded "newspaper". Julius Caesar, wanting to inform the public about important social and political happenings, ordered upcoming events posted in major cities. Written on large white boards and displayed in popular places like the Baths, the *Acta* kept citizens informed about government scandals, military campaigns, trials and executions.

In 8th century China, the first newspapers appeared as hand-written newsheets in Beijing. The newspaper as we know it today is a product borne of necessity, invention, the middle class, democracy, free enterprise, and professional standards. Pre-history "newspapers" were one-to-one in nature. The earliest variation on a newspaper was a daily sheet published in 59 BC in Rome called Acta Diurna, which Julius Caesar ordered posted throughout the city. The earliest known printed newspaper was in Beijing in 748.

In 1451, Johannes Gütenberg uses a press to print an old German poem, and started the era of the modern newspaper. Two years later Gütenberg printed a 42-line Bible—the significance being the mass production of print products, ushering in an era of newspapers, magazines, and books. By 1500, the genesis of a postal system can be seen in France, while book publishing becomes popular throughout Europe and the first paper mill can be found. Invention of printing press enabled the free exchange of ideas and the spread of knowledge—themes that would define Renaissance Europe.

During this era, newsletters supplied a growing merchant class with news relevant to trade and commerce. Manuscript newssheets were being circulated in German cities by the late 15th century. These pamphlets were often highly sensationalized; one reported on the abuse that Germans in Transylvania were suffering at the hands of Vlad TsepesDrakul, also known as Count Dracula.

In 1556 the Venetian government published *Notizie scritte*, for which readers paid a small coin, or "gazetta". Zeitung is a news report published in Germany in 1502, while Trewe Encountre becomes the earliest known English-language news sheet in 1513. Germany's Avisa Relation oder Zeitung, in 1609, is the first regularly published newspaper in Europe. Forty-four years after the first newspaper in England, the Oxford Gazette is published, utilising double columns for the first time; the Oxford/London Gazette is considered the first true newspaper.

The first North American newspaper, Publick Occurrences Both Foreign and Domestick, was published in 1690 in Boston. The 1700s was a century in which market elements were created that encouraged the development of daily newspapers: rising literacy, the formation of nation-states, a developing postal system, the proliferation of urban centers, a rising literary and philosophical tradition emphasising democratic involvement in government, and technologies that supported newspaper production. In short, it was a great news century.

The first daily newspaper was The Daily Courant in London, 1702. In 1754, The Daily Advertiser in London uses the first four-column format. France's first daily newspaper appears in 1777, Journal de Paris, while the first United States daily was the Pennsylvania Packet in 1784. In the first half of the 17th century, newspapers began to appear as regular and frequent publications.

The first modern newspapers were products of western European countries like Germany, France, Belgium and England. These periodicals consisted mainly of news items from Europe, and occasionally included information from America or Asia. They rarely covered domestic issues; instead English papers reported on French military blunders while French papers covered the latest British royal scandal. Newspaper content began to shift towards more local issues in the latter half of the 17th century.

Still, censorship was widespread and newspapers were rarely permitted to discuss events that might incite citizens to opposition. Newspaper headlines did announce the beheading of Charles I at the end of the English Civil War, although Oliver Cromwell tried to suppress all newsbooks on the eve of the execution.

In 1766, Sweden was the first country to pass a law protecting press freedom. The rise of the middle class transformed newspapers in the 1800s. A penny buys a New York newspaper in 1833, opening up the first mass market for newspapers. In 1847, the telegraph is used as a business tool, transforming far-away stories. In 1873, an illustrated daily newspaper can be seen in New

York. In 1878 the first full-page newspaper advertisements appear, and in 1880 the first photographs are seen in newspapers, using halftones. The invention of the telegraph in 1844 transformed print media. Now information could be transferred within a matter of minutes, allowing for more timely, relevant reporting. Newspapers were appearing in societies around the world.

Japan's first daily newspaper, *Yokohama Mainichi Shimbun*, appeared in 1870. With the basic technical groundwork for the modern newspaper in place by the late 19th century, the story of newspapers in the 20th century was about professional development and adaptation to changing consumer and media markets. The story also involved an evolving business model that rode an ever-growing wave of mass-market advertising.

Increased profitability and higher revenues attracted publicly owned corporations interested in buying newspapers from descendants of company founders, while simultaneously exposing newspapers to the whims of cash- and profit-hungry stock markets. By the middle of the 19th century, newspapers were becoming the primary means of disseminating and receiving information. Between 1890 to 1920, the period known as the "golden age" of print media, media barons such as William Randolph Hearst, Joseph Pulitzer, and Lord Northcliffe built huge publishing empires.

These men had enormous influence within the media industry, and gained notoriety for the ways in which they wielded their power. Newspapers have also played a role as disseminators of revolutionary propaganda. *Iskra*, published by Lenin in 1900, is one notable example. On June 21, 1925, *Thanh Nien* made its debut in Vietnam, introducing Marxism to the country and providing information on the revolution's strategic policies.

By 2000, newspapers were juggling priorities: fragmentation of news consumption, fragmentation of advertising investments, the advantages and disadvantages of being a mass medium, balancing the wants of the marketplace with the company's duty to provide the needs of the marketplace, a journalistic backlash against industry changes, the sheer physicality of ink-on-paper production and distribution versus digital distribution, increasing profit pressure surrounding the core print product, and extension of the company's core brand into other profit centers. Broadcast radio exploded onto the media scene in the 1920's. Newspapers were forced to re-evaluate their role as society's primary information provider.

Like the new media technologies of today, the development of a low cost, alternative media source produced rumblings that radio would topple the newspaper industry. To respond to this new competition, editors revamped the paper's format and content in order to broaden their appeal, and stories were expanded to provide more in depth coverage. No sooner had newspapers adapted to radio than they were forced to re-evaluate themselves in light of a new and more powerful medium: television.

Between 1940 and 1990, newspaper circulation in America dropped from one newspaper for every two adults to one for every three adults. Despite this sharp decline, television's omnipresence did not render the newspaper obsolete. Some newspapers, like *USA Today*, responded to the technological advancements by using colour and by utilizing the "short, quick and to the point" stories that are usually featured on television. The technological revolution of today is creating new challenges and opportunities for traditional media. Never before has so much information been so accessible to so many.

By the end of the 1990s, some 700 had web sites; today there are thousands. The amount and immediacy of information on the Internet is unparalleled, but it has not signalled the end of the newspaper's relevance. Newspapers in print remain a popular and powerful medium for the reporting and analysis of events that shape our lives. WAN estimates that one billion people in the world read a newspaper every day!

NEWSPAPER 400 YEARS YOUNG

The World Association of Newspapers has accepted evidence produced by one of the world's leading printing museums that 2005 marked the 400th anniversary of the birth of the first newspaper in print. Scholars have generally put the date at 1609, the year of the first preserved editions. According to The Gutenberg Museum in Mainz, Germany, which houses the world's first printing press, birth certificate' of the newspaper, 'Relation', was unearthed in the town archives of Strasbourg, now in France but at the time a part of the so-called 'Deutsches Reich'.

According to Martin Welke, founder of the German Newspaper Museum, who is also the 'father' of the discovery together with Professor Jean Pierre Kintz, a Strasbourg historian, the publisher of 'Relation' was a certain Johann Carolus, who earned his living at the turn of the 17th century by producing hand-written newsletters, sold to rich subscribers at very high prices, reproducing news sent to him by a network of paid correspondents." In 1604, he bought a complete printing shop from the widow of a famous printer,In the summer of 1605 he switched to printing his... newspapers, because it took him 'too much time copying by hand. Carolus also calculated that he could earn a lot more money "by printing a higher circulation for a lower price".

In October that year, Carolus wrote a petition to the Strasbourg city council asking for "protection against reprints by other printers". And the rest is history...Today, more than a billion people a day, across the planet, read a daily newspaper in print—a figure, not incidentally, that has risen nearly five per cent in the last five years.

So, We can say, we're not only 400 years old-or rather young-but we are globally enjoying great health and can presumably look forward to the next century or so, at least, with optimism".

A NEWSPAPER TIMELINE

- 59 B.C. *Acta Diurna* is published in Rome. Julius Caesar orders the major political and social events of the day to be made available to his citizenry. State appointed reporters, called "actuarii", gather information on everything from wars and legal decisions to births, deaths, and marriages.
- 713 *Mixed News* in Kaiyuan is first newspaper published in China. "Kaiyuan" is the name given to the year in which the paper is published.
- 1040 In China, Pi Sheng invents printing from movable woodblocks.
- 1392 Movable copper type is invented in Korea.
- 1447 Johann Gutenberg invents letterpress printing, a process that will enable the mass production of the printed word.
- 1501 Pope Alexander VI decreed that printed material must be submitted to clerical authority prior to publication in order to prevent heresy. Failure to do so could result in fines or excommunication.
- 1556 Venetian government publishes Notizie scritte, a monthly newspaper for which readers pay a "gazetta", or small coin.
- 1588 In Cologne, Germany, Michael Entzinger publishes a 24 page newsbook reporting on the defeat of the Spanish Armada. The newsbook's front page shows a woodcut representing the Spanish Armada sailing off the coast of England. Although the report came months after the actual event occurred, this is one of the earliest "first reports" of a significant historical event.
- 1605 Johann Carolus publishes the first printed newspaper, *Relation*, in Strasbourg, now in France but at the time a part of the so-called 'Deutsches Reich'.
- 1621 In London, the newspaper *Corante* is published.
- 1631 *The Gazette*, the first French newspaper, is founded.
- 1639 First American colonial printing press
- 1645 World's oldest newspaper still in circulation, *Post-och Inrikes Tidningar*, is published in Sweden
- 1690 *Publick Occurrences* is the first newspaper published in America when it appears in Boston. The editor, Benjamin Harris, stated he would issue the paper "once a month, or, if any Glut of Occurrences happen, oftener." The royal authority, wary of publications printed without its express consent, suppresses the newspaper after only one issue.
- 1704 Daniel Defoe, the author of *Robinson Crusoe* and often recognized as the world's first journalist, begins to publish the *Review*, a periodical covering European affairs.
- 1798 Alois Sedenfelder Invents Lithography. Although invented over

two centuries ago, offest lithography first gained popularity in the 1960's, and is now the industry standard.

- 1803 Australia's military government publishes the *Sydney Gazette and New South Wales Advertiser*, the country's first newspaper. This is only fifteen years after the colony of convicts had been established in Sydney Cove.
- 1812 Friedrich Koenig invents of the Steam Powered Cylinder Press. In 1814, John Walter, publisher of *The Times* in London, began to assemble the new press in secrecy, fearing that his pressmen might riot if they discovered his plans. On the night of November 28, 1814, Walter took his pressmen away from their hand presses with the excuse that he was expecting important news from the continent. He then used Koenig's presses to produce the entire print run of *The Times*—at an output of 1,100 sheets per hour.
- 1844 Telegraph is invented
- 1851 Reuters is established
- 1870s Charles Stewart Parnell uses the *Freeman's Journal* to promote the causes of his Irish Nationalist Party.
- 1880 First photographs appear in a newspaper
- 1900 Vladimir Lenin founds *Iskra*, in Leipzig, Germany. This revolutionary newspaper is to become a major tool for Communist propoganda.
- 1903 Alfred Harmsworth develops the first tabloid newspaper, the *Daily Mirror*, in London. The *Daily Mirror* introduced the concept of the "exclusive" interview. The first was with Lord Minto, the new Viceroy of India, in 1905.
- 1966 Behram "Busybee" Contractor begins publishing his column 'Round and About" in the *Evening News* of India. Running until 2001, the satirical column became the longest running column in the history of newspaper journalism.
- 1994 First independent on-line daily appears on the World Wide Web.

NEWSPAPER STRUCTURE

STRUCTURE OF NEWSPAPER STAFF

The structure of the staff changes from year to year depending on the strengths and weaknesses of the incoming group and the size of the class. Some years, I have had as many as 65 students in the class which means that I will have more editors and associate editors to handle the workload. Other years, the class has been 45-50 students and the number of editors will be reduced.

Students learn their role from the previous year's staff since they are in the programme for two years. They start when they are in tenth grade taking beginning journalism. Then in eleventh grade they are in page editor positions learning how to do layout, design and editing. The twelfth graders are the editors and so they have had opportunity to observe how and shadow their predecessors. Naturally, many seniors do not end up as editor, but continue on as page editors for another year. This has been somewhat of a problem in the past since these students frequently do not feel challenged enough and sometimes lose interest and do not perform as well as they could. It is incumbent upon the teacher to create meaningful positions for these students so they have new challenges for the coming year. I have been successful most of the time, but not one hundred per cent of the time. Some of the positions I have created include Section Editors who supervise the page editors; graphics editors, who supervise obtaining all graphic elements of the paper and additional page editors. For example, I added pages such as the Teen Health page, the Environmental Issues page and so forth. It is important for the teacher to be creative to meet the needs of the class and the students.

At the present time, this is the staff organization:

- Three editors-in-chief
- Three associate editors
- One technical editor-in-chief.
- Two to three page editors for each of the following pages:
  - News
  - Editorial
  - Opinion
  - Features
  - Entertainment
  - Reviews
  - People
  - Technology
  - Sports.
- Circulation Manager
- Business Manager
- Advertising Manager
- Ombudsman
- Photography Editor.

Each of these students learns his/her specific role from the section editor or from one of the editors. At the beginning of the year, students work in teams with one experienced page editor working with an inexperienced one. If there are not enough experienced ones, then the editors work with several page editors. It is an apprenticeship-like programme requiring specific procedures, layout skills, design skills, factual information, specific strategies for getting the job done. The organization of the staff and the organization of the class provides the necessary overall structure of the programme allowing the teacher to fade to an adviser or coach.

Everyone has a Different Learning Style

If a student does not learn as fast as another in any of the skills required, the editors are required to work with that student again until they learn. One important teaching philosophy stressed in beginning journalism is that all students learn at a different pace and in different ways. I say that repeatedly in class: no two people learn the same way. In advanced journalism I make it clear that students who do not learn certain skills right away are not "stupid." They just have a different learning style and that we all need to work with them until they understand. This is also reinforced by the revision process for the stories. Some people revise more than others, but eventually they will all learn how to write better. Students who are really poor writers and have consistent problems are helped by the teacher as well as the students.

Extra-Curriculars for Editors

The editors-in-chief and the associate editors may not have any conflicting sports or club obligations. If they want to maintain other extracurricular activities, they cannot be editor. This is to protect the staff from waiting for students to complete their other activity before devoting time and energy to the paper.

Changes over the Years

Over the years, I have made many changes to the operation of the staff. Initially, I had one editor-in-chief, but I found that they worked better in pairs because it was "lonely at the top." When the staff grew, I added more editors to balance the power at the top with the size of the class. I also added the technical editor-in-chief whose responsibility it is to be up-to-date on everything connected with technology and help implement it in the programme.

Everyone has a Defined Role

The fact that everyone has a defined role and the cycles are standardized makes it easy for students to function effectively in the learning community. In fact, they become experts in their own right, teach each other and a couple months into the semester, they can function well without teacher intervention.

Role of the Teacher as Adviser

The question is then so what does the teacher do when the students no longer need the teacher? The teacher transforms into an adviser and literally advises. I tell my students now that I am adviser my advice can be ignored; after all it is advise. If I switch from adviser to teacher and dictate what to do, which is rare, that means that they have in someway violated a basic law of the press: libel, obscenity or inciting to riot. Sometimes I have to intervene on the issues of obscenity or what can be called 'poor taste' or 'juvenile humour.'

However, since I ask them to censor themselves before I look over the paper, I rarely have to take any action.

The paroxysmal changes rattling the beleaguered newspaper industry have coincided with unprecedented declines in publishing companies' stock prices. The decimation has affected newspaper publishers regardless of size, geography, or prestige of their mastheads. Driving this decline is a structural shift of epochal dimensions that is fundamentally changing the way we generate, compile, disseminate, and consume news and information, manifested largely by the rise of the Internet and the proliferation of alternative digital media choices.

The effects of this shift are chipping away at the very business model by which newspapers have operated for decades. A cyclical downturn in business ad spending—driven by a credit crunch and subsequent consumer retrenchment—has accelerated the revenue declines at newspapers. The suffering this confluence of factors creates for newspapers is magnified by the suffocating effects of many publishers' debt-laden balance sheets, which leave them with diminished financial flexibility to navigate the treacherous industry environment and little margin for error should these companies hit a rough patch.

To date, newspapers have responded to declining revenue by implementing substantial cost cuts. With newspaper stocks having fallen so far, and costs being cut so aggressively, can these stocks go much lower? We think they can, and eventually will. We think the combination of their high fixed costs, substantial debt burdens, and poor growth prospects will continue to diminish newspaper publishers' profitability. In an environment of declining ad sales, newspapers' high fixed costs amount to a financial Achilles' heel. This combination makes it difficult for newspaper publishers to keep expenses in line with diminishing revenue. Besides owning and maintaining expensive printing plants and equipment, they must regularly buy commodities such as newsprint and ink, whose costs tend to fluctuate beyond publishers' control. Distribution expenses have also increased, as rising fuel prices add to the cost of running fleets of delivery trucks. Union contracts limit their ability to reduce labour costs, a reflection of newspapers' labour-intensive nature. Taken together, their limited ability to cut costs means that when newspaper revenue declines, profits decline even faster.

The resulting dynamic is a value-destroying feedback loop: Declining ad revenue and readership necessitates cost-cutting. Cost-cutting inevitably affects content. Diminished content, whether real or perceived, alienates readers, who become more likely to cancel their subscriptions and seek out alternative news sources. This accelerates the migration of readers to online sources and the decline in ad revenue, which will necessitate even more cost-cutting. We think the cycle will feed on itself. Newspaper CEOs expound on their efforts to build their publications' presence online. However, alluding to exponentially rising page views and double-digit growth rates in online ad revenue tend to mask a striker economic reality. Online advertisers refuse to pay up for Web site banner ads as they have for traditional print ads. This is because online readers are perceived as having truncated attention spans and being less engaged with the information. In contrast, paid subscribers' investment of time and money in the print product makes it more likely that ads will resonate with them than with online readers, thereby increasing their value to advertisers. Online ad revenues simply aren't substantial enough or growing quickly enough to stave off the breathtaking erosion in print ad revenue. Industrywide, for every $1 that newspapers lost in print ad revenue during 2007, online ads recaptured just $0.12. For most newspaper publishers, online ads still amount to less than 10 per cent of total revenue. By shifting their operations online, newspapers are literally trading dollars for pennies.

This is exacerbated by the deleterious effects of suffocating debt burdens. Several prominent newspaper publishers took on billions of dollars in debt in recent years to finance ill-timed acquisition binges that have only magnified the effects of declining revenues. McClatchy (MNI), Gatehouse (GHS), and Lee Enterprises (LEE) have balance sheets saddled with more than a billion dollars in debt each from dubious acquisitions. As declining revenue erodes profit margins, high fixed costs and debt service obligations siphon away diminishing cash flow, leaving little left for capital investment and innovation. As revenue continues to decline, some heavily leveraged publishers may find themselves straining harder to find the necessary cash to service their debt, forcing them to possibly liquidate assets at fire-sale prices. Others may be forced to reduce or eliminate their dividends. Gate House recently eliminated its own rich dividend, and we think McClatchy CEO Gary Pruitt is preparing shareholders for a likely dividend cut by the end of the year.

Newspapers' valuations may have cratered from the lofty levels of better times. However, cutting costs in the face of declining revenue is a survival tactic, not a buy signal. In the long run, the newspaper as we know it is unlikely to vanish completely. However, we think the publishing entities that survive the current tumult will be those that successfully morph into smaller, more nimble "multimedia information centres." Besides having lower cost structures and more modest cash flows, we think some of these entities will eventually be managed to satisfy bondholders at the expense of equity holders.

DAILY NEWSPAPERS AND THE NATURE OF VIRTUAL TEAMS

The nature of teams has changed significantly because of changes in organizations and the nature of the work they do. Organizations have become more distributed across geography and across industries. Relationships between people inside an organization and those previously considered outside (customers, suppliers, managers of collaborating organizations, other stakeholders) are becoming more important. Organizations have discovered the value of collaborative work. There is a new emphasis on knowledge management-harvesting the learning of the experience of members of the organization so that it is available to the whole organization.

All these changes in organizations have changed how teams are formed and how they operate. Teams have changed:

Although the technology that supports these new teams gets most of the attention when we talk about virtual teams, it's really the changes in the nature of teams-not their use of technology-that creates new challenges for team managers and members. Most "virtual" teams operate in multiple modes including having face-to-face meetings when possible. Managing a virtual team means managing the whole spectrum of communication strategies and project management techniques as well as human and social processes in ways that support the team. Managers of small and large organizations have known the importance of facilitation for successful team process, but few people have really grappled with the issues of trying to manage teams that are connected by distance in space and time. With increasing relevance of distributed communications systems (Internet, Intranets, groupware) in a diversity of working groups' everyday lives, innovators in the field will need to integrate these virtual practices into their current team building strategies as well as learn how to continually improve virtual group process.

There are several different kinds of virtual teams: Executive teams are made up of managers who are on the team because of their position in the organization. These teams are usually semi-permanent teams with responsibility for specific divisions or functions in the organization. Project teams are created around a specific task. Members of the team are selected based on their role and expertise in relation to that task. These teams are created for the life of the project. Community of practice teams support people who are working on common tasks or in the same professional field and who can benefit from sharing experience. Membership on these teams is voluntary. These teams don't usually have specific deliverables but instead are focused on learning.

While there are some obvious problems and disadvantages of distributed teams, these teams also provide some advantages such as:

- Developing and spreading better practices faster
- Connecting "islands of knowledge" into self-organizing, knowledge sharing networks of professional communities
- Fostering cross-functional and cross-divisional collaboration
- Increasing ability to initiate and contribute to projects across organizational boundaries

Some of the things that need to happen in order for organizations to make effective use of virtual teams include:

- Processes for team management and development have to be designed, defined, piloted, tested, refined

- Team managers have to be trained in new team management strategies
- Team members have to be trained in new ways of working
- The culture of the organization has to be reshaped to support new structures and processes
- Organizational structures have to be modified to reflect new team dynamics
- Rewards systems have to be updated to reflect new team structures
- New information technology (IT) systems have to be built to support teams
- New management, measurement and control systems have to be designed.

"The real basic structure of the workplace is the relationship. Each relationship is itself part of a larger network of relationships. These relationships can be measured along all kinds of dimensions-from political to professional expertise. The fact is that work gets done through these relationships."-Michael Schrage, No More Teams

In some ways, virtual teams are like the canary in the mine that detects life-threatening problems before anyone else realizes they are in danger. The issues raised for virtual team managers and members about managing people and projects at a distance are really the issues which need to be raised about all teamwork including; How do you achieve the right balance of top-down and self-organization? Between individual and collaborative work? Between manager-driven and team-driven work definition and assignment?

New technology requires us to rethink these dynamics because we don't have the option to use familiar approaches. It gives us an opening to change the way we manage the people and work process in general. The critical part of the question, "How can we manage teams operating at a distance?" is really "How do we effectively support the collaborative work of teams? Managing virtual teams is not about taking our old management techniques and transposing them for delivery using new media. Rather, it's about expanding our available tools to create new dynamics aligned with the best thinking about supporting collaborative work.

A NEW MANAGEMENT MIND SET

There are some critical aspects of a virtual team manager's mindset that must shift in order to be effective in contemporary organizations.

A New Management Style

Managing a virtual team meeting is not unlike managing a face-to-face team meeting: fruitful experiences don't happen by chance. There has been a lot of excitement about the potential of online networks to provide new environments for teams, communities of practice, and learning. But virtual meeting experiences can be frustrating and disappointing when interaction with others in the group results in information overload, topic drift, or conversations that are just not all that valuable.

When a face-to-face meeting doesn't "work" we tend to look at our meeting design and our role as facilitator for insights about why things didn't go the way we had hoped. When using groupware and other technologies, we tend to blame the technology. Instead, we need to extend our level of consciousness about group dynamics to include understanding of what happens when people interact using new media. Different media raise different sets of questions for managers. The important thing is to be sure that you are asking all the same questions you would ask yourself when thinking about the dynamics of any work team.

PURPOSE

Researchers agree that an explicit purpose is the most critical factor in determining the success of a virtual team. Whether you are meeting face-to-face or using some other media to connect, you can use familiar facilitation strategies to develop a shared understanding and commitment to the team's purpose. What may be different is the strategy for how the team will maintain alignment around the purpose over time when they are no longer able to meet together. Lacking face-to-face meetings, a virtual team may need more frequent and more explicit check-ins about their purpose. On the up side, the technology environment may provide some advantages because it provides multiple ways to remind team members about purpose (as well as goals, tasks, timings) as part of the daily fabric of their communication.

Roles

Managers need to help virtual teams identify roles in the same way required of all teams. Virtual teams need to define some additional roles related to their communication strategy. They may need technical support, knowledge archivists, and specialists in using different media. For all roles, virtual teams need to spend more time being explicit about mutual expectations for facilitators, managers, and members because the patterns of behaviour and dynamics of interaction are unfamiliar and it's easy to fall into misunderstandings and become frustrated with each other.

Culture

Whichever combinations of media you are using to support a virtual team, you need to think through how those media will affect the culture of the team's environment. What metaphors are you using for the environment and the interactions? How will these metaphors cue team members to think about where they are and what they are doing? Keep in mind that you are creating an environment to support relationships, not just to exchange information. How can you help the group create a mental map of the environment so that members develop appropriate expectations? What norms, styles and behaviours would help or hinder the atmosphere you want?

Conversation

Many people associate technology-particularly computer technology-with storing and exchanging data. Although you'll want to take advantage of the knowledge archiving features of new media, it's important to remember that conversation among team members is the most critical thing you need to support. Facilitators can contribute a lot by modelling ways of using different media conversationally. Assess the team's interactions often and you'll see considerable variation from day to day. At the end of each week, ask yourself about the pace and the scope of the interactions. Is the communication still interesting and engaging, or has it become stale?

Feedback

Since using technology as a primary means to communicate will be new to most team members, participants need to spend more time than usual talking about the quality of their communication. The facilitator can provide some feedback but it's even better if participants develop a norm of providing feedback to each other about communication style, quantity, frequency, clarity, etc. Facilitators can help team members access more of their own feelings and reactions to messages in different media.

Pace

In asynchronous environments, pace is an important dimension to facilitate. Different team members may access the virtual environment more or less frequently. This is what we mean by the term "rolling present." Generally, people consider material current if it has been entered since they last logged on. If you have several members who sign on four times a day, they may make it difficult for most group members to engage with the virtual team: it will all go by too fast. You may need to do some things to slow down the pace.

Entry and Re-Entry

One of the benefits of virtual teams is that you can bring in new members from anywhere in the organization as required by the project. But the problem of the rolling present is particularly critical for new members and for members who have been away for a period of time. Although new members can stimulate a virtual team, they may have problems figuring out how to enter a fast-moving discussion.

The facilitator needs to create strategies that make it easy for people to enter and re-enter the team in mid-stream, find out what's going on and feel welcomed and integrated into the team as a whole.

Weaving

Weaving is a networking term that refers to the process of summarizing and synthesizing multiple responses in a virtual group. The weaving item or response tells people where they've been, where they are, and where they might want to go next.

It can identify issues people agree upon or issues that still bring up many questions or require more information. This is similar to the kind of thing facilitators do face-to-face except that the ideas may have to be pulled from multiple different sources in multiple different media and it may be even more critical in virtual groups because members may find it hard to keep track of what's going on.

Participation

In a face-to-face group, managers watch body language and facial expression and lots of other signals to develop a sense of what's going on. Participants in virtual teams convey this same information in different ways. It's important to find ways to base your sense of what's happening on data. It's amazing how often your impressions of what's happening can be off base because we're not used to reading the cues people give out via new media.

Flow

There is no right answer to what should be happening in a virtual group-there may be times when you are more or less active. The key is to use the information about what's happening to learn, so that you can be a more purposeful facilitator. Facilitation is paying attention to what is happening in your group, as distinct from what you wanted or expected would happen. It is not unlike facilitating any group: if participants aren't participating as much as you'd hoped, don't admonish them (or blame the technology). Instead, you want to detect where members are now and work with that energy to move in the direction you need to go. Energy dynamics are greatly influenced by the nature of the media you're using so pay special attention to how interaction feels in different media. Does this sound familiar? The fact is, managing a virtual team requires all the finesse and skill of managing a meeting or project. When you get online, remember everything you've ever known about managing and facilitating group process. Just ask yourself: How can we move these virtual chairs into a circle so everyone feels involved? Some of the key ideas to keep in mind to make sure a virtual team works effectively include:

- Teamwork is fundamentally social

- Knowledge is integrated in the life of teams and needs to be made explicit
- It's important to create ways for team members to experience membership
- Knowledge depends on engagement in practice, people gain knowledge from observation and participation
- Engagement is inseparable from empowerment
- "Failure" to perform is often the result of exclusion from the process.

DEVELOPMENT OF BRITISH NEWSPAPERS

Regular newspaper publication in United Kingdom dates from the mid 17th century. Prior to then it was believed that the 'reckless' reporting of news might endanger the Crown and the country. A limit was placed on the printing of news other than of events abroad, natural disasters, royal declarations and crimes; there were weekly *corantos* published from the 1620s containing these kinds of news. Publication grew following the general relaxation after the ending of the Star Chamber in 1641.

During the Civil War there were regular news-sheets and then news books carrying general information along with propaganda. Following the Restoration there arose a number of publications including the *London Gazette*, the first official journal of record and the newspaper of the Crown. Publication was controlled under the Licensing Act of 1662, but the Act's lapse from 1679–1685 and then lapse in 1695 encouraged a number of new titles, there were twelve London newspapers and 24 provincial papers by the 1720s and by the early 19th century there were 52 London papers and over 100 other titles.

NINETEENTH CENTURY

As stamp, paper and other duties were progressively reduced from the 1830s onwards there was a massive growth in overall circulation as major events and improved communications developed the public's need for information. *The Daily Universal Register* began life in 1785 and was later to become known as *The Times* from 1788. This was the most significant newspaper of the first half of the 19th century, but from around 1860 there were a number of more strongly competitive titles, each differentiated by its political biases and interests. The *Manchester Guardian* was founded in Manchester in 1821 by a group of non-conformist businessmen. Its most famous editor, Charles Prestwich Scott, made the Manchester Guardian into a world-famous newspaper in the 1890s. It is now called *The Guardian*. The Chartist *Northern Star*, first published on May 26, 1838, was a pioneer of popular journalism but was very closely linked to the fortunes of the movement and was out of business by 1852.

At the same time there was the establishment of more specialized periodicals and the first cheap newspaper in the *Daily Telegraph and Courier*, later to be known simply as the *Daily Telegraph*. From 1860 until around 1910 is considered a 'golden age' of newspaper publication, with technical advances in printing and communication combined with a professionalization of journalism and the prominence of new owners. Newspapers became more partisan and there was the rise of new or yellow journalism. Socialist and labour newspapers also proliferated and in 1912 the *Daily Herald* was launched as the first daily newspaper of the trade union and labour movement.

TWENTIETH CENTURY

First World War saw the rise of the 'press barons' initially the Harmsworth Brothers and the Berry Brothers. A trend continued between the wars when the WW I barons were joined by Max Aitken and the newspaper industry took on an appearance similar to today's. The post-war period was marked by the emergence of tabloid newspapers, notably with Cecil Harmsworth King and his International Publishing Corporation. In the 1980s the powerful print trade unions were challenged and production moved away from Fleet Street, marked by the successes of Rupert Murdoch and the *Sun* in the 1980s and 1990s. Currently circulation is in a slow but steady decline but still comparatively high. More recently, the NUJ has complained of declining wages in the local press, which some claim are a result of increasing consolidation of the local newspaper industry.

In March 2006 Labour MP Austin Mitchell called for a debate on the matter and encouraged the UK parliament to enact legislation to regulate the sector. In the perceived gap left by local newspapers, many of which have closed 'district' offices in smaller towns, local news web sites are emerging. Examples of this include a web site for the town of Bourne, in Lincolnshire, which is run by former Fleet Street journalist Rex Needle, and RuberyVillage.co.uk, which is run by teenagers and provides news for the West Midlands village of Rubery.

DEVELOPMENT OF AMERICAN NEWSPAPERS

In America the first newspaper appeared in Boston in 1690, entitled *Publick Occurrences*. Published without authority, it was immediately suppressed, its publisher arrested, and all copies were destroyed. Indeed, it remained forgotten until 1845 when the only known surviving example was discovered in the British Library. The first successful newspaper was the *Boston News-Letter,* begun by postmaster John Campbell in 1704. Although it was heavily subsidized by the colonial government the experiment was a near-failure, with very limited circulation.

In the early years of its publication the News-Letter was filled mostly with news from London journals detailing the intrigues of English politics, and a variety of events concerning the European wars. The rest of the newspaper was filled with items listing ship arrivals, deaths, sermons, political appointments, fires, accidents and the like. One of the most sensational stories published when the News-Letter was the only newspaper in the colonies was the the account of how Blackbeard the pirate was killed in hand-to-hand combat on the deck of a sloop that had engaged his ship in battle. Campbell relinquished his stewardship of the paper in 1722 to Bartholomew Green, its printer. As editor, Green devoted less space to overseas events and more to domestic news.

When Green died after a decade as its editor, the News-Letter was inherited by his son John Draper, also a printer. Draper proved to be a better editor and publisher than his predecessors. He enlarged the paper to four good-sized pages, filling it with news from Boston, other towns throughout the colonies, and from abroad. Two more papers made their appearance in the 1720's, in Philadelphia and New York, and the Fourth Estate slowly became established on the new continent.

By the eve of the Revolutionary War, some two dozen papers were issued at all the colonies, although Massachusetts, New York, and Pennsylvania would remain the centers of American printing for many years. Articles in colonial papers, brilliantly conceived by revolutionary propagandists, were a major force that influenced public opinion in America from reconciliation with England to full political independence. At war's end in 1783 there were forty-three newspapers in print.

The press played a vital role in the affairs of the new nation; many more newspapers were started, representing all shades of political opinion. The no holds barred style of early journalism, much of it libelous by modern standards, reflected the rough and tumble political life of the republic as rival factions jostled for power. The ratification of the Bill of Rights in 1791 at last guaranteed of freedom of the press, and America's newspapers began to take on a central role in national affairs. Growth continued in every state. By 1814 there were 346 newspapers. In the Jacksonian populist 1830's, advances in printing and papermaking technology led to an explosion of newspaper growth, the emergence of the "Penny Press"; it was now possible to produce a newspaper that could be sold for just a cent a copy. Previously, newspapers were the province of the wealthy, literate minority. The price of a year's subscription, usually over a full week's pay for a labourer, had to be paid in full and "invariably in advance."

This sudden availability of cheap, interesting reading material was a significant stimulus to the achievement of the nearly universal literacy now taken for granted in America. However, the history of journalism reaches as far back as ancient Rome when current daily information was posted in public spaces to inform the citizenry of pertinent local news. Over time, societies used a variety of methods for news publications, but they were typically created for a highly specific audience, such as government officials.

Early prototypes of newspapers for the general public surfaced in Western Europe, England, and the United States in the seventeenth and eighteenth centuries. Authorities in many countries often censored information contained in early newspapers, but that began to change in the eighteenth century when countries such as Sweden and the US enacted legislation guaranteeing freedom of the press.

In the late 1800s, the term "yellow journalism" was applied to the headline wars between the New York City papers of Joseph Pulitzer and William Randolph Hearst. Yellow journalism employed sensationalistic, lurid stories and attention-grabbing banner headlines in order to increase sales. The decline of yellow journalism coincided with the rise of journalism as a profession. Early newspapers in the US were highly partisan and quick to attack politicians, including the president, but over time journalists understood their influence upon readers should be more socially responsible.

The first organization of journalists formed in England in 1883, and others were quick to follow. Professional courses in journalism began to crop up in universities, and the concept of responsible, unbiased reporting became the standard of quality, professional journalism. This more serious turn in journalism has remained a constant in the profession, even as technology has changed the way people access news.

IMPACT OF INDUSTRIAL REVOLUTION ON AMERICAN NEWSPAPERS

The industrial revolution, as it transformed all aspects of American life and society, dramatically affected newspapers. Both the numbers of papers and their paid circulations continued to rise. The 1850 census catalogued 2,526 titles. In the 1850's powerful, giant presses appeared, able to print ten thousand complete papers per hour. At this time the first "pictorial" weekly newspapers emerged; they featured for the first time extensive illustrations of events in the news, as woodcut engravings made from correspondents' sketches or taken from that new invention, the photograph.

During the Civil War the unprecedented demand for timely, accurate news reporting transformed American journalism into a dynamic, hardhitting force in the national life. Reporters, called "specials," became the darlings of the public and the idols of youngsters everywhere. Many accounts of battles turned in by these intrepid adventurers stand today as the definitive histories of their subjects. Newspaper growth continued unabated in the postwar years.

An astounding 11,314 different papers were recorded in the 1880 census. By the 1890's the first circulation figures of a million copies per issue were recorded. At this period appeared the features of the modern newspaper, bold "banner" headlines, extensive use of illustrations, "funny pages," plus expanded coverage of organized sporting events. The rise of "yellow journalism" also marks this era. Hearst could truthfully boast that his newspapers manufactured the public clamor for war on Spain in 1898.

This is also the age of media consolidation, as many independent newspapers were swallowed up into powerful "chains"; with regrettable consequences for a once fearless and incorruptible press, many were reduced to vehicles for the distribution of the particular views of their owners, and so remained, without competing papers to challenge their viewpoints. By the 1910's, all the essential features of the recognizably modern newspaper had emerged. In our time, radio and television have gradually supplanted newspapers as the nation's primary information sources, so it may be difficult initially to appreciate the role that newspapers have played in our history.

COLONIAL ORIGINS

It was James Franklin, Benjamin Franklin's older brother, who first made a news sheet something more than a garbled mass of stale items, "taken from the Gazetts and other Publick Prints of London" some six months late. James Franklin, "encouraged by a number of respectable characters, who were desirous of having a paper of a different cast from those then published,...began the publication, at his own risk, of a third newspapers, entitled The New England Courant."

These respectable characters were known as the Hell-Fire Club; they succeeded in publishing a paper "of a different cast," which, although it shocked New England orthodoxy pretty thoroughly, nevertheless proved vastly entertaining and established a kind of literary precedent. Instead of filling the first page of the Courant with the tedious conventionalities of governors' addresses to provincial legislatures, James Franklin's club wrote essays and satirical letters after the manner of The Spectator just ten years after the first appearance of *The Spectator* in London. As a result, the very look of an ordinary first page of the Courant is like that of a Spectator page.

After the more formal introductory paper on some general topic, such as zeal or hypocrisy or honour or contentment, the facetious letters of imaginary correspondents commonly fill the remainder of the Courant's first page. Timothy Turnstone addresses flippant jibes to Justice Nicholas Clodpate in the first extant number of the Courant Tom Pen-Shallow quickly follows, with his mischievous little postscript: "Pray inform me whether in your Province Criminals have the Privilege of a Jury." Tom Tram writes from the moon about a certain "villainous Post master" he has heard rumours of. Ichabod Henroost complains of a gadding wife. Abigail Afterwit would like to know when the editor of the rival paper, the Gazette, "intends to have done printing the Carolina Addresses to their Governour, and give his Readers Something in the Room of them, that will be more entertaining." Homespun Jack deplores the fashions in general, and small waists in particular.

Some of these papers represent native wit, with only a general approach to the model; others are little more than paraphrases of The Spectator. And sometimes a Spectator paper is inserted bodily, with no attempt at paraphrase whatever When Benjamin Franklin established himself in Philadelphia, shortly before 1730, the town boasted two "wretched little" news sheets, Andrew Bradford's American Mercury, and Keimer's Universal Instructor in all Arts and Sciences, and Pennsylvania Gazette.

This instruction in all arts and sciences consisted of weekly extracts from Chambers's Universal Dictionary, actually commencing with A, and going steadily on towards Z, followed by installments of Defoe's Religious Courtship, called by the editor "a scarce and delightful piece of History." Franklin quickly did away with all this when he took over the Instructor, and made it The Pennsylvania Gazette. The Gazette soon became Franklin's characteristic organ, which he freely used for satire, for the play of his wit, even for sheer excess of mischief or of fun. From the first he had a way of adapting his models to his own uses.

The series of essays called The Busy-Body, which he wrote for Bradford's American Mercury in 1729, followed the general Addisonian form, modified already to suit homelier conditions. The thrifty Patience, in her busy little shop, complaining of the useless visitors who waste her valuable time, is related to the ladies who address Mr. Spectator. The Busy-Body himself is a true Censor Morum, as Isaac Bickerstaff had been in the Tatler. And a number of the fictitious characters, Ridentius, Eugenius, Cato, and Cretico, represent traditional eighteenth-century classicism.

Even this Franklin could use for contemporary satire, since Cretico, the "sowre Philosopher," is evidently a portrait of Franklin's rival, Samuel Keimer. As time went on, Franklin depended less on his literary conventions, and more on his own native humour.

In this there is a new spirit,—not suggested to him by the fine breeding of Addison, or the bitter irony of Swift, or the stinging completeness of Pope. The brilliant little pieces Franklin wrote for his Pennsylvania Gazette have an imperishable place in American literature. It is none the less true that they belong to colonial journalism. The Pennsylvania Gazette, like most other newspapers of the period was often poorly printed.

Franklin was busy with a hundred matters outside of his printing office, and never seriously attempted to raise the standards of his trade. Nor did he ever properly edit or collate the chance medley of stale items which passed for news in the Gazette. His influence on the practical side of journalism was very small. On the other hand, his advertisements of books show his very great interest in popularizing secular literature. Undoubtedly his paper contributed to the broader culture which distinguished Pennsylvania from her neighbours before the Revolution. Starting with the custom of importing a stray volume or two along with stationer's supplies, Franklin gradually developed a book shop in his printing office. There was nothing unusual in this fact, by itself.

THE SOUTH CAROLINA GAZETTE

Franklin's influence in journalism was not confined to Pennsylvania. He often assisted young journeymen in the establishment of newspapers in distant towns. Thomas Whitemarsh, for instance, went to Charleston, South Carolina, in 1731, as Franklin's partner in a new enterprise, which soon included a new paper, The South Carolina Gazette. Naturally, Whitemarsh filled his front page with essays, sometimes reprinted from The Spectator, but often original, with a facetious quality suggesting Franklin.

Essays of one sort or another were always popular in The South Carolina Gazette. Here may be found interesting notices of the various performances of Otway's Orphan, Farquhar's Recruiting Officer, and other popular plays of the period which were given at the Charleston theatres for twenty or thirty years before the first wandering professional companies began to play in the Northern colonies.

THE VIRGINIA GAZETTE

Early theatrical notices may also be followed in The Virginia Gazette, a paper of unusual excellence, edited by William Parks in Williamsburg, the old capital of Virginia. Here The Busy-Body, The Recruiting Officer, and The Beaux-Stratagem were all performed, often by amateurs, though professionals were known as early as 1716 in Williamsburg. Life in Williamsburg in 1736 had a more cosmopolitan quality than in other towns.

A sprightly essay-serial called The Monitor, which fills the first page of The Virginia Gazette for twenty-two numbers, probably reflects not only the social life of the capital, but also the newer fashion in such periodical work. It is dramatic in method, with vividly realised characters who gossip and chat over games of piquet or at the theatre. The Beaux-Stratagem, which had been played in Williamsburg three weeks before, is mentioned as delightful enough to make one of the ladies commit the indiscretion of giggling. The Monitor represents a kind of light social satire unusual in the colonies.

POLITICS IN THE LATER NEWSPAPERS

After 1750, general news became accessible, and the newspapers show more and more interest in public affairs. The literary first page was no longer necessary, though occasionally used to cover a dull period. A new type of vigourous polemic gradually superseded the older essay. A few of the well-known conventions were retained, however. We still find the fictitious letter, with the fanciful signature, or a series of papers under a common title, such as The Virginia-Centinel, or Livingston's Watch-Tower.

The former is a flaming appeal to arms, running through The Virginia Gazette in 1756, and copied into Northern papers to rouse patriotism against the French enemy. The expression of the sentiment, even thus early, seems national. Livingston's well-known Watch-Tower, a continuation of his pamphlet-magazine The Independent Reflector, has already the keen edge of the Revolutionary writings of fifteen and twenty years later

REVOLUTIONARY AND EARLY NATIONAL ERA: 1770-1820

The Massachusetts Spy

Isaiah Thomas's Massachusetts Spy was constantly on the verge of being suppressed, from its establishment in 1770 to the American Revolution, it carried radicalism to its logical conclusion. When the Spy began to be reprinted in other papers, as "the most daring production ever published in America," the country as a whole was ready for Tom Paine's *Common Sense*.

The turbulent years between 1775 and 1783 were a time of great trial and disturbance among newspapers. Interruption, suppression, and lack of support so checked their growth that at the close of the war they were in most respects less thriving than at the beginning of it. Although there were forty-three newspapers in the United States when the treaty of peace was signed, as compared with thirty-seven on the date of the battle of Lexington, only a dozen had had continuous existence between the two events, and most of those had experienced delays and difficulties through lack of paper, type, and patronage.

Not one newspaper in the principal cities, Boston, New York, and Philadelphia, continued publication throughout the war. When the colonial forces were in possession, royalist papers were suppressed, and at times of British occupation Revolutionary papers moved away, or were discontinued, or they became royalist, only to suffer at the next turn of military fortunes. Thus there was an exodus of papers from the cities along the coast to smaller inland places, where alone it was possible for them to continue without interruption.

Scarcity of paper was acute; type worn out could not be replaced. The appearance of the newspapers deteriorated, and issues sometimes failed to appear at all. Mail service, never good, was poorer than ever; foreign newspapers, an important source of information, could be obtained but rarely; many of the ablest writers who had filled the columns with dissertations upon colonial rights and government were now otherwise occupied. News from a distance was less full and regular than before; yet when great events happened reports spread over the country with great rapidity, through messengers in the service of patriotic organizations. The newspapers made use of such assistance, and did service in further spreading the tidings, though they seldom overtook the flying word of mouth.

Naturally, reporting was still imperfect. The Salem Gazette printed a full but coloured account of the battle of Lexington, giving details of the burning, pillage, and barbarities charged to the British, and praising the militia who were filled with "higher sentiments of humanity." The Declaration of Independence was published by Congress, 6 July, 1776, in the Philadelphia Evening Post, from which it was copied by most of the papers; but some of them did not mention it until two weeks later, and even then found room for only a synopsis.

When they were permitted to do so they printed fairly full accounts of the proceedings of provincial assemblies and of Congress, which were copied widely, as were all official reports and proclamations. On the whole, however, a relatively small proportion of such material and an inadequate account of the progress of the war is found in the contemporaneous newspapers. The general spirit of the time found fuller utterance in mottoes, editorials, letters, and poems.

In the beginning both editorials and communications urged united resistance to oppression, praised patriotism, and denounced tyranny; as events and public sentiment developed these grew more vigourous, often a little more radical than the populace. Later, the idea of independence took form, and theories of government were discussed. More interesting and valuable as specimens of literature than these discussions were the poems inspired by the stirring events of the time. Long narratives of battles and of heroic deaths were mingled with eulogies of departed heroes. Songs meant to inspire and thrill were not lacking.

Humour, pathos, and satire sought to stir the feelings of the public. Much of the poetry of the Revolution is to be found in the columns of dingy newspapers, from the vivid and popular satires and narratives of Philip Freneau to the saddest effusions of the most commonplace schoolmaster.

The newspapers of the Revolution were an effective force working towards the unification of sentiment, the awakening of a consciousness of a common purpose, interest, and destiny among the separate colonies, and of a determination to see the war through to a successful issue. They were more single-minded than the people themselves, and they bore no small share of the burden of arousing and supporting the often discouraged and indifferent public spirit. Many of the papers, however, which were kept alive or brought to life during the war could not adapt themselves to the new conditions of peace.

Perhaps a dozen of the survivors held their own in the new time, notably the Boston Gazette, which declined rapidly in the following decade, The Connecticut Courant of Hartford, The Providence Gazette, and The Pennsylvania Packet of Philadelphia, to which may be added such representative papers as The Massachusetts Spy, the Boston Independent Chronicle, the New York Journal and Packet, the Newport Mercury, The Maryland Gazette of Annapolis, The Pennsylvania Gazette and The Pennsylvania Journal, both of Philadelphia. Practically all were of four small pages, each of three or four columns, issued weekly. The Pennsylvania Packet, which appeared three times a week, became in 1784 the first daily paper.

In the same year the New York Journal was published twice a week, as were several of the papers begun in that year. There was a notable extension to new fields. In Vermont, where the first paper, established in 1781, had soon died, another arose in 1783; in Maine two were started in 1785. In 1786 the first one west of the Alleghanies appeared at Pittsburg, and following the westward tide of immigration The Kentucky Gazette was begun at Lexington in 1787.

Conditions were hardly more favourable to newspapers than during the recent conflict. The sources of news were much the same; the means of communication and the postal system were little improved. Newspapers were not carried in the mails but by favour of the postmen, and the money of one state was of dubious value in another. Consequently circulations were small, rarely reaching a thousand; subscribers were slow in paying; and advertisements were not plentiful.

Newspapers remained subject to provincial laws of libel, in accordance with the old common law, and were, as in Massachusetts for a short time in 1785, subject to special state taxes on paper or on advertisements. But public sentiment was growing strongly against all legal restrictions, and in general the papers practised freedom, not to say license, of utterance. With independence had come the consciousness of a great destiny.

The collective spirit aroused by the war, though clouded by conflicting local difficulties, was intense, and the principal interest of the newspapers was to create a nation out of the loose confederation. Business and commerce were their next care; but in an effort to be all things to all men, the small page included a little of whatever might "interest, instruct, or amuse." Political intelligence occupied first place; news, in the modern sense, was subordinated. A new idea, quite as much as a fire, a murder, or a prodigy, was a matter of news moment.

There were always a few items of local interest, usually placed with paragraphs of editorial miscellany. Correspondents, in return for the paper, sent items; private letters, often no doubt written with a view to such use, were a fruitful source of news; but the chief resource was the newspapers which every office received as exchanges, carried in the post free of charge, and the newspapers from abroad.

Partisan Newspapers

The editor, usually reflecting the sentiment of a group or a faction, began to emerge as a distinct power. He closely followed the drift of events and expressed vigourous opinions. But as yet the principal discussions were contributed not by the editors but by "the master minds of the country." The growing importance of the newspaper was shown in the discussions preceding the Federal Convention, and notably in the countrywide debate on the adoption of the Constitution, in which the newspaper largely displaced the pamphlet.

When Alexander Hamilton, James Madison, and John Jay united to produce the Federalist essays, they chose to publish them in The Independent Journal and The Daily Advertiser, from which they were copied by practically every paper in America long before they were made into a book. When the first Congress assembled 4 March, 1789, the administration felt the need of a paper, and, under the influence of Hamilton, John Fenno issued at New York, 15 April, the first number of *The Gazette of the United States*, the earliest of a series of administration organs.

The seat of government became the journalistic centre of the country, and as long as party politics remained the staple news interest the administration organs and their opponents were the chief sources of news for the papers of the country. Partisan bitterness increased during the last decade of the century as the First Party System took shape. The parties needed newspapers to communicate with their voters. New England papers were generally Federalist; in Pennsylvania there was a balance; in the West and South the Republican press predominated.

Though the Federalists were vigourously supported by such able papers as Russell's Columbian Centinel in Boston, Isaiah Thomas's Massachusetts Spy, The Connecticut Courant, and, after 1793, Noah Webster's daily Minerva in New York, The Gazette of the United States, which in 1790 followed Congress and the capital to Philadelphia, was at the centre of conflict, "a paper of pure Toryism," as Thomas Jefferson said, "disseminating the doctrines of monarchy, aristocracy, and the exclusion of the people."

To offset the influence of this, Jefferson and Madison induced Philip Freneau, who had been editing The Daily Advertiser in New York, to set up a "half weekly," to "go through the states and furnish a Whig vehicle of intelligence." Freneau's National Gazette, which first appeared 31 October, 1791, soon became the most outspoken critic of the administration of Adams, Hamilton, and Washington, and an ardent advocate of the French Revolution. Fenno and Freneau, in The Gazette of the United States and The National Gazette, at once came to grips, and the campaign of personal and party abuse in partisan news reports, in virulent editorials, in poems and skits of every kind, was echoed from one end of the country to the other. Noah Webster, strapped for money accepted an offer in late 1793 from Alexander Hamilton of $1500 to move to New York City and edit a Federalist newspaper. In December he founded New York's first daily newspaper, *American Minerva*. He edited it for four years writing the equivalent of 20 volumes of articles and editorials.

He also published the semi-weekly publication, *The Herald, A Gazette for the country*. As a partisan he soon was denounced by the Jeffersonian Republicans as "a pusillanimous, half-begotten, self-dubbed patriot," "an incurable lunatic," and "a deceitful newsmonger... Pedagogue and Quack." Fellow Federalist Cobbett labeled him "a traitor to the cause of Federalism", calling him "a toad in the service of sans-cullottism," "a prostitute wretch," "a great fool, and a barefaced liar," "a spiteful viper," and "a maniacal pedant." The master of words was distressed. Even the use of words like "the people," "democracy," and "equality" in public debate, bothered him for such words were "metaphysical abstractions that either have no meaning, or at least none that mere mortals can comprehend." The first party newspapers were full of vituperation. As one historian comments, It was with the newspaper editors, however, on both sides that a climax of rancorous and venomous abuse was reached.

Of the Federalist editors, the most voluminous masters of scurrility were William Cobbett of Porcupine's Gazette and John Ward Fenno of the United States Gazette, at Philadelphia; Noah Webster of the American Minerva, at New York; and at Boston, Benjamin Russell of the Columbian Centinel, Thomas Paine of the Federal Orrery, and John Russell of the Boston Gazette.

Chief of these was Cobbett, whose control of abusive epithet and invective may be judged from the following terms applied by him to his political foes, the Jacobins: "refuse of nations"; "yelper of the Democratic kennels"; "vile old wretch"; "tool of a baboon"; "frog-eating, man-eating, blooddrinking cannibals"; "I say, beware, ye under-strapping cut-throats who walk in rags and sleep amidst filth and vermin; for if once the halter gets round your flea-bitten necks, howling and confessing will come too late."

He wrote of the "base and hellish calumnies" propagated by the Jacobins, and of "tearing the mask from the artful and ferocious villains who, owing to the infatuation of the poor, and the supineness of the rich, have made such fearful progress in the destruction of all that is amiable and good and sacred among men." Among the milder examples of his description of Jacobins was the following: "Where the voice of the people has the most weight in public affairs, there it is most easy to introduce novel and subversive doctrines.

In such States too, there generally, not to say always, exists a party who, from the long habit of hating those who administer the Government, become the enemies of the Government itself, and are ready to sell their treacherous services to the first bidder. To these descriptions of men, the sect of the Jacobins have attached themselves in every country they have been suffered to enter. They are a sort of flies, that naturally settle on the excremental and corrupted parts of the body politic.... The persons who composed this opposition, and who thence took the name of Anti-Federalists, were not equal to the Federalists, either in point of riches or respectability. They were in general, men of bad moral characters embarrassed in their private affairs, or the tools of such as were. Men of this caste naturally feared the operation of a Government embued with sufficient strength to make itself respected, and with sufficient wisdom to exclude the ignorant and wicked from a share in its administration."

This decade of violence was nevertheless one of development in both the quality and the power of newspapers. News reporting was extended to new fields of local affairs, and the intense rivalry of all too numerous competitors awoke the beginnings of that rush for the earliest reports which was to become the dominant trait in American journalism. The editor evolved into a new type. As a man of literary skill, or a politician, or a lawyer with a gift for polemical writing, he began to supersede the contributors of essays as the strongest writer on the paper. Much of the best writing, and of the rankest scurrility, be it said, was produced by editors born and trained abroad, like Bache of the Aurora, Cobbett, Cooper, Gales, Cheetham, Callender, Lyon, and Holt. Of the whole number of papers in the country towards the end of the decade, more than one hundred and fifty, at least twenty opposed to the administration were conducted by aliens. The power wielded by these anti-administration editors impressed John Adams, who in 1801 wrote: "If we had been blessed with common sense, we should not have been overthrown by Philip Freneau, Duane, Callender, Cooper, and Lyon, or their great patron and protector. A group of foreign liars encouraged by a few ambitious native gentlemen have discomfited the education, the talents, the virtues, and the prosperity of the country." The most obvious example of that Federalist lack of common sense was the passage of the Alien and Sedition laws in 1798 to protect the government from the libels of editors.

The result was a dozen convictions and a storm of outraged public opinion that threw the party from power and gave the Jeffersonian Republican press renewed confidence and the material benefit of patronage when the Republicans took control of the government in 1800. The Republican party was especially effective in building a network of newspapers in major cities to broadcast its statements and editorialize in its favour. Fisher Ames, a leading Federalist, blamed the newspapers for electing Jefferson: they were "an overmatch for any Government.... The Jacobins owe their triumph to the unceasing use of this engine; not so much to skill in use of it as by repetition.". The newspapers continued primarily party organs; the tone remained strongly partisan, though it gradually gained poise and attained a degree of literary excellence and professional dignity.

The typical newspaper, a weekly, had a paid circulation of 500. The growth of the postal system, with the free transportation of newspapers locally and statewide, allowed the emergence of powerful state newspapers that closely reflected, and shaped, party views.

Growth in Newspapers

The number and geographical distribution of newspapers grew apace. In 1800 there were between 150 and 200; by 1810 there were 366, and during the next two decades the increase was at least equally rapid. With astonishing promptness the press followed the sparse population as it trickled westward and down the Ohio or penetrated the more northerly forests.

By 1835 papers had spread to the Mississippi River and beyond, from Texas to St. Louis, throughout Ohio, Indiana, Illinois, Michigan, and into Wisconsin. These pioneer papers, poorly written, poorly printed, and partisan often beyond all reason, served a greater than a merely local purpose in sending weekly to the seat of government their hundreds of messages of good and evil report, of politics and trade, of weather and crops, that helped immeasurably to bind the farflung population into a nation.

Every congressman wrote regularly to his own local paper; other correspondents were called upon for like service, and in some instances the country editors established extensive and reliable lines of intelligence; but most of them depended on the bundle of exchanges from Washington, Philadelphia, and New York, and reciprocally the city papers made good use of their country exchanges. Meanwhile the daily newspapers were increasing in number.

The first had appeared in Philadelphia and New York in 1784 and 1785; in 1796 one appeared in Boston. By 1810 there were twenty-seven in the country—one in the city of Washington, five in Maryland, seven in New York, nine in Pennsylvania, three in South Carolina, and two in Louisiana. As early as 1835 the Detroit Free Press began its long career.

The Press Served the Second Party System: 1820–1890

The political and journalistic situation made the administration organ one of the characteristic features of the period. Fenno's Gazette had served the purpose for Washington and Adams; but the first great example of the type was The National Intelligencer established in October, 1800, by Samuel Harrison Smith, to support the administration of Jefferson and of successive presidents until after Jackson it was thrown into the opposition, and The United States Telegraph, edited by Duff Green, became the official paper.

It was replaced at the close of 1830 by a new paper, The Globe, under the editorship of Francis P. Blair, one of the ablest of all ante-bellum political editors, who, with John P. Rives, conducted it until the changing standards and conditions in journalism rendered the administration organ obsolescent. The Globe was displaced in 1841 by another paper called The National Intelligencer, which in turn gave way to The Madisonian.

Thomas Ritchie was in 1845 called from his long service on The Richmond Enquirer to found, on the remains of The Globe, the Washington Union, to speak for the Polk administration and to reconcile the factions of democracy. Neither the Union nor its successors, which maintained the semblance of official support until 1860, ever occupied the commanding position held by the Telegraph and The Globe, but for forty years the administration organs had been the leaders when political journalism was dominant.

Their influence was shared and increased by such political editors as M. M. Noah and James Watson Webb of the New York Courier and Enquirer, Solomon Southwick of the Albany Register, Edwin Croswell, who edited The Argus and who, supported by Martin Van Buren and others, formed what was known as the "Albany Regency." The "Regency," the Richmond "Junta," which centred in the Enquirer, and the "Kitchen Cabinet" headed by the editor of The Globe, formed one of the most powerful political and journalistic cabals that the country has ever known.

Their decline, in the late thirties, was coincident with great changes, both political and journalistic, and though successors arose, their kind was not again so prominent or influential. The newspaper of national scope was passing away, yielding to the influence of the telegraph and the railroad, which robbed the Washington press of its claim to prestige as the chief source of political news. At the same time politics was losing its predominating importance.

The public had many other interests, and by a new spirit and type of journalism was being trained to make greater and more various demands upon the journalistic resources of its papers. The administration organ presents but one aspect of a tendency in which political newspapers generally gained in editorial individuality, and both the papers and their editors acquired greater personal and editorial influence. The beginnings of the era of personal journalism were to be found early in the 19th century.

Even before Nathan Hale had shown the way to editorial responsibility, Thomas Ritchie, in the Richmond Enquirer in the second decade of the century, had combined with an effective development of the established use of anonymous letters on current questions a system of editorial discussion that soon extended his reputation and the influence of his newspaper far beyond the boundaries of Virginia. Washington Barrow and the Nashville Banner, Amos Kendall and The Argus of Western America, G. W. Kendall and the New Orleans Picayune, John M. Francis and the Troy Times, and Charles Hammond and the Cincinnati Gazette, to mention but a few among many, illustrate the rise of editors to individual power and prominence in the third and later decades.

Notable among these political editors was John M. Daniel, who just before 1850 became editor of the Richmond Examiner and soon made it the leading newspaper of the South. Perhaps no better example need be sought of brilliant invective and literary pungency in American journalism just prior to and during the Civil War than in Daniel's contributions to the Examiner.

Though it could still be said that "too many of our gazettes are in the hands of persons destitute at once of the urbanity of gentlemen, the information of scholars, and the principles of virtue," a fact due largely to the intensity of party spirit, the profession was by no means without editors who exhibited all these qualities, and put them into American journalism. William Coleman, for instance, who, encouraged by Alexander Hamilton, founded the New York Evening Post in 1801, was a man of high purposes, good training, and noble ideals.

The Evening Post, reflecting variously the fine qualities of the editor, exemplified the improvement in tone and illustrated the growing importance of editorial writing, as did a dozen or more papers in the early decades of the century. Indeed the problem most seriously discussed at the earliest state meetings of editors and publishers, held in the thirties, was that of improving the tone of the press.

They tried to attain by joint resolution a degree of editorial self-restraint which few individual editors had as yet acquired. Under the influence of Thomas Ritchie, vigourous and unsparing political editor but always a gentleman, who presided at the first meeting of Virginia journalists, the newspaper men in one state after another resolved to "abandon the infamous practice of pampering the vilest of appetites by violating the sanctity of private life, and indulging in gross personalities and indecorous language," and to "conduct all controversies between themselves with decency, decorum, and moderation."

Ritchie found in the low tone of the newspapers a reason why journalism in America did not occupy as high a place in public regard as it did in England and France. The editorial page was assuming something of its modern form. The editorial signed with a pseudonym gradually passed away, but unsigned editorial comment and leading articles did not become an established feature until after 1814, when Nathan Hale made them a characteristic of the newly established Boston Daily Advertiser. From that time on they grew in importance until in the succeeding period of personal journalism they were the most vital part of the greater papers.

Several of these changes are exemplified in the work of James Gordon Bennett, though he originated few of them. In more than ten years of unsuccessful effort as a political journalist he had become familiar with the increasing enterprise in news-gathering that had already distinguished American methods. He despised the journalism of the day—the seriousness of tone, the phlegmatic dignity, the party affiliations, the sense of responsibility. He believed journalists were fools to think that they could best serve their own purposes by serving the politicians.

As Washington correspondent for the New York Enquirer, he wrote vivacious, gossipy prattle, full of insignificant and entertaining detail, to which he added keen characterization and deft allusions. Bennett saw a public who would not buy a serious paper at any price, who had a vast and indiscriminate curiosity better satisfied with gossip than discussion, with sensation rather than fact, who could be reached through their appetites and passions.

The idea which he did much to develop rested on the success of the one-cent press created by the establishment of the New York Sun in 1833. To pay at such a price these papers must have large circulations, sought among the public that had not been accustomed to buy papers, and gained by printing news of the street, shop, and factory. To reach this public Bennett began the New York Herald, a small paper, fresh, sprightly, terse, and "newsy."

"In journalistic débuts of this kind," he wrote, "many talk of principle—political principle, party principle—as a sort of steel trap to catch the public.

We ... disdain ... all principle, as it is called, all party, all politics. Our only guide shall be good, sound, practical common sense, applicable to the business and bosoms of men engaged in every-day life." News was but a commodity, the furnishing of which was a business transaction only, which ignored the social responsibility of the press, "the grave importance of our vocation," prized of the elder journalists and of the still powerful six-cent papers. The Herald, like the Sun, was at once successful, and was remarkably influential in altering journalistic practices.

In a period of wide-spread unrest and change many specialized forms of journalism sprang up—religious, educational, agricultural, and commercial, which there is no space here to discuss. Workingmen were questioning the justice of existing economic systems and raising a new labour problem; the socialistic ideas of Cabet and Fourier were spreading; Unitarianism and Transcendentalism were creating and expressing new spiritual values; temperance, prohibition, and the political status of women were being discussed; abolition was a general irritant and a nightmare to politicians.

The subject of controversy most critically related to journalism was abolition. The abolitionist press which began with The Emancipator of 1820, and had its chief representative in William Lloyd Garrison's Liberator, first issued 1 January, 1831, forced the slavery question upon the newspapers, and there ensued a struggle for the freedom of the press more acute than any since that caused by the Alien and Sedition laws.

Many abolitionist papers were excluded from the mails; their circulation was forcibly prevented in the South; in Boston, New York, Baltimore, Cincinnati, Alton, and elsewhere, editors were assaulted, offices were attacked and destroyed; rewards were offered in the South for the capture of Greeley and Garrison; in a few instances editors, like Lovejoy at Alton, lost their lives at the hands of mobs.

Associated Press and Impact of Telegraph

This idea of news and the newspaper for its own sake, the unprecedented aggressiveness in news-gathering, and the blatant methods by which the cheap papers were popularized aroused the antagonism of the older papers, but created a competition which could not be ignored. Systems of more rapid news-gathering and distribution quickly appeared.

Sporadic attempts at co-operation in obtaining news had already been made; in 1848 the Journal of Commerce, Courier and Enquirer, Tribune, Herald, Sun, and Express formed the New York Associated Press to Obtain news for the members jointly. Out of this idea grew other local, then state, and finally national associations. European news, which, thanks to steamship service, could now be obtained when but half as old as before, became an important feature.

In the forties several papers sent correspondents abroad, and in the next decade this field was highly developed. The telegraph, in 1844 shown to be practical, and put to successful use during the Mexican War, led to numerous far-reaching results in journalism. Telegraphic columns became a leading feature; news associations grew as the wires lengthened; but the greatest effect on the journalism of the country at large was to decentralize the press by rendering the inland papers, in such cities as Chicago, Louisville, Cincinnati, St. Louis, and New Orleans independent of those in Washington and New York.

A change made in the postal laws in 1845 favoured the local circulation of newspapers. The country circulation of most of the large Eastern papers was so curtailed that only one or two, like the New York Tribune, were able to maintain through their weekly editions something of their national character; the organs in Washington, even Niles's Weekly Register, which had been a most useful vehicle for the disseminating of political information, were still further shorn of their usefulness and soon eliminated; and the already vigourous provincial press became numerous and powerful.

FATHER OF AMERICAN JOURNALISM: FREDRIC HUDSON

Hudson was born in Quincy on April 25, 1819 to Barzillai and Rebecca Hudson. Raised and educated primarily in Boston, Hudson spent two years at school in Concord—the culmination of his formal education—before heading to New York to seek his fortune in 1836, at age seventeen.

He worked first at Hudson's News Room, his brother Edward's news-gathering agency, where he came to the attention of James Gordon Bennett, who had begun publishing the New York Herald in 1835. Impressed by the competence and self-possession of the younger man, Bennett hired Hudson as a reporter for the Herald—the paper's third employee. Frederic Hudson had a talent for aggressively pursuing news. Early in his career, he made a name for himself in gathering shipping news. While working for his brother, he had spent time on the docks picking up information about incoming vessels. At the Herald, he went a step farther and sent boats out to meet ships on their way into port.

Under his influence, the Herald used the pony express, the railroad, and the telegraph to transmit information from faraway places to the newspaper office. Hudson's success in scooping the competition during the Mexican War caused rival papers also to adopt these practices.

Hudson Important to Rise of Modern Journalism

In 1840, Bennett promoted Hudson to a position which was at the time novel in the newspaper business—that of managing editor. In the early 19th century, the various tasks involved in putting out a newspaper—reporting, setting type, printing, and circulation among them—were frequently the responsibility of a single individual.

Bennett had ambitious plans for his paper, and was willing to hire staff to help realise them. As the *Herald* grew, he shrewdly understood that appointing a manager to coordinate the increasingly diverse activities of his employees would enhance the efficiency and effectiveness of his operation. Bennett's trust was well placed in Hudson, who was completely loyal to his employer and shared his hopes for the *Herald*. Hudson was a consummate professional.

He threw himself heart and soul into his work. A hands-on manager, he let no detail slide. Although James Gordon Bennett was not above editorial promotion of particular political agendas, Hudson was dedicated to the ideal of accurate, timely, and complete reportage as the primary obligation of a newspaper. He mulled over strategies to improve and refine the gathering of news. He sent out correspondents to observe and send back information about events as they unfolded. He made himself accessible to everyone who asked to speak with him at his office. Known as a gentleman, he was well-respected by those who worked for him and even by those who worked for competing dailies.

As second in command, he was left in charge of putting out the *Herald* for extended periods while Bennett traveled. In Frederic Hudson's capable hands, the *Herald* became the most widely read newspaper in America, with a reported circulation of 77,000. Bennett paid his managing editor the princely salary of $10,000. Nobody disputed that Hudson earned every penny.

The Associated Press Was Born

Beginning in 1846, the *Herald* combined its financial resources with those of other New York newspapers to defray the expense of telegraphic transfer of information. In 1848, the *Herald*, *Courier and Enquirer*, *Express*, *Journal of Commerce*, *Sun*, and *Tribune* formally established the New York Associated Press.

This syndicate leased its own telegraph line and chartered a steamer from Halifax. Frederic Hudson was on the executive committee for this forerunner of the Associated Press. During the Civil War, Bennett's and Hudson's mutual commitment to rapid dissemination of the news prompted the hiring of even more correspondents at the *Herald*. Hudson arranged for *Herald* correspondents to observe the war first-hand by traveling with the Union Army, and to send their graphic reports to New York by telegraph.

Hudson Returns to Concord

Throughout his years in New York, Frederic Hudson had visited Concord regularly. After the Civil War, James Gordon Bennett, Jr., took the *Herald* over from his father. In 1866, Hudson resigned and retired to Concord with his invalid wife Eliza Hudson and their son Woodward. The family lived on Main Street, in a house located where No. 252 stands today. He devoted his retirement to caring for Mrs. Hudson and to writing an exhaustive history of journalism in America, which is still consulted today.

LARGE AND SMALL NEWSPAPERS

At a routine story-assignment meeting, a newspaper editor hands a reporter a press release announcing a candidate's run for city council and tells the reporter to write a story for the next day's edition. The reporter looks at the press release and says, "Hey, the candidate is my next-door neighbour!" Although one assumes most editors, regardless of their newspapers' sizes, would recognize a conflict of interest in having a reporter cover the political campaign of a neighbour, it would be shortsighted to suggest that all editors would address the situation the same way. Which begs the very simple question: In terms of journalism practice, does size make a substantial difference? And, if so, what is the nature of those differences?

This study tackles those questions, using qualitative interviews with twenty-eight editors at American daily newspapers ranging in size from one of the most widely read in the United States to a few with circulations well below 10,000. They range in location from New England to the deep South, from the Midwest to the West Coast, from rural farming communities to major cities. Some are independent, family-owned operations; others are owned by the largest newspaper companies. Some editors have worked at a number of papers across the nation, and some work in the towns where they were born and raised. While not a probability sample, the papers studied are diverse and provide indicators about the ways editors of different-sized newspapers in different regions and communities might conceptualize ethical norms and approach distinct ethical dilemmas.

The study builds upon past research that considered circulation/community size as a possible influence on journalistic practices and procedures. The theoretical framework is "connectivity," or the concept that the level of intimacy journalists have with their communities can influence how journalists do their jobs. The qualitative method employed an interview schedule using a combination of non-directive, structural, and compare-contrast questions, such that editors were able to conceptualize and express their views about various ethics procedures and problems on their own terms with little or no prompting from the investigator.

From the outset, it should be noted that there is hardly agreement among journalists and scholars that newspaper journalism in the United States can be seen in terms of "big papers" and "small papers," although many researchers have documented such differences.

Small newspapers certainly outnumber large newspapers both in terms of total circulation and in the number of newsrooms (and, by extension, newsroom cultures). An analysis of circulation figures published in the 2004 Editor and

Publisher Year Book showed that of the 9,321 U.S. newspapers listed, 9,104 (97.7 per cent) had circulations below 50,000, a common benchmark used to distinguish "big" from "small" newspapers. Those 9,104 "small" newspapers reported circulations totaling 108.9 million, compared to a combined circulation of 38.2 million for the 213 "big" newspapers. The majority of all newspapers are weeklies, with an average circulation of slightly less than 7,500. Among the 1,456 dailies, 1,239, or 85 per cent, are small newspapers, and reach about 44 per cent of all daily newspaper readers. Those figures suggest that newspaper journalism in America is dominated by small newspapers, and that there are perhaps "two journalisms" in the American newspaper industry.

But are there significant differences between the newsroom practices and policies of those "two journalisms"? Some would argue "yes." For example, limited resources at smaller newspapers can make it difficult to invest in strong design, or to retain employees who want higher salaries, more benefits, and advanced training.

The level of intimacy between small-paper journalists and their audiences also can be a factor, as media ethicist Bob Steele noted when he argued small-newspaper editors were more courageous to run gay-wedding announcements than were editors at bigger papers because "The editors of smaller and medium-sized papers know they will hear directly from readers and advertisers, including some who will threaten to cancel subscriptions or pull advertising." Some empirical studies have found evidence to reinforce such anecdotal observations. Differences between "big" and "small" newspapers were found in terms of job satisfaction;8 assessments of newspaper business issues; and specific journalistic practices, such as the use of nonlinear story telling, staffing levels," and even how editors assess the quality of their journalism.

Studies of ethical considerations at both large and small newspapers abound, but primarily in the form of case studies or comparisons within circulation groups-and, as such, lack anything but speculation about the influence organizational size might have on newsroom ethics. For example, a 1996 case study considered the sensibilities of smalltown residents towards publication of a fatal accident photo in the local newspaper, but the author only speculated that the same photo in a metropolitan newspaper might have generated less controversy.

In another example, a comparison of how two small newspapers covered the same controversial issue led the author to conclude that even small newspapers have an ethical obligation to the journalistic ideals of balance, fairness, and accuracy, which the author considered "givens" at larger newspapers but without any evidence to support that claim. Of course, many studies of newspaper ethics focus on large newspapers exclusively and make generalized claims, but either reject or ignore the possibility that "small" newspapers might conceptualize ethics differently than do the "big" newspapers.

But there are a handful of research articles that do make such comparisons. One is a 2005 survey that found sports departments at small newspapers were less likely than their big-paper counterparts to use ethics codes, more likely to disagree that accepting "freebies" can influence reporters' objectivity, and more likely to support "boosterism" towards the home team.

In an older study limited to Pennsylvania, smaller newspapers were much less likely than larger newspapers to have published photos of a public suicide by a government official. Although not directly related to ethics, a 1993 study found that editors' sense of autonomy (from publishers) when making newsroom decisions (including, ostensibly, ethical decisions) was stronger at larger newspapers.

Some scholars have suggested that journalists at small newspapers might have more difficulty than those at larger papers when balancing community involvement with editorial independence. In terms of making ethical choices about content and professional activity, Viall suggested (but did not test) the concept that journalists at small newspapers might be more concerned with community perceptions of the newspaper, while "cosmopolitan" journalists might be more concerned with the professional reputation of the newspapers they work for.

Such a direct influence of community on newsrooms had been a key focus of the work of Tichenor, Donohue, and Olien, who argued that newspapers reflect the characteristics of the communities they serve, and that newspapers in smaller communities might serve different functions than newspapers in larger cities. There also is some evidence to suggest that smaller communities are more likely to trust their newspapers-for example, a study of twenty-one different media markets found that newspapers in smaller markets had higher credibility among readers than did newspapers in larger markets.

This study considers the "big paper-small paper" differences from another approach-how journalists in different-sized communities conceptualize and deal with ethical dilemmas. Journalism scholar Paul Voakes, using an adaptation of the work of Shoemaker and Reese, found that the small-group dynamics of newsrooms and organizational influence (*i.e.*, corporate ethics policies) had much more influence on journalists' conceptualization of ethical dilemmas than did their individual personal values, and "extramedia" influences (*i.e.*, audience and news subjects) had the least affect on those decisions.

However, Voakes did find that concerns about "extramedia" reactions were highest among journalists who expressed less willingness to approve of controversial tactics to gather and present news. Although Voakes did not make the connection directly, that finding is consistent with the arguments made by Tichenor, Donohue, and Olien nearly twenty years earlier about the heavier influence of community values on journalists working in small, relatively homogenous communities.

Although the study looks at how different newspapers conceptualize and approach ethics, it is not an "ethics study" per se. This study does draw upon ethics theory to differentiate between normative and situational ethics and to define the common types of ethical dilemmas journalists face (*i.e.*, conflict of interest, privacy vs. public's right to know, etc.), but it stops short at analyzing the "rightness" or "wrongness" of those differences.

Rather, its primary purpose is to explore the concept of "journalistic connectivity," or the suggestion that community size has an influence on all newsroom decisions, including ethics. This concept of "connectivity" is derived from two other theoretical frameworks-"imagined community" and "news work"-but in many ways builds upon the work of Tichenor, Donohue, and Olien regarding the influences of community structure on the press.

This study begins with two premises: that journalists routinely consider (or try to consider) their audience's desires when deciding "what news," and, second, that journalists' perceptions of what their audiences consider acceptable often do not match what those audiences truly believe, a premise also supported by past research.

Enter the process of "imagined community," Anderson's theory suggesting that members of large collectives (specifically, nations) cannot possibly know all of their compatriots, and as such their conceptualization of their "communities" is based largely on imagination. The concept can be extended to national subdivisions and subcultures-for example, "imagined community" certainly could be used to examine who is a "New Yorker" or a "Texan." Some scholars have applied this theory to analyse news media as members and facilitators of imagined communities, as manifest in the ways they cover immigration issues, their assumptions about culture and race in high-profile news stories, even how journalists see themselves as a community of professionals with similar values.

Tuchman perhaps recognized the role of newspapers in community-imagining, writing that newspapers "enable geographically dispersed individuals to know something about one another, one another's ethnic and neighborhood groups, and events in group life." Tuchman examined social aspects of news work and found an "insider" culture in which journalists and their sources formed a dosed circle of established institutions.

Some research has used "newswork" theory to analyse how journalists deal with ethical dilemmas: one study found that, when facing ethical dilemmas, journalists focus more on established tenets of journalism ethics than on guidance from people in their social settings. Even journalists who cover the media industry take a heavily peer-oriented approach to making ethical decisions.

"Imagining community" may be viewed as very much a part of the process of gathering, packaging, and distributing the news, and the process is influenced considerably by the size of the communities journalists serve. As Tkhenor, Donohue, and Olien suggested, "size and structure of the community are seen as major characteristics affecting newspapers." In their research on community-press relationships in Minnesota, they noted that the connections between journalists and their communities tend to become more impersonal in larger markets, whereas "the small-town journalist is more likely to have a multiplicity of interactions with sources, knowing them as citizens, members of social clubs, and/or as members of friendship groups in settings that make it difficult if not impossible to separate the professional from the purely social or personal relationship."

Thus, it may be posited:

- First, that journalists routinely "imagine" their communities in the process of gathering, packaging, and disseminating news;
- Second, that the process of "imagining" the comm-unity is more difficult and prone to detachment in large, pluralistic communities, and somewhat easier and more prone to attachment in small, homogeneous communities;
- Third, that in the process of "imagining community," journalists in all communities necessarily must compensate for their lack of personal knowledge about the community with their own imaginations of those communities;
- And fourth, that journalists compensate for their lack of personal connection by drawing on their own personal and professional values when they imagine their communities-the common "doing journalism for other journalists" phenomenon.

This study explores differences between "large" and "small" newspapers through interviews with editors from across the United States. The method is informed by the approaches to qualitative communication research suggested by Lindlof.

To ensure that informants would be in the best position to articulate their newsrooms' policies and practices, the study only includes interviews with senior-level editors.

Newspapers of varying sizes in varying parts of the United States were selected to ensure a diverse pool of research participants. States were grouped into fourteen geographic areas to ensure that there were several large newspapers (over 50,000 circulation) in each area (several states have only one or two large newspapers, so a state-by-state approach would have made recruiting and ensuring the anonymity of informants difficult). One large newspaper and one small newspaper were recruited from each area, for a total of twenty-eight interviews. Five newspapers had weekday circulations above 100,000; eight had circulations from 50,000 to 100,000; seven had circulations from 10,000 to 50,000; and six had circulations below 10,000.

During the interviews, informants were first asked to describe their communities, how they think the communities view their newspapers, and to describe the strongest supporters and critics of their newspapers. That first set of questions was intended to have a priming effect on the informants so that they would be thinking about their communities throughout the interviews.

The second set of questions had editors recount actions they had taken to address ethical dilemmas. Each was asked whether an ethical dilemma resulted in the editor making a personnel change, changing an editorial decision, or confronting co-workers in the advertising or circulation departments. Editors were asked to generally describe each situation and how it was resolved.

The third set of questions focused on specific types of ethical dilemmas and the policies/procedures used to deal with them. Each informant was asked to describe in his/her own terms the newspaper's procedures for dealing with dilemmas of "conflict of interest," "sensitivity," "privacy," "reporting practices," "accuracy," and "an oversight on the part of the newspaper." Again, the questions were such that they allowed the informants to define the concepts in their own terms, rather than the researcher defining them in advance.

Questions in the fourth set were open-ended. Informants were asked to describe the most common types of ethical dilemmas they deal with; dilemmas they had to deal with only once or twice; dilemmas they had not dealt with but expected to have to deal with at some point ("nightmare dilemmas"); and whether (and why or why not) they believed large and small newspapers face different types of ethical dilemmas.

Immediately after each interview, the researcher entered notes into a grid to facilitate analysis. Following in the tradition of the grounded theory approach to qualitative analysis, the researcher did not begin the process of categorization and coding until after all of the interviews were completed, and only then after giving the data several close readings.

Several themes that emerged from the analysis demonstrate ways in which the large and small newspapers differed. Some examples of informants' statements are provided, along with some frequencies to help give a sense of the strength of the themes within the "big" and "small" groups.

COMMUNITY VIEWS OF NEWSPAPERS

Most of the "big paper" editors (ten of fourteen) described their communities' views of their newspapers in terms of "institutional respect" (*i.e.*, "Overall, the community respects the newspaper even if they don't always like it") and/or "editorial-page ideology" (*i.e.*, "The community probably sees us as a little more liberal than we really are"), whereas most editors at the smaller newspapers (nine of fourteen) described community views in terms of "community connections" (*i.e.*, "The community embraces the paper. They look for it to connect different parts of the community," and "We have a growing population of people who are moving in and are not connected to the community, and they don't understand or appreciate the newspaper.").

Descriptions of "strongest critics of the newspaper" differed somewhat: The theme of "race/ethnic groups" as strong critics was found only among the large papers, and a theme of "readers wanting more professional journalism" was unique among newspapers at or below 50,000 circulation.

The description of "strongest supporters" also differed: editors at the largest newspapers (those with circulations of 80,000 or more) framed "supporters" in terms of social class ("business people," "working class," "highly educated") or in terms of politics/ideology ("liberals," "Republicans"); but below the 80,000 benchmark, two dominant categories emerged for "supporters"-long-time residents of the communities (mentioned by eight editors), and people who are interested in local news (also mentioned by eight editors).

ETHICAL DILEMMAS REQUIRING PERSONNEL OR EDITORIAL CHANGES

One of the most notable differences between large and small newspapers was the number of times editors made severe personnel changes due to ethical lapses. All but two of the large-paper editors recalled disciplining or firing reporters due to ethical dilemmas, whereas only half of the fourteen small-paper editors recalled such situations.

For the large papers, the most common problems were plagiarism or deceptive reporting/editing practices, and the most common response to those problems was formal discipline-six situations resulted in the firing of the employees in question, four resulted in suspensions, and two resulted in formal reprimands. Among the seven smaller papers that did make personnel changes, the most common "offence" was "conflict of interest" (three cases), followed by two cases of plagiarism and two cases of deception. Four of those were resolved by firing the employees, two resulted in warnings, and two were resolved with simple reassignments.

Two-thirds of the editors recalled having to change editorial decisions based on ethical dilemmas involving employees, and most of those (thirteen of eighteen) had to address some kind of "unethical" reporting practice by killing or holding articles, retracting articles, or writing apologies to their audiences.

PROCEDURES FOR SPECIFIC TYPES OF ETHICAL DILEMMAS

The three types of ethical dilemmas that generated notable differences were under the broad categories of "conflict of interest," "sensitivity," and "reporting practices." The other dilemmas mentioned in questions did not reveal any noteworthy differences.

The editors' most common definition for "conflict of interest" focused on personal relationships between staff members and news makers (twelve of twenty-eight editors used that definition, six in each size group). The second most common "conflict" identified by big-paper editors was freelancing by staff reporters (five of fourteen), a phenomenon not mentioned by any of the small-paper editors. Among the small-paper editors, the second most common type of "conflict" was having staffers involved in community organizations (seven of fourteen), which was only mentioned once among the big-paper editors.

Among the large newspapers, editors mostly dealt with "conflicts of interest" by informing staffers of the conflicts, issuing memos about policies prohibiting such conflicts, and expecting the conflicts not to be repeated. Among the smaller newspapers, however, editors seemed comfortable with the idea that such conflicts are inevitable, and they mostly dealt with the matters by reassigning staff to minimize the conflicts of interests.

For example, an editor at a 20,000-30,000 circulation newspaper said, "I know a lot of people in this town, and I also know what's right and what's wrong, so I don't get involved in the editing process in stories about people I know." And an editor at a 10,000-20,000 circulation newspaper said that turnaround among his reporting staff negates the problem: "We have a young, transient staff, and they're often not around long enough to develop relationships that might lead to conflicts of interest."

Editors' conceptualization of "sensitivity" as an ethical issue varied overall-three editors mentioned publishing controversial images, three mentioned publishing controversial words or phrases, four mentioned whether to identify juveniles accused of crimes, etc. But as with "conflict of interest," the approach to dealing with dilemmas of "sensitivity" differed noticeably by newspaper size. Among the big-paper editors, ten of the fourteen described their procedures as involving discussions within the newsroom focused on the journalistic standards of the information. As one editor of an 80,000-circulation newspaper put it, "We typically engage some number of editors in the discussion, and we each take turns articulating as thoroughly as possible arguments for or against. Then I make the decision based on my own news values."

But among the small-paper editors, the dominant theme (from seven of the fourteen) was to consider the community standards above journalistic standards. One small-paper editor stated, "We try to look at what's in the best interest of the community. We're part of the community, and we try to identify with the sensitivities of the people in this region." Another small-paper editor said he tries to "make sure the staff is aware of concerns in the community, especially among minority groups."

A blending of the approaches was seen in one mid-sized paper (of about 40,000 circulation), with the editor saying "we generally consider our readers to be big boys and girls, and so we don't try to protect them from information we think is important. We let them debate our choices in letters to the editor." In terms of unethical "reporting practices," large-paper editors mostly noted such dilemmas as arising from aggressive forms of reporting-inappropriate access to information, making "deals" with sources to get information, even investigating what reporters at competing media were working on. Small-paper editors, by contrast, complained of inexperienced or lazy (or both) reporters as causing the most problems-under-sourcing stories, withholding information about friends/family, and not doing enough background research on long-running stories.

Likewise, there were differences in the procedures for dealing with those situations. Big-paper editors seemed more attuned to punishing reporters-five of the fourteen said they disciplined the offending reporters, and three said they informally warned their reporters and issued memos to the newsroom reminding all staff about what is unacceptable. Small-paper editors, however, mostly took mentoring approaches-six of the fourteen said they used the situations to educate their (often young) reporters about acceptable practices, and only two said they had to discipline reporters who had repeatedly violated ethical standards.

One small-paper editor said, "Sometimes we have to cover basic reporting skills, like 'what is a quote, verbatim or close?,' or 'Is it OK to clean up the grammar for coaches and players of high-school sports?,' that you have to clearly identify yourself as a reporter in all situations, and so on." Another small-paper editor said her staff is dominated by "good reporters who are young, right out of college, and they ask things like 'Do I have to tell them I'm a reporter?' on matters of controversy in which they might be uncomfortable."

OPEN-ENDED QUESTIONS

The competing themes of "aggressive journalists" vs. "inexperienced journalists" carried over into responses to the open-ended questions. Most editors at the large papers described their "most common" ethical dilemmas in those same terms-many of them were particularly concerned about dealing with reporters who want to use anonymous sources, who use unorthodox means to obtain information, and who have strong opinions about the topics they cover.

Editors at the small papers, by contrast, identified their most common ethical problems in terms of reporters getting too involved in their communities or too close to sources.

One small-paper editor said, "Because this is a small town, most people on staff are involved in things outside of work, they have friends in the community, kids in the school, so it's hard not to have conflicts," and another said, "Many staffers have lived here a long time, some their whole lives, so they have friends and family in the news, and they hesitate to make new friends because they don't want to be too conflicted."

Differences also were apparent in how editors characterized their "rare dilemmas." Among the large-paper editors, plagiarism, fabrication, and deceptive reporting practices were nearly universal (twelve of the fourteen mentioned such problems), whereas only two of the small-paper editors mentioned such problems. But seven small-paper editors mentioned community pressures on reporters (such as officials asking reporters to withhold information or friends asking reporters not to put arrest records in the newspaper; one small-town editor recalled an incident in which a community leader innocently offered a reporter a gratuity for covering a fund-raising event, which the reporter respectfully declined).

Editors' views on "nightmare scenarios" also differed by newspaper size. Among the large-paper editors, nine of the fourteen anticipated having to deal with an issue of plagiarism/fabrication. One editor said, "I never thought it would be a problem here, but they told me (at a professional conference) that I'm naïve, that it happens all the time at big papers." A few of the small-paper editors (five) also mentioned plagiarism/fabrication, but mostly in terms of it not being something they worry about. One small-paper editor said, "If a reporter here fabricated a source, they would get caught. It's a small town, and everybody knows everybody else. People here would see a name they don't recognize and call us on it." Another small-paper editor said, "I'm not worried about plagiarism. I don't think you can get away with it in a small community. Somebody would catch you."

The small-paper editors were uniquely concerned about being manipulated by sources or having to write about misdeeds by well-liked community leaders. One small-paper editor said she fears a situation in which a birth announcement would be used to make a paternity claim; three were concerned that the local police would ask reporters to serve as witnesses or informants; four were concerned about situations in which the newspaper's coverage of criminal trials would upset victims and their relatives.

Are There Inherent Differences between Large and Small Newspapers? Most editors at large papers (nine of fourteen) answered that question with "no," essentially arguing that journalism ethics is the same for all newspapers. However, most small-paper editors (eleven of fourteen) said "yes." A common assumption among the few large-paper editors who said "yes" was that smaller newspapers face more pressures from advertisers-and, in fact, three small-paper editors said exactly that. A few editors also noted that a key difference is institutional structure-one big-paper editor bemoaned the bureaucracy of making ethical choices in a large newsroom, while three small-paper editors liked the informal, flexible approaches they could take to handling dilemmas. Four editors (two from each group) noted that bigger papers tend to do more investigative reporting, which involves more risky reporting and, as a result, more ethical dilemmas.

But the most dominant theme was clear-direct accountability to the community is the biggest difference. Just one big-paper editor mentioned that reason, but seven of the fourteen small-paper editors all mentioned differences that could be categorized as "community connections." "It's a lot easier to make hard calls in a big city where you aren't likely to know the people affected," said the managing editor of a 100,000-plus-circulation newspaper.

The editor of a 12,000-circulation newspaper echoed that concept: "At a metro paper, you almost never see the people you write about, but in a small town, you see those people in the grocery store or the hair salon. You walk out the door and face the readers. The public knows who you are, personally." And the editor of a 7,000-circulation paper put it this way: "You cover more local and personal issues about people you have direct contact with. You live in the aftermath of what you cause. You can't cover and run."

It would be folly to assume that, when it comes to "connectivity" in newspaper journalism, small-town journalists have stronger ties to their communities than do journalists in larger cities. Certainly, journalists in all markets-and all media-will have personal relationships, social activities, and off-duty interactions that connect them to the communities in which they work. And one certainly could find examples of small-town journalists who are largely detached from their communities and big-city journalists who know more about their cities than anybody might think possible. But when it comes to making ethical choices, this study suggests that small-town and big-city journalists perhaps start the process from very different levels of connectivity. At larger newspapers, the emphasis seems to be to preserve the reputation of the institution of the newspaper, whereas at smaller newspapers the starting point seems to be to manage journalists' individual connections with their communities.

For example, editors at the larger newspapers were much more attuned to setting ethical policies and disciplining violators, both of which suggest top-down, institutional approaches. Editors of the small newspapers were much more attuned to educating their reporters about ethical dilemmas without setting too many strict policies that would isolate reporters from the community.

Also consider how the two groups conceptualized "conflicts of interest": the editors at large newspapers were the only ones who mentioned freelancing as a prevailing dilemma in their newsrooms. Their concerns were very much based on monetary issues-that reporters might be "double dipping" by making additional money from work they were paid to do for their newspapers. And their general response to such situations was to set up prohibitions for such behaviour and to punish violators. For small-paper editors, conflicts of interest often were seen as situations in which reporters' voluntary involvement in community groups might be seen as influencing how those groups are covered. Rather than prohibit such external activity, the small-paper editors simply tried to avoid having conflicted staffers cover the groups or issues in which they are involved. Consider also the distinctions between the two groups in terms of "sensitivity" issues. For the larger papers, the process of determining how to handle controversial content mostly involved "within journalism" discussions, in which newsroom staffers-primarily editors of varying levels-weighed the journalistic value of the information. Although one could easily assume that "community values" would be part of such conversations, that concept was not overtly expressed by those large-paper editors. Among the small-town editors, however, community values were often given priority over journalistic values.

But the most telling differences came when the basic question of this study was put to the editors. The large-paper editors largely rejected the notion that ethics would be different for smaller papers, whereas the small-paper editors strongly supported that notion, arguing that small-town journalists are more connected to their communities than are bigcity journalists, and that connectivity drastically affects the ethical considerations they must make.

This study indicates that journalists at small newspapers perhaps see themselves as more connected to their communities than journalists at large newspapers, at least when it comes to identifying and dealing with ethical dilemmas. Whether the degree of connectivity is stronger in smaller communities can only be tested by additional research. The findings do support the idea that, when tackling ethical dilemmas, small-town journalists may be more deferential to what they see as community values, whereas big-city journalists may be more deferential to what they see as institutional values. Professional standards still come into play at all levels. Both big and small papers are concerned about unethical reporting practices, for example. But even there differences emerged (consider: larger papers seemed more concerned about overly aggressive reporting, smaller papers about inexperienced or sloppy reporting).

Obviously, these findings cannot be generalized to all newspapers, but they do challenge research that aims to make broad claims about journalism practices from data gathered only from large newspapers. While there certainly must be some professional standards that all journalists share, there also are clearly standards and approaches that differ. As teachers and researchers of journalism, we must all be more cognizant of the fact that size can make a difference, and that the distinctions between big and small newspapers very well may be distinctions that matter.

6

Electronic Publishing

INTRODUCTION

The scope of the term 'electronic publishing' can be interpreted in many different ways. For example, it could be considered to include all forms of electronic aids to authors, from simple word processing capabilities to actual typesetting and/or mark-up tools as well as networking support to collaborative authorship and electronic communication among authors, editors, referees, and other participants in the publishing process.

Since, 'publishing' implies production and distribution, however, the term refers most obviously to the generation of publications in electronic form or, at least, with the aid of electronics. In this more restricted sense, electronic publishing can be considered to have evolved gradually over a period of about thirty years, the evolution having the following manifestations. Use of computers to generate conventional print-on-paper publications. This development can be traced back to the early 1960s.

The use of electronics to print on paper is not a completely pedestrian application since, it allows new capabilities such as printing on demand and even the production of customised publications tailored to individual needs:

- The distribution of text in electronic form, where the electronic version is the exact equivalent of a paper version and may have been used to generate the paper version. For secondary publications, electronic distribution began early in the 1960s. For primary journals, the development occurred somewhat later. Today there is considerable activity and interest in projects that make electronically accessible the text and/or graphics of journals that are also sold in print-on-paper form. Major projects of this kind include ADONIS, Red Sage, CORE, and TULIP. Moreover, the full text of a significant number of journals is now made accessible online by vendors such as DIALOG.
- Distribution in electronic form only but with the publication being little more than print on paper displayed electronically. Nevertheless,

it may have various 'value added' features, including search, data manipulation and alerting capabilities.

- The generation of completely new publications that exploit the true capabilities of electronics. This phase of development can actually be subdivided into:
  - The presentation of existing text and graphics in innovative ways, and
  - The production of publications designed *ab initio* to exploit full electronic capabilities.

PUBLISHING—SOME BACKGROUND ISSUES

A HETEROGENEOUS COMMUNITY

It is almost always misleading to talk about 'publishing' as if it were a single industry; there are many different publishing industries, loosely grouped together by their use of a common medium for dissemination—print on paper. 'Publishing' is conventionally broken down into major sub-categories—newspapers, magazines, books, journals. Even at this high level of granularity, some significant problems begin to appear at the margins—in defining when a magazine becomes a journal. Our major focus in this report is 'book and journal' publishing—but this categorisation masks considerable differences between different sectors.

There are at least four major categories of book publishing: consumer; educational; professional; and academic. Each of these has very different business models and very different businesses. As we move further into the network environment, various aspects of our approach to categorising publishers must start to change. There is considerable convergence between different types of content as they come together for the first time in a common distribution environment. However, the differences between the different markets to which each of these types of publisher disseminates are in some ways further highlighted by the different ways with which different communities of users are adopting electronic dissemination. There are, for example, some interesting sectoral differences already beginning to emerge in attitudes towards e-books. The publishers to whom we spoke for this report are primarily in professional and academic publishing; however, we included some publishers who publish educational content and some who publish for general consumers. As suggested, draw out such differences as we observe between these groups, although we must again stress that our sample size in insufficient for drawing statistically significant conclusions.

PUBLISHING AND THE PRODUCTION PROCESS

We often observe a tendency to equate 'the publishing industry' with the process by which an author's raw material is converted into a consumable product; this is the aspect of publishing that we mean when we talk about the 'production process'. Although the origins of publishing and printing may have been very closely linked, for the greater part of the twentieth century at least, the majority of publishers took very little interest in their production process. Production was a relatively unimportant part of their activity; most or all of it has been subcontracted to external suppliers, and the technical aspects of the process are of little interest to publishing management.

In recent years, those publishers who have felt the greatest impact of the digital revolution—particularly those in professional and STM publishing—have greatly increased their technological expertise. The type of larger publisher to whom we spoke for this report now employ people who can speak with some degree of confidence about SGML, for example. This would not have been uniformly the case five or ten years ago. Nevertheless, publishers themselves emphatically do not equate publishing and production.

What is more, we have spoken to a somewhat non-representative sample of the publishing industry as a whole. Most publishers do not have the kind of expertise that exists among our target group, and have no desire to acquire it. They will publish in digital formats as the market demands that they do so; but they will continue to depend entirely on outsourcing for all the technological aspects of the production process.

The significance of this, from the point of view of libraries with an interest in digital deposit and preservation, is that the people with whom they will find themselves dealing will not have much understanding of the technology involved. They will not manage their own content, but will depend on third parties. In an era of increasing globalisation, those third parties are as likely as not to be elsewhere in the world. This is likely greatly to complicate dealings relating to the management of digital deposit.

PUBLISHERS' MOTIVATION FOR ADOPTING STANDARDS

As suggested, introduce immediately here one theme that will be–implicitly if not explicitly—recurrent throughout our report. Publishers' motives in adopting standards are the same as those that drive all of their decision-making; they are strictly commercial. The decision on whether or not to adopt a standard will be driven entirely by perceptions of their own commercial advantage. In general, publishers do not produce their publications with an eye to their long-term preservation. They produce publications to sell them at a profit; long-term preservation may become significant to them, but only when the failure to accommodate its requirements in some way looks likely to have a significant impact on their commercial interest.

As one publisher revealingly said to us:

- "I am not particularly optimistic if you take the long- term view. I don't think publishers are well equipped or even well motivated to manage the long-term availability of their material—any material is only going to be cared for if it's financially viable. Once we can't get any money for something, we're not likely to worry about it. We should deliver whatever we can to the preservation libraries, but then it's over to them."

Several of our other respondents explicitly stated that they considered long-term preservation to be 'someone else's problem'. In the recent history of print-on-paper publishing, we can observe the direct analogy of the adoption of 'acid-free' papers. When publishers of scholarly monographs were first asked to produce books on acid-free paper, the response from larger academic publishers was generally slow and uninterested. Acid-free paper tended to be more expensive and difficult to source.

This remained the case until competition in paper manufacture eliminated the price premium from acid-free stocks. At that point, when it became entirely painless to make the transition, publishers were happy to adopt acid-free paper and to earn whatever public relations value there was from being able to advertise the fact that they had done so. There was no commercial disbenefit and possibly a small commercial benefit. The decision became an easy one to make. Commercial motivation is now driving publishers of one specific type of content—scholarly journals—to think harder about preservation issues. Major publishers have made a commitment to moving their primary publication platform from print-on-paper to electronic publication in the very near future.

It has been widely posited that a possible reason for academic authors' reluctance to publish in 'electronic-only' serials is their concern for the long-term preservation of the academic record. Certainly, there is anecdotal evidence that such a concern stands behind some academic librarians' reluctance to move to an 'electronic only' strategy for their serials collection. This has pushed some publishers of journals publicly to acknowledge that the development of an active policy relating to the deposit of their journals with national libraries is becoming an essential element of their long-term commercial strategy.

In this context, it is notable that major journal publishers in the Netherlands and Germany are already depositing electronic versions of their journals on a voluntary basis with their national libraries. At this stage, it seems to us to be unlikely that in any other sector of the publishing market either authors or customers will be found to be so concerned about issues relating to longterm preservation; this is likely to be reflected in publishers' attitudes towards the deposit of many of their digital publications. While they may be entirely happy to deposit their publications they are unlikely willingly to take on substantial additional cost or effort in order to facilitate long-term preservation.

The adoption of standards for electronic publishing will be driven by other factors. Any benefit that this may bring to the business of long-term preservation will be purely serendipitous. Some specific examples may deserve exploration here. A simple one relates to the adoption of standard identifiers. The near universal adoption of the ISBN was driven by the commercial demands of the channel of distribution. A significant subset of the STM journal publishing community has recently found a similar commercial driver for the widespread adoption of the Digital Object Identifier (DOI) at the individual article level, in reference linking. However, a recent conversation with an electronic publisher in another sector suggests to us that some publishers see common identification standards as being at odds with their commercial interests.

It will be a long time before that sector adopts a similar solution. A more significant example may be the adoption of PDF. Despite fierce competition between proprietary page description languages during the 1980s, Adobe's success in establishing PostScript as the *de facto* standard in the graphics arts industries has been complete. The close relationship between PDF and PostScript allowed a few publishers quickly to adopt PDF as an electronic publishing platform very simply and at comparatively low cost.

The 'network effect' rapidly created a community of producers and consumers that has increasingly expected PDF to be used for the dissemination of page-based electronic publications. Despite the claimed superiority of other formats, it is very notable that all but one of our respondents who are delivering page-based images are using PDF to do so. Where information from multiple sources has to be combined into a single resource, the drive towards standardisation is strongest. The recent announcement of NewsML, an XML-based standard for managing and interchanging multimedia news, is an obvious case in point. NewsML will allow the easy distribution of syndicated news in conformance to a standard XML DTD. For the time being, we can foresee no similar developments in other areas of content, since, the need to interchange content has not proved strong enough to generate real enthusiasm for the adoption of standards.

PUBLISHERS AND METADATA

The generation of bibliographic data by publishers has been notorious for its inaccuracy and inconsistency. Publishers have generally depended on third-party bibliographic agencies for the maintenance and dissemination of information about their products—and indeed have often re-purchased information about their own products. However, recent developments are making it increasingly clear—to some publishers at least—that accurate and consistent metadata is an essential aspect of their business in the network environment.

One element of BIBLINK, a European project that involved several deposit libraries as partners, tested the principles of the interchange and 'improvement' of simple metadata records between publishers and libraries. Dialogue between libraries and publishers during the course of that project revealed that many publishers—particularly the smaller and 'newer' ones—are becoming increasingly aware of the fact that their metadata is inadequate. They are actively seeking appropriate standards for the management and interchange of metadata. Libraries involved in the project, aware of the proven difficulties involved in cataloguing electronic publications, made considerable efforts to raise the awareness among publishers of the need for 'electronic title pages' to be included in their publications.

In the electronic publication of academic journals, publishers realised from the outset that article level metadata would be an essential element of any online delivery service; as a result, even where the primary delivery format has been PDF, article 'headers' have consistently been provided in SGML. These now have the benefit of being produced as part of the production workflow and should therefore be consistent with the published document.

The most significant current driver of metadata developments in the book publishing community is the pressure from online booksellers for more extensive descriptive information. The development of the EPICS data dictionary and even more so its subset, ONIX International, have been strongly motivated by the need to provide information in a consistent form to the online bookselling community. ONIX International provides a data dictionary and a standard XML DTD as a mechanism for the electronic interchange of a limited bibliographic metadata record. Although the initial release is focussed on conventional print on paper books, future releases are expected to cover not only e-books but also other media.

The extent to which all publishers will prove able to manage their metadata to a sufficiently high standard to meet market requirements remains to be seen. However, it is notable that a growing number of publishers, certainly in the US and the UK, are making significant systems investment in this area. The adoption of the ONIX International standard appears to be moving ahead with surprising speed in the US and the UK; and there is a real possibility that it could move towards rapid global acceptance in the publishing industry. We believe that publisher-generated metadata will be particularly significant in the whole area of deposit of electronic publications; otherwise the conceptual and technical difficulties of cataloguing will be extremely difficult to overcome.

To what extent does ONIX International meet libraries' cataloguing needs? A forthcoming conference presentation by Priscilla Caplan suggests that libraries should:

- "...Begin thinking about basic bibliographic metadata as a commodity, produced and exchanged by a number of communities in order to serve a number of purposes.... As suggested, soon be in an environment where most metadata is exchanged in XML: the publishers have already adopted it, and library systems are moving in that direction.

> In this context it makes very little sense to think that libraries, publishers, booksellers, distributors and vendors will all be creating incompatible, non-reusable bibliographic metadata...I do urge librarians to take a serious and objective look at the metadata schemas emerging in the publishing community with the long-term goal of maximising the interchangeability of data.".

Caplan goes on to suggest that libraries should "work proactively with publishers to establish enough commonality between respective rule sets to allow meaningful exchange and reuse of metadata." This co-operative approach was also endorsed during a workshop on digital preservation and deposit held in London in July 2000. For example, it became apparent during the conference that the technical data that publishers are gathering for the management of their own internal content repositories is essentially identical to that required by libraries for the long-term preservation of the same resources. There is nothing to be gained from recreating essentially identical data.

The EPICS data dictionary is designed to be extensible in ways that will encompass the necessary technical description of resources and it is anticipated that co-operative work between publishers and librarians will enable the development of such an extension. However, it is important to remember that only a small minority even of large publishers currently have sophisticated digital content repositories; most are continuing to outsource their content management requirements. This can only make the protocols for metadata exchange more complex to manage.

PURPOSE OF ELECTRONIC PUBLISHING

For the purposes of this resource guide electronic publishing is defined as:

- Making the content of the journal available online.

This chapter will also address the use of electronic tools to facilitate the processes of, publication, for example online electronic editorial processing.

WHY DO ELECTRONIC PUBLISHING AT ALL

Many journals around the world struggle to attract authors and readers, and frequently suffer from a lack of resources—both human and financial. In addition, research habits are changing and researchers increasingly expect any information to be found online, which means that a journal which cannot be located on the web may be effectively invisible. Online publication can help to address some of these issues. At the same time, many readers still seem to prefer print so you may not feel you can stop producing a print edition as well.

Publishing a journal electronically sounds very attractive. There are a number of good reasons for doing so, but it does have disadvantages too. Before committing yourself and your organisation to the effort and expense involved, it is sensible to look carefully at both the advantages and disadvantages. In the end, the decision will depend on what your main objectives are, so it is important to be clear about why you are publishing, or planning to publish, in the first place: what information you want to disseminate, and to whom. Electronic publishing is often considered to have six advantages over print: international reach, speed, additional capabilities, lower cost, new publishing opportunities and sustainability.

INTERNATIONAL REACH

If a journal is available on the Internet, it is true that readers all over the world can obtain and read your journal; you do not have to arrange for printed copies to be mailed to different parts of the world, which can be both expensive and slow. However, if readers are going to obtain and read your journal they need to know of its existence, and they must want to read the articles you publish. To enable readers to discover your articles/journal, you need to be visible on the main search engines and to encourage use, you really need to carry out some international promotion to raise awareness and trust in your publication.

SPEED OF PUBLICATION

An online journal has a great advantage over a print journal, as it is possible to publish an issue as soon as it is ready, and not wait for it to be printed and bound, then despatched. What is more, you do not need to wait until you have enough articles to make up a complete printed issue. You can, if you wish, publish articles individually as soon as they are ready. These time savings can be very helpful to authors, particularly in fast-moving subjects such as some of the sciences where speed of publication is extremely important. Many of the important processes of publication, however, cannot be speeded up if you want to produce a quality journal. If it is a research journal, you will still need to arrange for peer review to be carried out—and peer review is often the most time-consuming step between submission of an article and its eventual publication.

The transmission of papers to referees, and of their reports to the editorial office, can be done instantly by electronic means, and make some time savings, but the reading, thinking and writing of reports will take exactly the same amount of time. It is also important to recognise that even online publication is not instantaneous; preparing the files correctly, loading them online and maintaining the online service all take time—further time is inevitably introduced if you are working with a third party host.

ADDITIONAL CAPABILITIES

The online environment offers the potential to provide readers with more functionality. One key feature of online publications is the ability to search for articles—at a minimum within one journal, and frequently across multiple journals Another feature commonly added to online journals is that of linking. This refers to the ability to go from one place online to another, at a click of a button—the most common example being the link from a citation within the body of an article to the relevant reference at the end of the article, and from there to the actual article which is being referenced.

Reference linking in scholarly journals is now increasingly being undertaken using DOIs, which are unique identification codes assigned to online articles, and which provide permanent links for the user. This is one of the international standards being developed to assist different systems to communicate and link with each other, to help with visibility and discovery of online material. The methodology of using DOIs in scholarly journals is being managed by an organisation called CrossRef. Electronic publication also makes it possible to include material which you would not include in a print journal, either for space reasons or because the material is difficult, costly or even impossible to print.

Research articles online can be accompanied by the full data-sets from which the results were reached—ideally in a form which readers can manipulate for themselves. Colour illustrations may be prohibitively expensive in a printed journal, but present no such problems in an electronic journal. Moving images, sound, or animations may also be included, although relatively few authors automatically think of providing such material at present and the technical comple-xities may outweigh the benefits. Before introducing any additional features within the online journal, you must consider whether your readers are likely to have the necessary software to make use of the additional material.

It is also worth noting that linking is generally rated very highly by readers, who find it an invaluable way of enhancing their research; however, other additional features are much less highly valued. It may, therefore, not be worth spending a great deal of time and money on these. One final consideration is that the additional capabilities which online publishing can offer may be of particular relevance to you, as the publisher, and not so much use to the user. These may involve the ease with which you can upload your content, and streamline your working practices.

One particularly important new facility which online publishing can provide you with, is a tool to measure and monitor online use. Most commercial hosts will automatically offer sophisticated usage statistics, and most of these will be COUNTER compliant, which is another increasingly important international standard which online publications should comply with.

REDUCED COSTS

It was originally assumed that publishing online introduced immediate cost savings. However, this is only true if the journal is no longer printed at all;

continuing to print even a few copies removes most of the cost savings.. If you decide to cease printing altogether, you may save a significant percentage of your total direct costs, although many costs will be unchanged—however, most readers still seem to want print copies. The cost of administering an electronic version will also be considerably lower if you are able to make it available to everyone, free of charge.

Depending on the way the journal is funded, however, you may need to replace subscriptions income by raising author-side charges; this will require an administration system, which will reduce the savings. The costs of publishing a journal can be split into direct costs and indirect costs. Direct costs are those where an invoice is received from an external supplier, and the journal needs to find the money to pay them. Indirect costs are those costs which are covered by the parent organisation, and the journal may be unaware of them. Introducing online publishing may provide an opportunity to reduce direct costs but is likely to increase indirect costs.

NEW PUBLISHING OPPORTUNITIES

It is perfectly possible for an online journal to work in all respects exactly like a print journal. However, the online medium does make possible new ways of doing things—new ways of publishing, new ways of covering costs, and new processes—which may help to address the problems of a struggling journal.

NEW WAYS OF PUBLISHING

Publish Often, Print Infrequently

This approach may be particularly attractive if you have difficulty publishing issues on time, whether this is due to lack of funds to pay for printing and distribution, or to a shortage of articles. Online issues would be published regularly and frequently, but you might only produce one, archival, print issue per year. This can help to improve regularity of publication, whilst at the same time saving some of the print and distribution costs.

Article-by-article Publication

This approach may be even more attractive if rapid publication is important to authors in your subject area. Articles would be published online individually, as soon as they are ready. In addition to offering fast publication for authors, this will bring readers back to the online journal frequently, thus increasing usage.

Separate Online and Print Content

Some journals have separated their print and online publications so that they are almost different journals—an example of this is 'electronic long, paper short' used in the British Medical Journal. This model publishes the full article online, but only publishes a shorter version of the article within its print journal. Some journals include additional sections within their online journal, and some exclude some materials from online version that appear in the print journal. However, if you decide to publish different content in the print and the online publication, this brings extra complexity into the way of dealing with your content, which is likely to increase your editorial costs overall.

New Publishing Processes

Open Peer Review

The Internet makes it easy for readers to comment on papers after they are published by the journal. This may be done once papers have gone through the normal peer review process, or it may precede or even replace it. Some journals then allow authors to modify their articles in the light of feedback. However, this makes for considerable extra complexity, and makes it essential that readers know which version of the article they are actually reading; this approach may not be welcomed in all disciplines, as scholars differ in their willingness to expose their unfinished work to their colleagues, so it is important that you know your reader/author community before making a decision.

Index

You may be able to do without an index if the web site allows searching of the full text of articles, particularly if it also allows searching by specific fields. However, human indexers add considerable value-electronic searching will only find the exact word you are looking for, whereas an indexer can think of synonyms, and will not index irrelevant occurrences of the word. If you can afford it, many publishers believe that a human-compiled index is still worth having.

CHALLENGES IN ONLINE PUBLISHING

Although publishing online presents many opportunities for journals, it can also present some challenges. Two of the most important challenges are presented here.

PERPETUAL ACCESS AND ARCHIVING

This is an issue which is worrying publishers and libraries the world over. In the print environment, a library which has subscribed to a journal in the past will always have the copies to which it subscribed, even if one day it has to cancel its subscription. However the same may not be true in the electronic environment, where the library does not ‘purchase’ the online journal, but merely ‘rents access’ for a specified period of time. Thus the library never holds the content locally, but relies on third-party servers to deliver the content. Many publishers have now changed their agreements with libraries so that the library has perpetual access to any journal issues to which it subscribed; however, this means that the publisher needs to ensure good records and administration of online access to make sure that this works smoothly over time. Print journals are relatively easy to archive but there is no easy way of archiving an electronic-only online journal. Even if the archiving library makes backup files of the journals, these may need to be updated over time as technology changes.

Links to other sites—one of the most attractive features of online journals—may become inactive due to the impermanence of World Wide Web addresses. Some publishers have signed an agreement with archiving organisations to preserve their journals permanently; this has the advantage that they can also provide ongoing access to customers after they have ceased to subscribe, or even in the event of the publisher's own service failing, or of the journal or publisher going out of business.

Much work is going on in various countries to extend their legislation to provide for legal deposit of electronic materials in the same way as is currently required for print. For example, the UK law was updated in 2003, and in 2004 the British Library started a pilot project to test deposit of online journals. Another related consideration is the digitisation and online publishing of your historical print content. Although it is costly, there are benefits to placing all issues of your journal online so that they can be searched; there is evidence that usage of older issues increases. Some organisations will fund the digitisation on the condition that subsequent access is free.

CITATION AND DEFINITIVE VERSION

Electronic publication gives rise to a whole range of new questions, such as: How do you cite a reference in an electronic-only journal? Or to an article pre-published online? What do you give as the publication date for an article which is published online before the print issue is available? What is the definitive version of the journal—the online or the print? There are more fundamental issues, too, about what counts as 'publication' in an environment of potentially continually updated documents; these are all difficult and, so far, largely unanswered questions.

One issue that has been problematic for journals wishing to move to online-only publication has been the way that these journals are perceived by the research and academic community. In the past they have not always been recognised as credible publications by the relevant authorities when considering tenure and promotion based on publication. Fortunately this attitude is changing, and it has been assisted by the acceptance of online-only publications within indexing services, giving them recognition within the journal publishing community. Citations can be made far more useful, in online journals, by linking directly to the cited item. This is facilitated by the Digital Object Identifier which provides a much more permanent link than a URL. The DOI/CrossRef system is now being used extensively; it does not in fact require sophisticated publishing although there are charges, these are relatively small.

An illustration of how DOIs may be used in citations can be found on the BMJ web site, in the area called 'Online First' which contains articles that have been accepted, but are not yet published, or assigned an issue. On this web page, the readers are instructed to cite the articles using their DOIs and the date of publication online. In some communities this has become an accepted method of citation, but it is early days and it is still to gain acceptance in many areas of academic publishing and research.

NONFICTION PUBLISHING IN THE NEW CENTURY

There are new writing opportunities today. For example, the online news and electronic publications industry has evolved rapidly. Writing positions have opened at online newspapers, print and electronic magazines, print and electronic newsletters, and online broadcast outlets.

In this age of media convergence on the World Wide Web, a growing number of news organizations require staff and freelance writers who can produce feature content involving multimedia, not just print content.

News organizations that have taken their publications to the Internet also offer original content on those sites, creating a need for writers and editors. There were 1,468 morning and evening daily newspapers and 913 Sunday newspapers in the United States in 2001.

The vast majority was small, with circulation less than 20,000 copies. There were 7,689 weekly newspapers with an average circulation of 5,857 copies in 2000, including paid and free circulation newspapers. The largest daily newspapers circulate more than 1 million copies daily.

These are *The Wall Street Journal* and *USA Today*, both nationally and internationally oriented publications with circulations about 1.7 million each. *The New York Times* and *The Los Angeles Times* are both very large, each with a circulation of more than 1 million copies per weekday.

There are plenty of small newspapers, also. These are often the best markets for beginning feature writers because they have small staffs, limited resources, and welcome contributions from student and freelance writers.

Weekly newspapers publish from once every 2 weeks to as many as 3 times a week. Their circulation sizes vary considerably, too. Most weeklies are very small—in the 1,000 to 4,000 copies per issue category—but there are several dozen weeklies each with circulation more than 100,000 copies per issue. It is a large market, when considered all together. The almost 7,700 weeklies in the United States publish almost 71 million copies each week.

However, newspapers are experiencing relative hard times. Circulation is flat, even dropping in some markets, but the U. S. population continues to grow. This means fewer people are reading newspapers, preferring to get their information from television or other more immediate sources. Some experts have already labeled newspapers as "irrelevant".

Other authorities think it is an overstatement to call newspapers irrelevant. But the point is well taken: No one seems to know what the future of the newspaper will be for the next generations of writers and editors. Publishers are unsure of content and form in the generations ahead. But for now, there is some optimism, especially if newspapers can adapt and use new technologies, such as the Internet.

Some major news and information and telecommunications companies that publish newspapers and other news products are developing such bold changes as electronic versions of their products. This, of course, is not a new idea because such services have been available for a decade or more.

However, these companies are exploring new ways to use computers, telecommunications, and other common consumer technology to deliver news to customers. This not only means personal computers, but such innovations as pocket-sized wireless computer receivers or such things as personalized newspapers printed within the home of subscribers. The implications for all writers, not just feature writers, seem to be massive.

There are many more magazines than daily and weekly newspapers. There are as many as 17,800 U. S. periodical titles, according to compilations of the Magazine Publishers of America. This total includes more than 8,100 consumer magazines.

In terms of editorial pages, the largest single subject category is culture and humanities. Entertainment and celebrities publications constituted the second-largest number of pages. Other leading categories included food and nutrition pages, sports-hobbies-recreation, wearing apparel, home furnishings, national affairs, and health.

The largest magazines in the country reach older, or retirement age, citizens. *NRTA/AARP Bulletin* and *Modern Maturity* are the two largest periodicals according to independently audited paid circulation figures in 2002. *NRTA/AARP Bulletin* distributes about 21.7 million copies per issue and *Modern Maturity* circulates 17.5 million.

Reader's Digest and *TV Guide* both publish more than 11.5 million and 8.1 million copies per issue, respectively, and *Better Homes and* Gardens distributes 7.2 million issues each month. *National Geographic* publishes almost 6.6 million copies per month. The top 50 magazines in the United States circulated more than 160 million copies per edition, or an average of about 3.2 million per periodical.

The top 113 magazines in the United States in 2000 circulated more than 258 billion pages. Almost two-thirds of the top 100 magazines experienced circulation gains when comparing 2001 and 2000 circulation figures. Although many magazines are dependent upon subscriptions for sales, some sell more single-copy issues than subscription issues. For example, two-thirds of

Cosmopolitan's three million copies circulation is single-copy sales. The biggest magazines continue to be very big. However, there are thousands of smaller monthly, bimonthly, and quarterly publications. And some of the smaller national or regional magazines, such as *VeloNews* (competitive cycling; circulation about 48,000) or *Videomaker* (video camera users; 89,000), are comparatively small, but are growing very fast. They are smaller because they reach more specialized audiences, but they offer marvelous opportunities for serious feature writers.

A smart feature writer seeking freelance markets will not overlook newsletter journalism. There are small organization-based newsletters, large public subscription-based newsletters, and lots in between. In this decade, careers are developing in this new and growing field.

Newsletters are not all small "mom and pop"-type editorial operations. Commercial business-to-business newsletters have become a major industry with thousands of editions each business day, week, month, or quarter. It may be impossible to estimate the number of newsletters regularly published in the United States.

With so many new publications beginning each month and others closing down because funding becomes difficult to find or interests change, the numbers are difficult to estimate.

Many newsletters are organizational and not widely circulated. Others are distributed to the public or to private groups free or for sale, but their circulation numbers or simple existence are not regulated or monitored by any national organizations. It is safe to say, however, that there are thousands of such periodicals, and the figure is growing with the recent development of inexpensive production and printing technology. Some are large and some are small.

People who need to communicate something publish these thousands of newsletters. Gale's directory of newsletters, *Newsletters in Print*, lists more than 11,300 newsletters with about 4,000 different key word or subject terms in the United States and Canada, but this total does not include many of the smaller circulation newsletters for internal corporate, institutional, organizational, or other proprietary purposes. Other estimates, such as that of the Oxbridge directory, go as high as 21,000 newsletters in the United States.

For writers, the newspapers, magazines, and newsletters today depend on technology. Because of computers, fax machines, and other modern hardware, you are able to gather information in ways impossible for a generation before you.

You are able to work on machines that make preparation of manuscripts much easier than before. Publications are sophisticated in production techniques. This means feature writers on deadline can produce stories faster and closer to printing deadlines and supplement the usual news coverage of an event, whether it be for a daily newspaper, a daily fax newsletter, or a weekly newsmagazine. Newspaper and magazine group ownership trends have changed the nature of the business. The largest newspaper groups, such as Gannett and KnightRidder, have purchased many major and medium-sized dailies.

Other companies have gathered up available small dailies and weeklies. Magazines have experienced the same phenomenon, with many ownership changes in the past decade. Companies have bought up independently owned magazines to form new or larger groups.

The effect has been less independent management of publications. At times, staff positions have been eliminated to create more profitable operating costs. It has meant a harder time making a living for feature writers in some markets and some specializations. It has also meant greater resources and new ideas. It has meant some publications near failure got a second chance, which has helped writers.

Newspapers are in the midst of significant change. They are using feature material in larger quantities. Because of this, they seek better quality from writers to keep the high demand for their editions.

Reacting to television and other electronic media vying for growing entertainment and leisure time of Americans, newspapers are offering material once found only in magazines such as longer in-depth profiles and analyses. Stanford University Professor Emeritus William Rivers labeled this phenomenon the "magazining of newspapers". Some newspaper feature sections have shown interest in shorter, tightly written pieces with the same "television story" flare of *USA Today*.

Television, film, and other influences changed newspapers and magazines in the 1960s and 1970s. Newspapers began to develop regional, or zoned, editions and to look at other dissemination techniques. General interest consumer magazines closed when operations became more costly than circulation and advertising revenues could cover.

In an effort to segment the general audience, more specialized magazines evolved in the 1960s and 1970s to replace general interest publications. Suddenly, readers interested in health and medicine did not have to depend on newsmagazines or the coffee-table magazines of another era. They, instead, subscribe to *Prevention, Vibrant Life, Vim and Vigour*, or other similar magazines.

Magazines, like newspapers, have changed as well in the past three decades. In some cases, there have been very difficult times, forcing basic survival decisions by editors and publishers, for magazines, and the problems are not always caused by their choice of content.

Magazines such as *Psychology Today, Savvy Woman, Fame, Taxi*, and *Smart* were forced to close in the harsh realities of advertising slumps caused by an economic recession in the early 1990s. It has been a case of "too many titles chasing too few ad pages," according to magazine industry consultant George

Simpson. Some magazines have survived on sound fiscal management and other rare publications have existed on subscriber and newsstand sales alone. The bimonthly *Ms.* magazine, for example, did not suffer as much as other publications during the same recession period because it does not accept advertising. It has not depended on advertising since it debuted in 1972.

One key area of growth has been in "alternative newsweekly" publications. These are magazine-like hybrid periodicals that are often published on newsprint in tabloid format. The alternatives are often monthlies or biweeklies and usually serve specific geographic markets such as a metropolitan area.

Tennessee's *Nashville Scene* is one example. *New Times* draws thousands of readers in the Miami, Denver, Dallas, Houston, San Francisco, Los Angeles, and Phoenix metropolitan markets. *Creative Loafing*, which is an Atlanta-based alternative, publishes editions in seven cities in the southeastern United States.

The *San Francisco Bay Guardian* circulates about 135,000 copies each issue. The news and feature-based content of alternative publications is often magazine length and magazine quality and offers writing assignment opportunities for both freelance and staff feature writers.

These publications are popular with young adults who seek information and listings about the arts, current events, local nightlife and music, young adult life-styles, movies and local theater, and other forms of entertainment. However, these publications often do not stop with that—they also offer in-depth features such as profiles and investigative reporting on current issues.

The publications often fill a void left by the more mainstream newspapers and lifestyles magazines of their markets. Typical alternative readers tend to be young, between 18 and 45, and they live an active lifestyle. These readers are well educated news readers with a good income. Sports-oriented magazines have given themselves a new look in recent years. The very traditional *Sporting News* underwent a 5-year multimillion dollar re-launch between 1997 and 2002. The biggest change was towards a magazine look. The publication had been a newspaper tabloid. *Sports Illustrated* also reinvented itself, including a new logo, in 1998. And ESPN, the television sports cable network, started its own magazine, called *ESPN Magazine*, in 1998, to compete against the sports magazine category leaders. In addition, sports magazines oriented to women have been growing in recent years—publishers and advertisers realise that valuable market is still up for grabs.

Women's magazines remain popular and successful at most levels. New titles are announced each year. Although some do not generate the advertising support to continue, others flourish in the era of specialty publications. Two recent new titles will illustrate the point. *More* is a recent bimonthly magazine that is geared towards women ages 45 to 64. *Lucky* magazine is a monthly magazine about shopping that began in 2000. And still another specialty magazine is *Mamm*, a bimonthly magazine that targets women living with cancer, especially those women ages 40 to 55. Breast cancer is the top cause of death for women in that age group. Each publisher has identified a market niche and has filled it with their publication.

One category of magazines showing encouraging growth is magazines geared to children and young teens. These include *Disney Adventures, Sports Illustrated for Kids, Nickelodeon Magazine*, and *Family Life*.

Articles focus on indoor and outdoor activities, travel, food, the environment, basic science, television programmes, clothing, toys such as video games, and activities designed to enhance quality time with parents. One subset drawing attention is magazines oriented to teenage girls. *Seventeen* is the oldest, with roots back to 1944. Geared to high school females, *Seventeen* has been successful and emulated much over the past 50-plus years. Today, there are dozens of magazines aimed at the same market, but there are many other popular teen publications, which include *YM* and *Twist*. Time Inc. debuted *Teen People*, a spinoff of its highly successful *People*, in 1998 to attract young readers as well. It includes articles on celebrity teens, but also on noncelebrity teens. Endeavors such as these show the continuing evolution of the magazine market.

Writers, as well as editors and publishers, have to keep track of the evolving industry. Lifestyle publications are popular today. Leading the parade to the newsstand are a collection of specialty books called city and regional magazines.

HOSTING ISSUES IN ONLINE PUBLISHING

Where a journal is published online can affect its success or failure as the online site can help or hinder the journal by the technical facilities and visibility that it offers. The price of online hosting is another important consideration. There are various options open to the journal publisher.

OWN/ORGANISATION WEB SITE

The benefit of publishing your journal on your own web site is that you have complete control over the web site—the design and the 'look and feel' of the site. Although there are, of course, costs associated with this option, no external supplier is involved. However, there are also disadvantages to publishing online this way. These may include a lack of technical skills and support for the journal, and a lack of current awareness of online publishing standards and compliance with new protocols. In addition maintenance and updating of the web site may not receive enough attention if it competes with the other requirement of the institution's own web site. In addition, the journal may suffer from low visibility, since, it may be difficult to locate within the institution's web site, and visitors will not be attracted to discover it.

COMMERCIAL HOST

Several commercial companies are now hosting scholarly journals on behalf of their publishers. They also frequently provide value-added benefits, for example file conversion, and supply of metadata to abstracting and indexing services, as well as all the benefits of a sophisticated system which is continually being developed. They are also experienced in dealing with subscribers and access-controlled environments, and ensuring security of the online journal from hackers and unauthorised access.

Against this, there are some disadvantages. The prime one, for a journal with little access to funding, is that they charge for their services, and although most of them offer a price which is reasonable within the budgets of western journals, they may be too costly for journals from the developing world. It should also be remembered that commercial hosts may only provide a hosting service; although they can offer advice on matters relating to online publishing, they are unable to take on the role of a publisher. However, some do offer marketing services—for additional payment—to help increase subscriptions and visibility through promotion.

SUBSCRIPTION AGENTS

Some subscription agents also now offer to host online journals on behalf of publishers. Again, they offer a high level of technical competence and value-added benefits. However they are unlikely to take your online journal unless they feel able to earn sufficient revenue from sales. They will deduct the fee for their hosting from revenues that they obtain, in which case you would not have to find the money up-front.

Another potential disadvantage is that they may not be effective at increasing the journal's visibility outside their own customer base.

AGGREGATORS

A number of companies will put your journal content online as part of a large package which they sell in its entirety to libraries.

OTHER ONLINE HOSTS

There are a number of organisations set up specifically to support the online hosting of journals from developing and transitional countries.

Further information about online hosts can be found on the web site of the Association of Learned and Professional Society Publishers, and the International Network for the Availability of Scientific Publications:

- African Journals OnLine (AJOL) is an initiative originally established by INASP, and now managed within South Africa, to host African-published journals. The web site contains abstracts only for most journals, but in addition it has been developed to host full-text journals where required. Currently there is no provision for charging for access but this is likely to be offered in future for journals which require it.
- Bioline is an initiative set up by the Electronic Publishing Trust to host online versions of journals from developing countries around the world.

They will convert print journals into electronic format; however, Bioline also supports training to help publishers prepare their own e-files. Bioline only supports journals that are willing to publish under the Open Access model.

- CLACSO provides support for a digital library of social science journals from member institutions within Latin America. Its digital library site hosts the full text of journals and other publications from the member organisations; the site currently operates under the Open Access model.
- Hrcak is a project of the National and University Library in Zagreb, Croatia, to host Croatian journals online.
- Sabinet is a South African company which hosts and sells African-published journals as a single package–access is thus restricted to subscribers, but this model does provide some revenue to the journals.
- SciElo is another Latin American initiative which hosts full-text, Open Access journals within the biomedical and applied sciences. This platform only accepts journals which are judged to be of high enough quality—so it provides both support for publishers and also quality assurance for users.

MULTIPLE HOSTING

You can–of course–host your journal on multiple web sites, using different hosting services. Although full-text hosting on more than one web site is unusual and probably unnecessary, a common model is for your own web site to host a homepage for the journal, with detailed information about the journal, the editorial board, guides for authors, etc., but to use a commercial host for the full text content. You may, however, wish to consider also including your content in the collection of one aggregators as well.

CHOOSING AN ONLINE HOST

Choosing an online host is an important decision for all journals, and although it is quite possible to change hosts, the decision of which to go with should not be undertaken lightly.

There are many considerations to be taken into account, which are described more fully in a recent publishing Guide Sheet from ALPSP but the first two questions to be asked are:

- What technology and resources do you have within your organisation, and what do you need to buy in from external companies/suppliers.
- How much can you afford to pay for online hosting.

WHAT CHANGES DO YOU HAVE TO MAKE TO YOUR PROCEDURES

Whether you decide to do it all yourself or not, electronic publication will require you to change the way you do things. It is important not to overlook this aspect. You may need to re-examine all your processes—from receipt of submitted manuscripts to final publication—in order to make sure they are as streamlined, and in as logical an order, as possible. In fact, this exercise is often highly beneficial in improving both cost and time-efficiency!

EDITORIAL

The peer review, revision, and editing of articles, as already pointed out, does not become any less important if they are to be published electronically. In addition, editors may need to add electronic links within the article, within the journal, to other publications and to additional material. The majority of authors may be able to submit their articles in electronic form, and should be encouraged to do so, as this will facilitate the editorial processes. Electronic editorial processing software is available to manage the entire editorial process from online author submission to article acceptance. These software packages can help to streamline the editorial process, but are not essential to online publishing.

They have several advantages:

- There are no postal delays for authors submitting articles, or for the editorial office, editors and reviewers during the editorial processes, since, everything is managed and held online.
- The systems automate much of the correspondence, which can assist the editorial office.
- Most systems maintain and generate records of article progress, which may be accessible to authors as well as the editorial office. In addition, systems generally provide for a database of reviewers; this assists the editorial team in choosing the most appropriate reviewers for each manuscript.
- Since, the packages operate online, the editors, reviewers, and authors can all access the database and upload or download articles from any Internet connection worldwide, thus facilitating work when they are not in the office.

However these systems also have some disadvantages:

- They require everyone involved in the journal to have online access.
- They only save the time spent in postal delays—they do not reduce the time required to review, correct or finalise the articles.
- They require the authors, reviewers and—especially—the editorial team to be competent in using online systems, since, they are not always very user-friendly.
- They require reviewers and the editorial team to have adequate computer equipment, and either to work entirely online, or to be able to print out articles locally for reviewing, etc.
- Unless the majority of authors, reviewers and editors do make use

of the software, such systems can actually increase the workload of the editorial office, who will need to load articles online themselves.

- And of course, most of them also cost money—usually in the form of a software licence fee.

Copyright

It is essential that, when acquiring copyright or the right to publish from your journal contributors—which you should always do—you make sure that you have also secured the electronic rights. It is also important to double-check that you or the author have obtained electronic rights for any other material you wish to include, such as illustrations or quotations from other publications. Examples of appropriate agreements have been produced by ALPSP and INASP.

PRODUCTION

Your methods of production are unlikely to be entirely suitable for publishing in the online environment, and this area of your activities is the one to be most affected by the introduction of online publication. It is sensible to get the articles into electronic form as early as possible; all the subsequent processing should then be done on the electronic version, and both print and electronic version should be output from the same file at the very end of the process. It is highly inefficient to work on a paper version, and then convert it to electronic at the very end.

The first change is that the final articles will need to be in suitable format for online as well as print publication. The most efficient approach is to process all articles in a 'neutral' format from which both print and electronic outputs can be produced. PDF files are adequate for straightforward journals, and of course this does preserve the appearance of the printed page; some systems may require the header information in other formats to enable searching and indexing. For more sophisticated electronic publication, PDF files are not sufficient—HTML or XML will be needed.

To produce appropriate files, you will need either to train staff and purchase appropriate software and computer equipment, or to identify and recruit suitable external suppliers to undertake this work; if it is done in-house, you will need to adapt the existing journal production system to ensure that the correct files are produced. If you decide to introduce additional functionality within the online version, you will also need to introduce production systems to implement this. Illustrations may cause problems if authors cannot supply them electronically, since,—at some point–they need to be converted into digital files for electronic publication. If the authors cannot supply e-files for all artwork, either you or the printer/typesetter/designer need to be able to scan the artwork so that the appropriate e-files can be created for online publication.

The electronic files must be carefully checked for accuracy, as it is surprisingly easy for errors to creep in when they are converted. You will need to devise—and stick rigourously to–a system for naming the electronic files for each article, and for every table or illustration associated with that article; it is sensible to include a version numbering/dating system so that you do not use an earlier version by mistake. When deciding to publish online you need to consider carefully whether your existing staff have the necessary level of skills to undertake the work required, and whether you have the hardware and software needed.

To produce the files required you may need to outsource the work that was previously done by departmental/journal staff, or you may need to change your existing suppliers if they do not have the skills, experience and equipment to provide what you need. Alternatively, the online host may undertake some or all of the file conversion work. If you decide to have different content in the print and online versions you need to ensure that the production set-up takes this into account, and that you are able to manage the administration of different versions.

MARKETING AND PROMOTION

Marketing, in the true sense of discovering what your market wants and then providing it, is every bit as necessary for electronic journals as it is for print journals. Many journals are not sufficiently visible—*i.e.*, not enough people know about them, or are able to discover them—and although publishing online may help, it is vital that some promotional activity is undertaken if online publication is to achieve the goal of making the journal more visible, and thus more used. For any journal—in print or online—conducting market research to identify what readers and authors want is essential.

In addition to talking to as many potential authors and readers and possible, try to carry out systematic surveys by questionnaire. If you see electronic publication as being a way to make your journal more international, your market research should be international too. This may cost money, but not as much as you could lose if your journal fails. An electronic journal will not sell itself, any more than a print journal. You will need to make sure that those who should be interested in reading it, and writing for it, are aware of its existence. This is not simply a matter of mailing a leaflet.

If you can obtain suitable lists of e-mail addresses, this is much cheaper than a postal mailing; be careful, however, about sending 'promotional' messages to e-mail discussion lists, as this is considered unprofessional, and may generate a strong negative reaction, although straightforward information about journals is welcomed on many lists. You should always check the 'rules' for posting to a listserv with the listserv manager.

In addition, you could involve the editorial team in promoting the journal by, for example:

- Referring to the journal within their e-mail signature;

- Handing out leaflets at relevant meetings, and
- Ensuring that their institutional library is not only aware of the existence of the journal, but also makes it visible to users.

Online publication relies on readers coming to the web site, rather than sending the print journal to their library or their desks. Bringing people back to a web site is particularly important if the journal is published infrequently or irregularly. E-mail alerts are a good way to tell people about the latest issue when it becomes available online, and can be set up manually or you could offer the facility to sign up to an automated alert on the journal's web site.

Linking to and from abstracting and indexing databases, and citation linking using DOI and CrossRef are also important ways to bring readers to your content. To ensure visibility to researchers and librarians you must make sure your journal is covered by the major Internet search engines. Another very important way of ensuring visibility to your community is to make sure your journal is included in secondary databases. The major services used to be resistant to including electronic-only journals, but this is no longer the case.

The one often considered most influential is ISI although their acceptance procedures are quite stringent and the number of journals they include is restricted. However, you cannot include your journal in too many such databases; identify as many as you can which are relevant to the subject matter. You may be asked to provide a free subscription, but this is a very small price to pay. If you can supply 'headers'—bibliographic details and, ideally, abstracts—in electronic form, so much the better; unfortunately, however, there is as yet no standardisation about the format in which they require them.

You should also make sure that your journal is listed in Ulrich's International Periodicals Directory, which is the major reference source for librarians. Some abstracting and indexing databases—such as Medline—require the journal's header information in XML format. If you are unable to obtain these files from your supplier, INASP have a template available for use which simplifies generation of these XML documents. Once a journal is made available online, the process of gathering feedback from readers and authors can be much easier than for a printed title, as the Internet facilitates two-way communications. Online feedback forms, direct links to e-mail addresses, and discussion forums all permit much more effective exchange of information.

SALES

Printed journals need little or nothing in the way of salesmen. Libraries decide which journals they want, and then choose their preferred channel for buying them. However, site licensing of electronic journals does require detailed discussion and negotiation with each customer; this is time-consuming, and if you decide to do it yourself you are likely to need extra staff with the appropriate skills. The alternative is to have someone else, such as a subscription agent, do it for you—but you need to be willing for someone else to negotiate prices on your behalf. Bear in mind that the price for a single library may represent several subscriptions; if libraries join together to form consortia, this is even more likely to be the case. Selling to library consortia is a particularly difficult and time-consuming process, and the publisher with only a small number of journals can easily get squeezed out.

Initiatives are, however, being developed to help smaller publishers work together to sell a single, larger collection of journals in these circumstances. It may be beneficial to try to work with other publishers, whether internationally or in your own country or region, to overcome these problems. In some countries, the tax situation will be made more complicated if you are selling electronic journals; they may attract tax where printed journals do not. You will need expert local advice on this.

SUBSCRIPTIONS ADMINISTRATION/CUSTOMER SERVICE

If you decide to restrict access in any way you will need to administer this process, providing passwords or other access controls to new users, disabling those which have come to an end, and ensuring that your system can identify authorised users when they try to access the system. All of this will entail even more complicated administration than is required for a printed journal, and will require considerable technical expertise. Customers do not need any help to use print journals; however, the situation is different with electronic journals. Some customers will forget their passwords and you will need to reissue them.

Others will be unable to get access even though apparently using the correct password. Even if you make your journal available free of charge, you will find that some of your customers have technical problems in accessing or using it.

Thus you will need to provide some kind of helpline for customer support, whether on the telephone, on e-mail or both; customers will become very frustrated if help is not available at the exact moment when they need it, so the helpline should ideally be manned full-time during working hours, even if not for 24 hours a day. Of course, if you decide to use an intermediary to provide access to your electronic journal, all of these problems will be taken care of, although naturally at a cost.

MEDIA PUBLICATION

OFFLINE PUBLICATIONS

In the offline category, as suggested, consider only CDROM publications: only one of our respondents mentioned any other offline media in their publishing. Seven of our respondents are publishing ‘stand alone’ CDROMs.

For us, perhaps the most striking response to our questionnaire is the very rapid decline in interest in CDROM publishing among most of the publishers in our sample. Several of those we spoke to have established very satisfactory CDROM-based publishing businesses and some publishers use CDROM as an adjunct to online publication.

Most did not expect to be publishing many if any new products on CDROM in future. Increases in the available bandwidth are simply rendering this style of publication, dependent on a physical supply chain, unnecessary and rather clumsy. Most publications previously published on CDROM seem likely to migrate primarily to online publication, although some migration to ebook publication must be a possibility. This decline in offline publication seems to us in general terms to represent good news from the point of view of libraries managing digital deposit. Although protocols for the physical deposit of offline publications may be a great deal easier to manage, the process of managing the long-term preservation of their content seems to us to be likely to be rather more complex.

This is partly because of the lower degree of standardisation of their content, when compared with web-based products. CDROM products deliver their content through proprietary user interfaces. Our respondents named a number of such interfaces; of these, only FolioViews and DynaText received more than one mention. Many, indeed most, CDROM user interfaces are specific to a particular product. All of these CDROMs are typically Windows products; only four of our respondents produce products for Macintosh; two specifically mentioned that some of their products also run under UNIX.

The other complication with the preservation of offline publications is that, frequently, the content is encrypted. Publishers themselves, because they do not manage the production of their own CDROM publications, often do not have easy access to non-encrypted versions of the content.

ONLINE AND HYBRID PUBLICATIONS

All fourteen of our respondents publish either online or hybrid publications. All twelve of the larger publishers publish products that are entirely online. Seven of the fourteen publishers publish hybrid products. Among almost all the publishers we spoke to, the trend is again away from hybrid products towards pure online delivery. As we mentioned in respect of the offline publications, the requirement to deliver 'high band width' content offline is seen to be of decreasing importance as available bandwidth increases.

All the online publications in our sample are delivered using standard Web browsers for their user interface; many, though, require users to have additional software for access to some content. Commonly, this is a requirement for the PDF Reader plug-in, but the lack of standardisation of formats for sound and audio-visual means that a variety of interfaces are needed for these elements.

One publisher in our sample is also, for example, using a specific ASCII-based format for rendering chemical structures. Publishers often provide supplementary material in their online content; it appears that the commonest file formats for such material are mainstream Microsoft applications.

Among academic publishers, there is very rapid growth in the publication of author-supplied supplementary material, alongside journal articles; this is seen as a significant value added of electronic publication and is typically published in whatever file format the author may provide. Access to this supplementary material therefore requires the user to have a copy of the specific application. While these may most frequently be in the form of research data, published as mainstream Microsoft application files, this is not controlled. For example, two publishers mentioned that raw PostScript was used for some supplementary material.

Two publishers mentioned TeX, and we are aware of audio-visual materials also being submitted for publication in this way. Standardisation of this supplementary material is therefore only achieved only to the extent that standard applications are adopted within the author community at large. Security of content in online applications is usually achieved through access control, rather than encryption. Although the content may be inaccessible to Web harvesting techniques, it is very much easier for publishers and libraries to manage deposit processes with essentially unprotected content.

7

Strategy of News Editing

Although many video production and editing texts deal with the development of the more expansive and the far more artistically licensed techniques of fictional video editing, the trends evident in the more restrictive evolving conventions and practices of broadcast journalists have received little scholarly attention.

Fang's early television news texts typically provided a few short paragraphs devoted to the concepts of montage and continuity editing. More recent broadcast news primers offer entire chapters on contemporary journalistic shooting and editing techniques.

These texts convey considerable guidance for video graphers and editors, as well as reporters and producers, on continuity sequencing techniques and advice on avoiding jump cuts and keeping from crossing the axis. These sections in broadcast journalism texts are consistent with the even more detailed continuity guidelines found in the aforementioned video production and "editing" texts written for non-journalists.

But in spite of the careful pedagogical attention paid to continuity techniques, contemporary texts offer little or no guidance on the extent to which expansive synthetic montage editing strategies augment continuity techniques.

Indeed, only one form of "montage" technique—the fast paced editing of similar images that is often set to music—appears to have become part of the common vocabulary of American broadcast journalists and many journalism scholars. Hence, judging from the allocations of space in contemporary broadcast journalism primers, readers might assume that continuity techniques had come to be an increasingly important aspect of broadcast journalism in recent years.

This study tracks the extent to which that assumption has been valid with regard to the presentation of pre-recorded materials in network newscasts from 1969 to 2005.

MOSAIC JOURNALISTIC CONSTRUCTIONS

A number of scholars have debated the point at which faithfully recorded actuality images stop functioning as a "camera of record" index of an event and begin to function primarily as symbolic building blocks in the hands of skilled journalists who construct arguments the way artists use tile fragments in a representational mosaic. Nowhere has this debate been more evident than in the many studies that track television journalists' use of soundbites.

Longitudinal methodologies with content analyses were used to study soundbite and quote usage. The researchers generally saw steep declines in the length of sources' soundbites, as well as more juxtapositions of the increasingly short bite fragments. Barnhurst and Mutz and Patterson used similar longitudinal techniques to depict Twentieth century U.S. journalism as decreasingly "event centered." They maintained that contemporary journalists were less interested in covering specific events or even re-presenting interviewees' most significant arguments, and more interested in covering trends, issues, and historic understandings—themes for which the shorter, more fragmented bites were better tailored.

In some rare instances these fragmenting techniques even violated network norms. In an analysis of network documentary editing techniques, Schaefer noted that on a few rare occasions CBS producers violated journalistic norms by juxtaposing soundbites and realistically coded visual imagery in ways that misrepresented specific interview "events." A few CBS producers did this by editing snippets from the interviewees in ways that clearly went beyond the more guarded statements made by any one of the many interviewees the documentary producers had filmed or taped.

Stein used a similar methodology to analyse the tenuous nature of the arguments made by the visual and verbal tracks in reports from CBS's 60 Minutes. In both studies, juxtaposing short soundbites helped eliminate the caveats and nuance evident in the source's original comments, and allowed the decontextualized soundbite excerpts to become the building blocks for an argument that the various sources never actually stated, either individually or collectively.

Based on the various lines of prior research, as well as commonly held intuitive assumptions, five hypotheses were developed to track changes in the formal characteristics of network news editing from 1969 through 2005.

H.sub.1: Shot lengths would decline from 1969 through 2005.

H.sub.2: Sound bite shot lengths would decline from 1969 through 2005.

H.sub.3: Realism and continuity editing techniques would decline and montage editing would increase from 1969 through 2005.

H.sub.4: The use of straight cuts would decline and special effects transitions would increase from 1969 through 2005.

H.sub.5: The relative amounts of synchronous primary audio would decline and asynchronous audio would increase from 1969 through 2005.

Support for [H.sub.1] and [H.sub.2] would buttress earlier assertions that the pacing or editing rate of pre-recorded news imagery had increased. High cutting rates suggest adoption of more fragmented editing strategies, whereas very low cutting rates suggest a less fragmented approach to realistic representation.

[H.sub.3], [H.sub.4], and [H.sub.5] together specifically test Schaefer's case-study-derived speculations regarding the decline of continuity realism and the ascendancy of synthetic montage as network journalistic strategies. [H.sub.3] is premised on the motivation for each edit. Sequences of shots recorded at a single site and lacking any apparent breaks in the action were considered realistically coded continuity edits. Continuity edits (invisible edits) implied the presence of "camera of record" strategies, whereas the broad range of montage edits presumably pointed towards traditional formalist or more symbolic editing strategies.

Frequent use of special effects visual transitions in [H.sub.4] would typically convey a sense of manipulation of imagery and reduce the sense of classic continuity realism that straight cuts have implied since the earliest days of feature filmmaking. Indeed, Grabe, Lang, and Zhao describe the use of flash-frame edits and audio and musical transitional effects as hallmarks of a new "tabloid style" of journalistic editing that undermines journalistic realism and negatively affects recall while it also diminishes the credibility of news reports. This may explain why it is far more commonly used in local and cable news and entertainment news programmes and documentaries than by the more staid U.S. network newscasters.

[*H.sub*.5] is premised on the notion that synchronized sound reinforces realistic interpretation of imagery, as is the case with most continuity-edited feature films. In contrast, voice-over narration and other sounds that appeared not to have been recorded on location, and which appeared to have been attached to particular visual images only in the editing process, were categorized as asynchronous. The presence of overlaid asynchronous sounds, such as narration or music, is another indicator of synthetic montage constructions and complex symbolically oriented editing strategies.

This investigation aggregated pre-recorded footage and graphics from the ABC, CBS, and NBC half-hour evening newscasts, drawing upon a purposive convenience sample from June 17, 1969; June 21, 1983; June 17, 1997; and June 7, 2005, to examine changes in network editing techniques. The dates for the broadcasts were deliberately chosen to avoid ratings sweeps periods, and days on which the news could have been dominated by a single major story.

All the chosen newscasts occurred on a Tuesday in June when a copy of the broadcasts from each of the three major U.S. commercial networks (ABC, CBS, and NBC), as well as the cable and non-commercial newscasts (BBC, PBS, CNN, and Fox) were available.

Newscasts from 1969 and 1983 were obtained from the Vanderbilt Television News Archive, whereas those from 1997 and and 2005 were recorded off-air as they were broadcast in the Albuquerque market. However, for the sake of consistency, only the three longstanding U.S. commercial networks—ABC, CBS, and NBC—were used because they alone produced national newscasts throughout the 36-year span of the study.

The three periods analysed in this study, which begin after the mid-1960s when the networks expanded their nightly newscasts to full half-hour formats, allowed for tracking the two great technological changes in network news gathering: the shift in the 1970s from 16mm filming and editing, to the use of analog video techniques, followed by the transition from analog to digital video shooting and editing between 1997 and 2005.

The programs' pre-produced news footage (VOs, prerecorded bites and packages) and pre-produced news-oriented graphics were coded on a visual shot-by-shot basis, following the techniques used by Schaefer. The content analysis excluded ornamental graphics, such as newscast opens and tease "bumpers," which were not intended to convey news information.

Live anchor images and live shots were also excluded from this analysis, because the live shots were not "pre-edited" material. Hence, within the carefully selected convenience sample of aggregated network edits from each of the four time periods, a maximum of 1,825 shots eventually fit the criteria of pre-edited news footage, or full-screen news graphics. The following four variables were tracked for each visual edit, as well as for shots that were specifically coded as news source "soundbites":

Shot length: The duration in seconds and tenths-of-seconds of each visual image. This variable indicates cutting rate, or how many seconds each visual shot lasted.

Style of edit: This was operationalized as a dichotomous variable dealing with whether the visual edit could be realistically coded or would otherwise be coded as any type of synthetic montage. Those 77 shot changes that seemed to lack any meaning altogether were coded as "missing," producing a total N for this variable of 1,748.

Since continuity techniques have been well discussed in contemporary journalism texts and were, therefore, easier for people with broadcast journalism training to recognize and identify than were the various permutations of synthetic montage, any edit that could possibly have been construed as having a continuity component was considered a "continuity edit" for the purpose of this study.

Two undergraduate broadcast journalism students served as coders, and they were instructed to include in this continuity category any shot changes that had both continuity and montage overtones, as well as the few shots across the years that were initially coded as jump cuts or crossing the axis. This latter characterization was used because even jump cuts and axis crosses could potentially represent an attempt to convey a "realist" editing strategy. For the purposes of this study, it was deemed that it was better to over-represent continuity/realism techniques than to run the risk of possibly under-representing them.

This approach was adopted because it was considered far easier and practical to attempt to make the case that realism and continuity had declined than it was to make the case that the various permutations of montage strategies might have increased. This was due in large part to the more nebulous, complex and pervasive aspects of interpretation associated with the theoretically challenging synthetic montage categorization.

Therefore, it was important for any transition with elements of realism and continuity to have been coded into the realism/continuity category, since the null hypothesis would depend more on the decline of realism and continuity than on the more contestable coding of synthetic montages.

For shot changes that clearly lacked a continuity or realism component, the coders were asked to determine if the shot bore a thematic relationship with prior shots, or recently prior, or current audio contents.

Since this more complex interpretive frame is far less theoretically developed and not as consensually recognizable, and because thematic sense-making appears to be an extremely pervasive human activity, it should not be too surprising that fully 1,748 shot changes were coded as either continuity or montage edits. Indeed, even if an anchor lead-in to a package had been preceded by an over-the-shoulder pre-produced graphic that bore a thematic relationship to the first image in the package, that first transition into the package would have been coded as a "synthetic montage" transition.

Transition type: Whether visual transitions utilized straight cut edits or more elaborate special effects, such as dissolves, fades, wipes, and digital video effects (DVE). Only the 1,746 of the 1,748 shots that were coded for style of edit were used in the table presenting combined data on the style of edit and transition type, as two of those transitions at the head of shots were so difficult to interpret that they were coded as "missing."

Audio-visual synchronization of the primary soundtrack: Whether or not the primary audio track was edited with synch sound that appeared to have been recorded at the scene with the visual image. The primary audio track is the one that is loudest and most clearly audible.

Syncrhonized sounds typically include soundbites, narration from pre-recorded reporter standups, music, and loud natural sounds that appeared to have been recorded at the same time and the same locations as the pre-recorded visual images. Synch sound in the background of pre-recorded visuals is an important aspect of contemporary news editing, but it was not coded for this study because such sounds are often quite soft and difficult to consistently interpret from one shot to another, and videographers and editors now routinely include background sounds in their work. Furthermore, analysis of this additional variable would have added another layer of complexity while contributing little to the theoretical thrust of the present study.

The four listed variables were chosen, in part, for their relative simplicity of coding. Copies of the original broadcasts were time coded, and reviewed on television monitors and professional video machines that accommodated half-frame (one field) shuttling so each shot and transition could be coded. The two students who had been trained in continuity techniques, did the initial coding after approximately 40 minutes of coding instruction.

A random sample of sequences from the four time periods that contained 181 shots (approximately a tenth of total prerecorded material that was coded) were recoded by a third coder to determine the reliability of the students' content analysis. Coefficients of reliability tests for categorical agreement on the sample of dual-coded segments for the four variables broke down as follows: shot length (agreement to plus or minus 0.1 sec.).934; transition type.989; style of edit (a 3-category variable of realism/montage/missing).818; audio-visual synchronization.956.

The ANOVA calculations for significance were performed with the Dunnett's T3 test because the calculation works for categories with non-equivalent variances, and the MANOVA calculations utilized the similarly robust Lambda statistic.

OWNERSHIP BY BIG BUSINESS

The early, intimate connections with the world of finance deepened as each European wire service became a public company in the i86os and 18705. In February 1865, julius Reuter reorganized his firm as Renter's Telegram Company (Limited), a joint-stock undertaking capitalized at £250,000. Of the £80,000 realized by the sale of shares, £65,000 went to Reuter personally.

He was kept on as managing director at a handsome salary, and his contract guaranteed him "the sole and entire management" of the telegraph business, with which "no other Director or Shareholder shall be entitled to interfere."

The new Reuters board, which had only four members, included not one publisher, editor, or journalist. Rather, it was made up of bankers and traders in India and China.

Reuter wanted to expand his business to the East, and his backers shared his interest in swift and reliable intelligence from Asia.

He used the capital raised from the sale of shares in his company to finance the construction of a cable connecting Lowestoft, England, to Norderney on the north German coast, the first link in an overland telegraph route to Asia.

Renter's newly raised capital also fueled a joint effort with Havas to buy up Wolff's. In March of 1865, Wolff appealed to no less an authority than the king himself for help in resisting the takeover. Wolff stressed the political importance of keeping the wire service Prussian: should Havas and Reuters succeed, Prussia would become dependent on foreigners for its political intelligence. Wolff alone could not compete with foreign companies, particularly joint-stock enterprises.

He urged that "patriotic financiers" ensure a more secure footing for his agency. Wilhelm I was receptive, noting, "I would be very pleased if patriotic financiers like the gentlemen v.

Oppenfeld, v. Magnus and Bleichroder would come to an agreement with you over the business in question." The king sent the desired endorsement to these Berlin bankers, including the man who would become principal backer of a new holding company for the firm, Gerson von Bleichroder.

It is difficult to avoid melodrama when describing this colourful, powerful figure. An ingenious financier, Bleichroder was the personal banker of the Iron Chancellor himself, an intimate of the Rothschilds, an adviser, lobbyist, kingmaker, and secret agent.

He achieved a glittering political and social success, becoming the first German Jew to be raised to the ranks of hereditary nobility. With the assistance of one of the richest men in the world, Wolff's resisted the Reuters-Havas bid of 1865. On May 20, 1865, a new joint-stock holding company, the Continental Telegraphen-Compagnie (Continental Telegraph Company), was founded to pump capital into Wolff's. As Reuter had done, Wolff remained the general manager of the new firm. Editing and distribution went on exactly as before, by the same personnel.

The Agence Havas, too, fell into the hands of a financier. In 1873, Auguste Havas, the son of founder Charles-Louis, withdrew, childless, from the agency at the age of fifty-nine. Jacques-Edouard Lebey, long instrumental in the advertising end of the firm, assumed its direction.

Lebey's fashionable and elegant son, Edouard Leon, had joined Havas in 1871, at twenty-two; at twenty-four, he now cast about for the means to secure his own domination of the company. Young Lebey needed someone to buy up the agency from Auguste Havas and name Lebey lead director of the firm. He found a willing ally in the Baron Frederic-Emile d'Erlanger.

Here was another legendary figure of nineteenth-century finance. Frederic-Emile's father, Raphael von Erlanger, had been an agent of the Rothschilds, but struck out to found his own maison financiere at Frankfurt, frequently allying with rivals of the Rothschilds and incurring the wrath of the powerful dynasty. In 1853, Frederic-Emile became an associate in his father's business.

In 1854, he joined Ferdinand de Lesseps during his exploratory voyage for the future Suez Canal. In 1858, Erlanger came to Paris, armed with the experiences of his father's business and his travels. He created a new firm on the model of the Frankfurt bank. During the American Civil War, he became the appointed banker of the Confederacy. In 1870, Erlanger opened a branch in London, putting his powerful organization in direct communication with the world's most important financial centre. Like Lesseps, Erlanger became a leading Saint-Simonian. These champions of industrialization envisioned a single world bound together peacefully and profitably by trade and technology-by letters of credit, steel, steam, and copper wire. They achieved notoriety for their ambitious and imaginative promotion of transportation and communication projects: railways, canals, dockyards, and shipping. Erlanger's fascination was telegraphy. he created France's telegraphic links to Algeria, Egypt, India, Australia, China and Indochina, and the Americas.

Erlanger aimed to control both the hardware and the "software" of French telecommunications. he promised Edouard Lebey the direction of the Agence Havas if Lebey could bring about the sale, en bloc, of the entire business. Though relinquishing the family business to a foreign financier made Havas uncomfortable, he was offered a generous sum by Erlanger: 634,000 francs for Havas, 574,000 for Lebey Sr., and a comparable sum for the three remaining partners. In july 1879, the Agence Havas incorporated at 8.5 million francs, of which Erlanger took 637,000 francs.

Even the Associated Press, a nonprofit newspaper cooperative, was not without its connections to the world of high finance. When it reincorporated in the 1890-5, its new general manager was Melville Stone, formerly a Chicago newspaper proprietor and editor and most recently president of the new Globe National Bank-though he gave up this position when the Associated Press offered him a higher salary.

Perhaps the most explicit connection between the worlds of telegraphic news and finance was the establishment of a Reuters Bank in 1910. In his later years, julius Reuter had become something of an audacious financier in his own right. he laid the Norderney cable to Germany in 1865. He cosponsored a French transatlantic cable with Erlanger in 1869. And, in 1872, he secured a breathtaking seventy-year concession from the Shah of Persia for the development of the entire country. The profits and losses of the concession and the Atlantic cable occupied increasing shares of Renter's time, but he deliberately kept them separate from the news business: they were the baron's own personal property. But his son and successor, Herbert de Reuter, was not so squeamish about staking the fortunes of the firm in the world of high finance.

The bank was an attempt to recoup the agency's failing profits. Between 1894 and 1910, Reuters' dividends remained a paltry 5 per cent. In 1910, Reuters therefore launched a banking department, reconstituted in 1913 as Reuter's Bank, Ltd. The wire-service firm was the sole stockholder of the £510,000 worth of shares. Even when further shares were created and distributed, Reuters retained its control over the bank. The board of the bank was composed entirely of members of the board and the managing director of the wire service.

The bank was managed by a Hungarian, Arnold J. Hadjuska, who opened a branch in Australia and plunged into investments in continental Europe. At first, the venture appeared to pay off. In 1913, Reuters reported gross revenues of almost a million pounds-four times the sum for 1912-and a profit of £46,046.

All four international wire services not only served financial and commercial clients but were also owned or managed by important bankers and financiers. But simply because the wire services served financial clients and were in turn controlled by financiers did not prove that their news reports were tainted. The personnel and direction of the services was unchanged, despite the corporate reorganizations and buy-outs.

Nevertheless, throughout the late nineteenth and early twentieth centuries, the wire services endured accusations of "occult relations" with financial circles. There were allegations that they offered privileged information to, and skewed their news coverage in favour of, the financial interests that lay behind them.

WORKING ONLINE—THE ONLINE NEWS EDITOR

Online news may represent a revolution in news delivery, but writing for the medium requires much the same skills as any form of journalism. This is the view the news editor at *The Age Online,* Hamish Fitzsimmons, who defines the main requirements for reporting online as "strict accuracy, clarity and speed". He says, "It's most akin to writing for radio or wire services so there's that need for speed because you do want to turn stories around quickly."

Online news stories also have to be concise. At *The Age Online* that means an average length of 30–40cm or about 14 pars. The site's news staff see their role as "value adding" to the masthead *The Age* by giving people who read the newspaper in the morning the chance to get the latest news plus a bit of light entertainment as the day progresses.

That means catering to an audience that wants "an instant fix". I think people reading stories online want to be told straightaway. People are not so much impatient—they're very choosy about what they will look at. And, with one click, they can be on another site so you've got to really maintain people's interest.

We find people want the top stories of the day but they also want some sort of entertainment so we do put up a lot of stories that are quirky or amusing. The strength of online news is the speed with which it can be delivered. But high-speed delivery imposes a series of disciplines on journalists.

The main thing is the time factor. People are used to having one deadline a day. Some of my colleagues who've come across from newspapers find the absence of a deadline quite easy. But coming from a broadcasting background, I find the absence of a deadline a bit scary because if there's no deadline it's a deadline of remit. There's a sense of urgency when you come from a broadcast background and I do think that helps with breaking news quickly and getting it up on the site. Of course, one of the pitfalls of working at high speed is the extra risk of making a mistake. The online environment is one in which errors can be corrected quickly. But, as Hamish notes, that's not something reporters would want to rely on. It's important to be right the first time.

As with other media, news online has its own requirements about the way material is *presented* to make it accessible to the audience. There is such a thing as information overload. People are very susceptible to that online. I think you have to be very careful in the way you lay out a web site as well so it's not too cluttered. I see some news web sites where there's just too much going on. If it's too busy you can't focus on the one thing. It's too confusing for the reader.

At *The Age Online,* they see a future in video rather than audio, not least because the audio segments they have run have received little traffic. But they also see a future in the blending of stills, audio and text to produce stories that are told in a way which is unique to the medium.

We're using stories from the paper but we're adding more. We just picked up an award for a story about a cancer sufferer, which was a beautifully written piece (in the newspaper) to start with, but we were able to get every photo from the photographer and just fade up quotes from the story. It was a remarkably touching piece and it was so well suited to the medium.

So that's really what we're trying to do, to add value to what's in the paper. I guess a good way of looking at different ways of telling a story using the Internet is that it's a story-telling medium so you've got to be able to think: "How is this medium going to be able to help me tell the story?" "What can I do that's different or more interesting?" I think the use of multimedia packages is a good way to go.

Within the Australia media, online news is not a large employer. Many news sites rely on wire service material and *The Age Online* is unusual in that it has journalists writing exclusively for the site. But the skills required for working online point to the broader changes in journalism that will eventually affect more and more journalists. I speak to friends who are with CNN and they've got the complete integration of TV and online so I think having video shooting and editing skills would be a real advantage. I don't know how soon it will happen but I think that's where journalism is definitely heading ... I mean AAP reporters are taking digital stills and recording digital audio. So that's a fair indication that it's not a luxury to be multiskilled anymore. It's a necessity.

Being comfortable in front of a microphone or camera is an obvious requirement of working in broadcast news. It's also an increasingly useful skill for print reporters, for several reasons:

- Some may have to contribute to an online arm of their organisation, either by recording interview segments or appearing on camera to deliver short, spoken reports.
- Reporters covering a particularly significant story often find themselves appearing in other media, either to promote the story or

explain it to a wider audience. This is especially true when there are only one or two Australian reporters in a particular location.

- Learning to report in broadcast style forces print reporters to learn to tell their stories in the briefest possible form, because brevity is particularly important in broadcast news. Reporters who develop their story-telling techniques in this way often find it improves their writing technique too.

The types of presentation skills that are useful for all reporters include being able to conduct an interview for broadcast, being "good talent" in an interview for broadcast, and being able to present stories directly to camera.

APPEARING ON CAMERA

Even in television, reporters don't spend a lot of time in front of the camera unless they are studio-based presenters. When television reporters appear on camera, it's usually either to pre-record a short piece to camera as part of a packaged story or take part in what's called a "live cross" into a programme being broadcast.

This is usually to update an ongoing story. The first of these is a skill specific to television news. Our concern here is the type of presentation skills that might be required of other reporters and these are:

- Short, self-contained pieces to camera for use on air or online.
- Q and A interviews from a news scene.

It's relatively common for broadcasts to include short QandA segments with reporters at a news scene or remote location. In these cases, the reporter is there to introduce, update or comment on a picture report, or provide a full report in cases where there are no pictures available. And very often the first question from the studio presenter will be something straightforward, along the lines of "what's happening", allowing the reporter at the scene to carry most of the segment.

It's very difficult to memorise more than a couple of sentences and there's not a lot of point in trying. It's permissible for a longer report to look ad-libbed as long as it's done fluently.

It's also permissible for the reporter to glance at notes occasionally, as long as it's done briefly. If a report like this is live, you have to slide over any glitches since there's no opportunity to go back and do it again.

And even if the report is being pre-recorded, it should probably be treated as live because of time constraints. Aim to get it right, first time.

If the report is a live broadcast, the reporter will need to know in advance:

- The cue to begin speaking.
- The amount of time they have for speaking.
- The words that will signal the end of their segment so that the studio presenter can resume talking.

Experienced television or video reporters make addressing the camera look effortless. Needless to say, it's not, especially if you're just starting out.

Some of the more common mistakes are:

- Obvious nervousness.
- Spending too much time looking at notes.
- Staring goggle-eyed at the camera.
- Talking too fast or too slow.
- Mumbling.
- Moving around.

Fluid presentation takes practice, like so many other things. There are also some techniques that can help your performance.

The first is preparation. You will sound so much more confident and knowledgeable if you really do know your material. Being generally well informed is also a great confidence booster, which is one more reason why reporters need a good general knowledge and grasp of current events.

Second, you need to learn to look beyond the camera itself to the audience.

Of course, thinking about a vast audience out there watching you can be a bit daunting. So think of just one audience member.

Think of the camera as a friend to whom you're relating a piece of news. You won't want to stare at your electronic friend without blinking. On the other hand, you won't want to let your gaze wander away, distractedly. You will want to maintain eye contact, with the occasional glance down.

Use natural body language and gestures but remember that the camera magnifies gestures, so avoid being too theatrical.

Some people become very self-conscious about their hands and don't know what to do with them. Television reporters recording a short piece to camera for a story usually keep their hands fairly still and out of shot. But when someone is in front of the camera for longer and framed wider, this is not so important.

Plenty of people "speak with their hands" as a natural way of communicating and it works on camera as long as the gestures are not too expansive. If you want to minimise the degree to which you move your hands, try holding a notebook or pen (but *not* one that clicks off and on), just for something to do.

Try to keep your head erect and fairly still. Try not to tilt your head or bob about too much. In fact, your entire body should remain fairly static unless you *need* to move, for instance to point out something. Don't shift your weight from foot to foot. Unless the subject of your report is extremely lighthearted, don't smile. You want to convey an air of professional detachment. Equally, you don't need to frown or look concerned during a serious report. You're not there to act out the news.

TIPS

- You will sound and look more natural in front of a microphone and/or camera if you think of the device as a friend to whom you're telling a story. Relax.

- Anyone involved in a live report should remain quiet and still just prior to and immediatelyafter the interview itself, in case the microphone and camera are switched to air earlyor switched off air late. Don't relax your expression immediately after a TV report is over because often the camera will stayon you for an extra second or two.
- If you are pre-recording a report and you do it more than once, identify each "take" of the piece to camera by number and a short pause—that is, "take one", "take two' etc. Note the camera's counter or time-code setting for the take you plan to use. It will save time later.

WHAT TO WEAR ON CAMERA

The issue here is that you should dress and behave in a way that does not distract from the story. You are not the story. The story is the story.

That means it's generally best to avoid chunky jewellery (especially if you're a bloke). Ties and necklines should be conservative. In a casual environment, casual clothes will probably look more suitable. These are the stylistic requirements.

There are also some technical ones:

- Avoid clothes with fine stripes or tight checks.
- Some very shiny fabrics should also be avoided.

This is because these types of clothes can cause the image to strobe and, once again, this is distracting for viewers. The easiest way to check whether an item of clothing will strobe is to hold it in front of a camera and check the screen.

In years past, reporters and presenters were advised against wearing white on camera. Modern cameras can cope with white, so that's no longer a problem, except that too much of any colour—especially white or black— can look bland and boring.

These days everyone has access to a video camera. You can either tape yourself or get a friend to help. Practise recording pieces to camera and reviewing the results. You can usually tell for yourself what your strengths and weaknesses are.

TIP

If you are recording a piece to camera—whether for broadcast or practice—remember that doing more and more "takes" won't make your performance better. After about half a dozen, you will begin to look and sound fed up with yourself. Aim to achieve your best performance in the first few takes. That means learning to slide over tiny imperfections rather than needing to stop and do it again. But big mistakes will mean another take. Reporters, who are accustomed to asking questions rather than answering them, sometimes find themselves on the other side of the microphone or camera. There are a number of circumstances in which this might happen. A reporter might be expert in a particular field, making their views particularly valuable to other journalists. Alternatively, they might have written an exclusive or controversial report, which has itself become the focus of news reports.

There are also stories—such as stake-outs—where there is no one else to interview except other reporters. This is considered a pretty poor form of journalism, but sometimes there's no other choice. Oddly enough, working in the media doesn't automatically make journalists good interviewees, particularly when they are print reporters being interviewed for radio or television.

There are some simple strategies for effective communication during a broadcast interview. The following can be used if the interview is not going to be combative—in other words, if you're being asked to provide information or expert comment rather than defend yourself against aggressive questioning.

- Ask the reporter what they're after, especially if you're not familiar with the format of the programme. Will the interview be used as a QandA (*i.e.* with questions and answers) or does the reporter just want a soundbite? If they just want a soundbite, about how long can it be? These days, soundbites in television news rarely run beyond 15 seconds and most are between seven and 10 seconds (that's between 21 and 30 words). But current-affairs programmes run longer segments as do online sites.
- Focus on the reporter, don't be distracted by the camera operator or by the camera or microphone. But remember that the reporter is just a conduit to the audience. Don't call the reporter by name unnecessarily —you're talking to the audience.
- Is the interview live or pre-recorded? If it's pre-recorded, it will probably be edited. That means if you feel you could have given a better answer, tell the reporter. They might give you another go at it. Don't make a habit of this.
- If you're being interviewed for audio only—that is for radio or Web audio—you will find that your voice will sound much warmer and more friendly if you smile as you're speaking. Try it and see. Obviously, this would not be suitable if the topic were very grave, and this technique doesn't work for television or other video interviews where the audience can *see* you unless the topic lends itself to your smiling. With video, you have to be careful not to appear to be smirking or grinning.

We've already touched on those circumstances where a studio presenter interviews a reporter at a news scene or some other location.

Sometimes this is just an opportunity for a reporter to give a report to camera after an initial prompt from the presenter, but it can also involve a longer Q and A interview.

Keen observers of television will have noticed that an occasional feature of remote interviews—where the interviewer is in one place and the interviewee somewhere else—is that the "talent" seems to be a bit distracted. Their eyes wander and, at worst, they look confused. The reason is usually that they can't see the person they are talking to. It is possible to set up a monitor in front of the interviewee to carry the return vision from the studio.

But this adds to the cost of the satellite or microwave link. So, very often, interviewees have to look into the camera, take their questions via an earpiece, and imagine the person at the other end of the signal. It's hard. But if this happens to you, remember that while you can't see the person in the studio, they—and the audience—can see you. So you have to avoid letting your gaze wander and maintain a suitable expression until the interview is over.

Reporters being interviewed by other reporters can usually expect a fairly easy time of it. But there are occasions in which the interview can be combative; for example, if the interviewee has written a controversial report or done something likely to be challenged by other areas of the profession.

In these cases, journalists need to undertake the same level of preparation as any other interviewee facing a tough interview. As a reporter, you already know that you can't control the line of questioning and that even attempting to do so is likely to backfire. So your strategy in approaching the interview should be to: Work out the likely line of questioning and prepare answers. You might want to workshop the interview with colleagues. Get them to pitch questions and assess your response. Do this in front of a video camera and check your reactions.

UNDERSTANDING AND CAPABILITY OF EDITING

In addition to the time crunch and issues that contribute to it, a second broad influence on editing quality, from the vantage point of some copy editors, is the experience and ability of editors itself.

Four of the copy editors interviewed cited this factor as the biggest influence on editing quality on the desk. One editor noted that turnover in recent years had brought many new editors to the central desk. In addition to being new to the desk, some editors had relatively little experience in copy editing as a specialty. One experienced editor said problems sometimes showed up in headline breaks, local style and story trims.

Several other factors emerged through interviews and observation as real or potential influences on editing quality. Some of them, such as good content editing by city editors, represent immediate and direct influences on quality. Others, such as role-switching among various desk jobs, do not have a directly visible effect on quality but appear likely to influence it in the long run.

Several potential negative factors emerged:

- Lack of communication by the photo department about when photos are put in the AP Leafdesk system used for photo storage and selection.

One inside layout editor said it was a consistent problem that she was not told when local photos had arrived - or would arrive - in the system (especially photos used without accompanying stories). Another editor noted the photo people put photos on the archive Leaf system, rather than the live system the desk normally uses. It is slow for the desk to switch to that system and search, this editor said.

- Relationship (mostly absent or negative) between the central desk and reporters.

The predominant view among central and city desk editors interviewed was that, in most cases, little or no relationship exists between reporters and central desk editors - or the relationship is not positive. As one city editor put it, "I think they look on each other as people from another planet, some of them." Four editors were somewhat positive about relations, at least among some staffers. And two of them pointed out those individual efforts to establish relationships can change the picture.

- Morale on the central desk.

Central desk editors who discussed morale were mixed in their assessment. One said morale seems to go in cycles. "Now I would call it just kind of a plugging-along time - no one's real pumped or excited about work or anything." Another saw morale as mostly good, with good relationships among editors and good management on the desk helping out. But the night shift is a permanent barrier to good morale because central desk editors must juggle their personal and professional lives more deftly than daytime workers. In addition, the absence of perks available to daytime workers - such as the fitness center, credit union and cafeteria, and CD/book/movie-ticket grabs - creates frustration for some editors.

- Repetitive strain injury.

With one central desk editor having had surgery and another showing RSI symptoms, the threat of this problem to editing on the central desk was real. Choices sometimes had to be made between more and less important editing changes to avoid keystrokes that might prove painful.

Although editors pointed to several negatives, they also noted factors that have a positive influence on quality or may in the long run:

- Good relationships among central desk editors.

It was clear from numerous visits to the desk that the editors worked well together and generally enjoyed one another's company. Their cooperation made the night shift more bearable. It also removed a potential barrier to good editing.

- Good relationship between central desk and city desk (though some on each desk saw areas for improvement). Several editors on both desks spoke highly of the relationship between the desks, and one mentioned this as the most important quality factor. One central desk editor who often worked closely with the city desk praised city editors for their willingness to answer questions and to give updates about the progress of stories.

However, two editors thought the city desk could sometimes be more receptive to proposed changes in copy. Another central desk editor thought editing would improve if reporters were available more often to talk in person with copy editors about stories. Some, but not all, city editors said copy editors too often made assumptions about meaning in rewording or trimming stories, resulting in mistakes that could have been averted if they had asked the city desk.

- Good content editing by city editors.

Content questions about city desk copy were the second most frequently mentioned problem during the nightly short interviews, but these were noted only eight times by a total of five editors during the 110 conversations. Central desk editors were generally positive about the condition of copy when it came from the city desk, though quality varied by reporter and one copy editor saw problems in stories as a key factor in quality. Copy editors still read critically for factual problems but said these problems usually involved clarity or detail, not major holes.

- Division of early and late Page One work, including pre-reads of Page One stories by the city edition Page One person.

The Daily Oklahoman circulates statewide and publishes three daily editions. Makeover between the first and third editions had been heavy since summer 1996, when management decided to put greater emphasis on state news in the first edition and city news in the final. On most nights, a different editor was assigned to work on Page One for each of these two editions. Each Page One person designs and paginates the page and slots the copy. The division between early and late Page One work enables the city edition Page One editor to read Page One copy for all editions before it goes to the rim.

Two editors noted that these early reads had reduced the number of fixes that need to be made from page proofs. The additional read enables content problems to be caught early and provides the opportunity to do needed tightening before the length of the story is locked in during pagination. And because more editing is done early, the rim editor has more freedom to focus on writing a good headline.

- Division of early and late slot work.

Just before the study began, the highest-volume slot job (handling most copy other than Page One) had also been divided for most nights between early and late editors. The split grew out of slots' complaints about stress. The slot editors interviewed agreed that the division of work was making life easier. Doing the job for all editions allows little relief because fixes need to be done between first and second editions. When the late slot person takes over, he or she comes to the copy fresher and more likely to give the copy a good read.

- Role-switching among editing and layout jobs, and in and out of slot.

One of the notable features of the Daily Oklahoman's central desk is that editors - slots and others - often switch roles from night to night and even within the same night.

Some editors saw these benefits:

- Continued mental sharpness from switching between word-oriented jobs (such as slot) and visually oriented jobs (such as inside layout), and from job-switching in general. One editor said role-switching may help avert mistakes that result from a lack of concentration.
- Understanding of the constraints editors face in other jobs on the desk. For example, rim experience can help a layout editor avoid requesting a headline that is too tight to write or a trim that is too large to do in the available time.
- Sharpening of editing skills when rim editors take on slot responsibilities. Working slot requires editors to focus even more on catching style and other problems, and it exposes them to the different approaches colleagues take to editing.

Some editors had mixed feelings about role-switching. One noted that quality might improve if people were able to specialize in their areas of strength. Another suggested allowing some people to rotate while others specialize.

- Feedback mechanisms available for copy editors. Get in Style, a weekly memo written by an assistant managing editor and edited by a central desk editor, has provided feedback on writing and editing to copy editors and other staffers. After Deadline, a periodic report assembled by a central desk editor, has offered more comments on desk work (good and bad), especially headlines. Other feedback to the rim sometimes comes in e-mail from slots.

The absence of a dominant problem in the nightly interviews suggests there were no crises on the Daily Oklahoman's central desk at the time of the study. But the nightly and longer interviews, coupled with observation, did point to a number of quality issues - some immediate and others likely to influence quality over time.

Some common threads run through the negative and positive factors. Several involve communication, including late arrival of copy (aggravated by lack of communication with reporters about deadlines), inaccurate classified estimates (which might improve if newsroom managers talked to classified managers), and lack of communication about photos (again a matter of communication between departments).

On the positive side, feedback mechanisms such as in-house memos represent communication that is directly aimed at improving quality - and may help address concerns about less experienced editors. The fact that several communication issues emerged underlines the potential benefit if copy editors and other staffers and managers would simply talk about problems. The importance of communication issues also suggests that communication patterns should be studied further at the Daily Oklahoman and other newspapers. Several other factors involve relationships - both the largely absent or negative relationships between the central desk and reporters, and the more positive ones between the central desk and city desk, and especially on the central desk itself.

The state of relationships is potentially connected to job satisfaction and burnout - as are the divisions of labour and the problem of repetitive strain injury. The findings on communication and relationships suggest that human factors must be considered along with technological ones in any broad attempt to assess or improve editing quality. The problems in copy desk-reporter relations are consistent with the concern about tensions that Gene Foreman expressed in the 1996 ASNE report on copy desk concerns.

In addition, editors' reports of relationship troubles - coupled with morale concerns - seem to line up with the finding in another study that copy editors showed higher levels of emotional exhaustion and depersonalization than reporters.

One interviewee said copy editors feel invisible because they work nights and holidays while losing the perks of day workers (such as the fitness center and credit union). Although previous research on job satisfaction and burnout did not try to measure a link to editing quality - nor did this study - the expressions of dissatisfaction in this study underline the need to systematically investigate how job satisfaction relates to quality.

Also worthy of further investigation is the long-term impact on quality of rotating copy editors through desk roles. At a time when the industry is trying numerous organizational forms for traditional copy desk functions - including team organizations with no copy desk and separate copy and design desks - the Daily Oklahoman has retained a traditional rim-slot editing format and kept the page-design function on the copy desk. But most desk editors are cross-trained and scheduled to change roles several times during their work weeks, sometimes switching jobs within the same night.

Most do both editing and design. Interviews suggest both real and potential benefits to editing quality from this rotation, but the impact of this organization over time - as well as the quality impact of various desk organizations in other newsrooms - needs to be explored in further studies. A final issue for research is the impact of changes in editing and pagination systems. At the time of this study, the Oklahoman, which has been paginating since 1985, was preparing to install its third-generation pagination system. Discussing the computer system in use at the time of the study, both editors who paginated on it and those who merely edited and checked stories criticized its speed. The time some reported losing to slowdowns and crashes posed an unavoidable cost to editing quality - apart from the potential cost of editors' pagination time itself, as suggested by other studies. It would be worth exploring whether the current system has led to better quality. Studies at other papers would further help to explore how the evolution of editing and pagination systems affects the quality of editors' work.

There is some shame in editing which is perhaps why there is so much abuse among editors. To be discovered doing it now is like being found with the cross-word puzzle rather than the news section of literature. The shame makes many of us underestimate the pursuit or rather tack wildly between embarrassed apology - "I am only editing, you are writing criticism" - to more confrontational encounters in conferences and symposia; there the textual emendation is urged against an entire argument or the footnote used to destabilize a tall and elegant edifice which one's own editorial obsession prevents one from creating. It is not editors who are asked to be plenary speakers at general literary gatherings, one notes sourly.

Editing is the dullard's end of scholarship, refused the allure of gender, race and class and denied the glamour of poststructuralist or new historicist criticism that soars beyond the comma and absent colon. Long-term, obsessive editing of the sort of works that only the equally obsessed or the ambitiously scholarly would ever read, which has as its aim the establishment of an author and his or her works, a kind of brief for canonization, is out of kilter with the modern mode of cultural studies.

The tendency at the moment is to shift from the study of a particular writer to concentrate instead on large socio-cultural movements, genres or discourses. In this sort of enterprise, works or texts may be discussed but they usually become the product less of an individual author, however he or she may be conceived, than the construction of a general culture. The book trade rather than the book is currently of interest, the body in the text rather than the body of the texts.

And yet so frequently the literary text which is being reduced or moderated or mediated by the other "discourses" is none the less subtly but clearly the centre of the study, the originary work which is oddly enough simply assumed to be the only thing not shifting. So, if the text exists in some sort of pre-eminence, however modified and unacknowledged, there may be a place for our old-fashioned business.

Perhaps it was a mistake to go it alone and not try to form a panel or advisory board. But having tried to work with large groups of people on both sides of the Atlantic on projects like encyclopaedias I decided it might, given my geographical position on the extreme edge of England and its transport system, be the least difficult option. In fact, however, the people working textually on Behn have been quite remarkably helpful and would I suspect have been splendid colleagues despite logistical difficulties.

But they are unlikely to have agreed to participate, since all are much engrossed elswehere. Their general amiability may have two causes: Aphra Behn is such a mystery that curiosity overtops any possibility of academic rivalry: we all simply want to know on a rather basic unreconstructed level who she was and what she wrote. Also it is an ageing preoccupation. On the whole younger scholars in the new historical or gender-race-class mode are not much interested in editing in any area in which - unlike in Romanticism - there is, so far, little relation with critical theory. So it tends to be rather age-specific.

On one level she would certainly have found such an enterprise ridiculous. I am conscious of reading, editing and footnoting what Behn herself tossed off in a tavern or a friends house in company or what took its final form because an actor had a cold at rehearsal or failed to turn up. My efforts at fixing a reading, a spelling or a meaning could well be regarded as a ludicrous attempt at controlling literature by insisting on categories and rules, and Behn had a tart way with university-educated people who criticized from an academic stance and were quite incapable of composing what they picked apart or denigrated:

Method, and Rule - you only understand; Pursue that way of Fooling, and be damn'd. Your learned Cant of Action, Time and Place, Must all give way to the unlabour'd Farce. Her business in her plays, as she pointed out in the preface to The Dutch Lover, was with pleasing an audience and imitating life. If she copied well the trivia of the moment she was doing her job, a job which an uneducated woman could do quite as admirably as a learned man.

She harped on the same string in her vindicatory address "To the Reader" printed before Sir Patient Fancy, a cheeky preface which formed the written equivalent of the rather impertinent prologues spoken before Restoration plays. In this address she insisted again that she was not writing for her own enjoyment or for literary self-esteem but for public entertainment. Thus her method was to study what the spectators desired and then give them what they had shown by their patronage they wanted. It could not have mattered less what happened to her texts in the eighteenth or twentieth centuries and she would have mocked the care with which a modern editor placed her work in the tradition of, for example, female or libertine writing.

And she would have felt irritation, even anger at that aspect of editing that demands mention of allusions, borrowings and echoes. She had had quite enough of people accusing her of plagiarising. Against those who "cryed [Sir Patient Fancy] was made out of at least four French Plays" she declared categorically that she "had but a very bare hint from one, the Malad Imagenere... but how much of the French is in this, I leave to those who do indeed understand it and have seen it at the Court". No doubt she hoped this was a small group and one consisting of likeminded royalists who would have agreed with the political tenor of the play and be prepared to overlook other aspects. The defence against stealing from Moliere was much the same as that she had made to her purloining of a great part of Killigrew's Thomaso for her most famous play The Rover and was as blatantly false - it was not a "bare hint" that she had taken from Le Malade Imaginaire. But happily for her no one seems to have pursued the point in the 1670s or taken her to task in print.

The theatre moved on and no play remained a sensation for long. She would not have expected a scholar with more time than sense and no connection whatsoever with a court to place the play beside Moliere's and note the similarities. If she had she would, I imagine, have suggested that we in our age no longer knew how to please a public and were inventing tasks for ourselves. But, as the years of her life went by, another desire peeped through her irate prefaces. Indeed it was already beginning to emerge at the end of the address before Sir Patient Fancy.

This followed the preface to The Dutch Lover in declaring her piece was written to be popular, made no claims to being great art, and aimed at money. But a different, sourer tone has crept in. She declared that she was obliged to write as she did because the age demanded it, but then, curiously, she added, "though it is a way too cheap for men of wit to pursue who write for Glory, and a way which even I despise as much below me." This snobbish attitude was hardly an advertisement for the play that followed, and the petulance and change in tone suggest how touched she had been by the charges of bawdiness and plagiarism, how deeply tired she was of being criticized. On one level, this irritation at seekers for echoes is not encouraging for an editor, but on another it shows quite clearly that she wanted fame.

This desire in her is connected with her increasing valorization of the notion of the professional author. Early in her publishing life Behn stated she "wrote for Bread" and was not ashamed of the fact; later she seems to have felt some pride not beside amateur and talented aristocrats like the Earl of Rochester but beside would-be poets of mediocre ability who prided themselves on not writing for money. In the 1680s she clearly had a sense of herself as a professional author of some dignity who did not write for "a thirde day only," and she was scathing about a rival court poet who tried to steal a march on her by declaring himself a gentleman amateur.

Her growing concern with her work as her work may have been implicated in her movement towards prose fiction in her last writing years. To some extent no doubt poverty or professional necessity pushed her in this direction because, after the amalgamation of the two patent dramatic companies, there was far less call for new plays than there had earlier been. None the less her move towards prose fiction at this time may also have been a move made through inclination; perhaps she had some desire to own her own text in a way she had not been able to do with drama which involved so many other people.

Yet one should not overstress the solitariness of prose composition. The only reference to Behn's writing of prose suggests that this, like her drama and much of her poetry, was communal. Oroonoko was written in a room full of people and recorded on paper only after it had been told many times as a tale within a social setting. She was, then, recording the telling of a tale as much as creating a new fixed form of literature. In the last year of her life Behn made explicit what she had hinted at before: that she wanted fame. In her translation of the long sixth book of Cowley's Latin poem Of Plants she wrote, addressing the laurel, that sign of fame and acclaim:

There is too a personal purpose for the editor. As a method Leavisite close reading has lost favour and there is no other obvious method that pushes a reader close to the text. Editing forces such closeness in a rather different way and it has its uses. For a writer so quickly appropriated as Behn it is necessary to read attentively and try to listen to the voices of the past which speak through her works when in Dominick La Capra's words they "qualify the interpretation we would like to place on them."

Editing does not merely let one assume that this is a good thing but it forces the point by the insistence on looking up, historicizing, guessing the word. The differences between the present and the past are constantly stressed and, though the desire to see current interests intrudes, one is pushed onwards to go beyond echoes of ones own age. At the same time ones sense of what the words did or must mean can be as jolted by present concerns as by an unexpected historical definition in the OED.

But, in general, for us now - ignoring the desire of the author and the benefit of the editor - is textual editing at all important? If Behn's Oroonoko can enter anthologies as a pure anti-slavery tract and John Barton stage one of the few large-scale productions of a Behn play, The Rover, with a hefty portion of its lines changed, who needs authentic texts? And where does authenticity in authorship lie when Restoration authorship is so very loose and dubious? The notion of Bakhtinian heteroglossia becomes less exciting before evidence of multiple composition and compositorial insertions.

The one holograph manuscript of a Behn poem makes it clear that the very baroque punctuation of the printed version is in fact the compositor's not Behn's. That after her death a "G. J." could meddle with the text of her important play The Widdow Ranter, omit political material he regarded as old-fashioned, and eliminate the whole scene of the Indian King's ghost, renders slightly absurd any careful editing three hundred years later of every word Behn may not have written. But, if one has decided to edit and has a contract to do so, the next questions and problems are technical: choice of copy text, editorial practice, and attribution. How is the copy text of an Aphra Behn work to be decided on? It sounds straightforward enough when Philip Gaskell postulates a tidy line of descent from the authors manuscript, a first edition set from that manuscript, a second edition set from a copy of the first which had been corrected in a few places by the author, and finally a third edition set during the author's lifetime but without further revision by him from the copy of the second. The copy text is, Gaskell declares, that printed edition which is closest in line of descent to the authors manuscript and it should be followed in accidentals and substantives unless there is evidence that the author's intentions would be more closely represented by other readings.

Alas, the situation of Aphra Behn is not so simple. Should the copy text be the first edition or the first edition over which one might speculate that the author had some control? That is, for example, in her collections bearing her name or in an earlier broadsheet. How much control might she have had over her works printed with or without her name on the title pages? What is an edition when the book as we know it was unknown and a bookseller would have had loose sheets bound if a buyer was found, so the possibility of odd sheets forming a new work would have been great indeed.

A good example from Aphra Behn is her series of six-line poems for Aesop's Fables commissioned by Francis Barlow to supersede those of a previous writer, Thomas Philipott. The habit of putting books together at the last minute here results in numerous composite copies where Behn's poems are interspersed with the old leaves from Philipott. Then there is the problem of works that have come out in one form in collections edited by her while occurring earlier in another form in works by or edited by other authors.

This is especially problematic in the case of the dedicatory poem to the translator Thomas Creech where Creech, fearing the response to publication in English of so dangerous a figure as Lucretius, may have toned down his friends daring enthusiasm for classical materialism and her urge to praise reason over religion. Or she may herself have written two versions, one for Creech's purposes, one for her own. Or between 1683 when she wrote the poem for Creech and 1684 when she published a version in her own collection Poems on Several Occasions - over which I assume she had some control - she may have changed her mind about philosophical matters and become more irritated with contemporary Christianity, keener to reveal herself as a follower of a liberating Ancient.

Does the existence of a letter mentioning her "resentment" towards Creech indicate the first? Whether it does or not, which should be the copy-text? Or are there two separate poems requiring two separate copy texts? So too with verses that came out first under other peoples names like the rather bawdy poems printed as Rochester's but then later claimed by Behn, or those which appeared first, often unsigned, as broadsides. Since these prior publications might have been tampered with, added to or altered by others, should they have the same status as works appearing more conventionally under her signature or in a work in whose production she probably had a hand?

Having decided, however hesitantly, what copy texts to choose, the next decision is what to emend if anything. What should be done about errors? Have we the liberty to call anything with certainty an "error"? Should what seem to us absurdities be left? If sideways letters and very odd spellings are changed, is this a slippery slide to complete modernization of spelling, punctuation and print, so producing a modification of the work that destroys its original integrity - if there is such a thing? If one goes for some "authenticity," should the punctuation be left as it is, with semicolons at the ends of speeches in the plays, for example, or between subject and verb in the prose? This certainly affects a modern reader's reading and understanding. What then should be done with the Restoration typography, arguably the most flamboyant of any age? Is its flamboyance part of the message? How much is acceptable? And when was it the author's intention, when the compositors? If it is seventeenth-century practice for compositors to set proper names, adjectives formed from them, words of emphasis and foreign words in italic form, should this be followed? Should a text be close to a facsimile, reproducing gothic and italic scripts and capitals of all sizes and dimensions? The obsessed editor leans towards it I fear. Where does authenticity overcome common sense and the author become buried in the past?

At the now almost illegible black letter or the possibly misplaced capitals or the probably mistaken inverted or sideways letter? On the one hand, if we modernize for the sake of easing comprehension, have we prevented something - which we ourselves may have failed to grasp - from being communicated? On the other, how far is the modern readers perception of the work dulled or obscured by the editors retaining of the original punctuation? Editors cannot demand that readers make an effort rather than stop reading and throw the book aside. Behn wanted to be popular: will we be ruining her chances if we retain all this old-fashioned orthography which she herself perhaps regarded as the height of modishness?

Would the fainthearted be hindered from continuing with The Fair Jilt by the intrusive use of semicolons after phrases and commas between subjects and verbs? If capitals and punctuation are kept and the text rendered as close as possible to the original, are we treating the author with proper reverence? Or is this practice a kind of irreverence since it is the "new" writer like Behn who will appear only in a scholarly text where the much edited Shakespeares and Drydens appear in both scholarly and "popular" format, thus remaining accessible to a general reader?

Then we come to the great obsession of the editor: footnoting. Much of this footnoting of necessity directs the reader to other texts. It points out similarities and echoes in an effort to make a rich texture for the work being edited, especially if that work is a play which exists so closely in relation to other contemporary plays.

But is there not something unkind about footnoting to allusions, especially if as editors we forget to speak of intertextuality and refer instead to copying and plagiarism? Aphra Behn was spirited about people digging for parallels and echoes in her texts, as her response to the furore over Sir Patient Fancy attests. She disliked those who showed "their breeding" by finding sources on her plays.

None the less she faced the issue head-on and several times drew attention to the reports circulating in town, composed either by the very malicious or the very ignorant, that what she wrote was such and such a play altered. In the case of Thomaso and The Rover she admitted "I have stolen some hints."

Is it not a disservice when with editing one shows that she was economical with the truth, that, although she changed Killigrew's setting from Madrid to Naples and added a carnival, cut down on the number of whores and scenes and let Angellica Bianca stay bitter and unrepentant at the end, at the level of the word, phrase, and line it is difficult to avoid observing that The Rover has taken something more than "hints" from its original.

Does a reader want to know that Thomaso II, 2.1 is the original of Hellena's spirited lines: "this man you must kiss; nay you must kiss none but him too - and nuzel through his beard to find his lips," or that when Behn's hero exclaims "does not my fortune sit triumphing on my brow! dost not see the little wanton god there all gay and smiling. Have I not an air about my face and eyes that distinguish me from the crowd of common lovers!" he quotes Thomaso who asks "Do's not the little god appear upon my Brow to distinguish me from the Common Crow'd of Lovers"?

The Rover is not the only play of Behn's which is close to an unacknowledged original; yet all are published as her own works. Indeed many of her plays are closer to their sources in English drama than her "translations" are to the foreign works from which they purportedly derive. The Voyage to the Island of Love, for example, was said to have been taken from the French, and yet it turns Paul Tallemant's bare and simple salon allegory told in a jog-trot series of verses framed in flat prose narration into a detailed and evocative baroque poem encompassing a much wider range of moral, social, emotional and sensual possibilities.

The work becomes recognizably Behn's as the hero, simply a charming person in the French, is provided with wit, energy and sexual attractiveness, while the ugly ridiculous old women who chase after handsome young men are balanced by ugly ridiculous old men chasing beautiful young girls. Her political obsessions creep in too, as the once conventional city on the banks of the River of Pretension has a Princess Hope who beguiles a young hero full of smiles and joy, deceived by shouting rabble and faithful flatterers, dazzled by the image of a crown. This Monmouth passage, twenty-four lines long, has no precedent in Tallemant. Elsewhere ten lines of the French will commonly yield forty lines of English despite Behn's statement that English is far terser than French. Yet this work is labelled a "translation."

What should happen when the pedantry of the present outstretches that of the past and the editor notes that the reference or quotation is not accurate? Should reference be made to the present state of scholarship in classical texts or myths or should the "mistakes" of the seventeenth century be lovingly respected? How much should be explained of oaths and mumbo-jumbo words? Were they nonsense at the time? Certainly French writers like Moliere make use of combinations of syllables to express the absurd. Is it ridiculous to struggle to find in, for example, The Widdow Ranter that the word Quiocto might refer to the Indian god of the Qiocos? Would anyone of the time have known this?

This is especially problematic with a work like Oroonoko, which has been thrust into the limelight of cultural studies as a classic early text of gender, class, and especially race. How this to be edited since it no longer is lives only in the world of talking trees, indolent swains, and the "black" Stuarts, but also in the brightly lit world of modern criticism and subaltern culture? Because it concerns slavery and we are interested in slavery, should it be cushioned round with contemporary accounts of slavery, detailed descriptions of the New World colonies, and noted African habits? Does this give the work a factual authenticity that separates it from all Behn's other short stories which, touching on convents and masquerades, have less relevance to modern readers although she makes similar autobiographical claims in them and attests to their "truth" to history?

And thus the dangers of inauthenticity, even falsehood are greater. But so are the imaginative possibilities. So an image, a biography begins to take shape from authenticated works, from the tenor of the proposed ascriptions, the image depending, like the ascription on which it is partly based, on the present and the present notion of what the past was like, on what identity one puts on Behn's period and how its subjectivity is imagined and recreated.

And here again is critical fashion, the fashion that was at work in allowing one person to be accorded a full-scale critical edition and another not.

In both edition and literary biography there has to be some assumption that the subject says what we want to hear and that he or she can be in dialogue with the present in terms that can relate to the present. She did not know her date of death would be a few days into the new reign, one might argue in extenuation, and a professional court poet needed a court. Should the response to this realization of trimming or apostasy be the horror that early biographers of the great republican Algernon Sidney felt when they learnt that their hero had been in the pay of ultra-monarchical France?

The editor/footnoter obviously has nothing to feel smug about. The terrible truth is that one can put into footnotes all the lumber that should have remained in the attic of notecards and never have been allowed near the word processor. Yet, all this lumber may be relevant. There is some humility as well as arrogance in overloading footnotes, for unsuccessful connections allowed by this excess of material may await another's connecting. If the uncharitable might see this fullness as an anal problem, the charitable might murmur potential fecundity and plenitude.

NEWSPAPER COPY EDITORS' PERCEPTIONS

Newspaper copy editors have long been known as "the last line of defence" against errors because they do their work near the end of the production cycle. That also means they have the potential to be a last line of defence against violations of ethical standards. In fact, many editing textbooks say copy editors should be prepared to raise questions about potential ethics-related problems, such as a lack of balance or fairness, and to watch for obvious breaches of ethics like plagiarism. There is anecdotal evidence that many copy editors take this role seriously. In recent years, copy editors have been credited with detecting lifted quotations, plagiarized stories and columns and letters to the editor, and fabricated material.

There is also anecdotal evidence, however, that copy editors' ethics-related concerns are not always taken seriously. For example, a copy editor reportedly raised questions "about the level of truth" in Patricia Smith's Boston Globe columns three years before she was forced to resign under fire for fabrication. Similarly, "growing newsroom unrest" resulted when managers ignored a copy editor's concerns about stereotyping in a Houston Chronicle section on juvenile justice that pictured only minority youths. Articles based on depositions of Atlanta Journal-Constitution copy editors indicate that some tried unsuccessfully to get senior editors to reconsider the fairness of a 1996 column likening security guard Richard Jewell-who was never charged with bombing Atlanta's Centennial Olympic Park and was eventually formally cleared-to Wayne Williams, convicted in 1982 of murdering two people and implicated in the deaths of twenty-two others. The column was published and Jewell filed a 1997 libel suit against the paper that was still pending in late 2005." More recently, John E. McIntyre, managing editor for the copy desk at the Baltimore Sun and former president of the American Copy Editors Society, wrote:

In the endeavor to head off plagiarism and fabrication in news stories, and to ensure the reliability and accuracy of stories... the ranking editors and the copy editors are on the same side. The problem is that the ranking editors don't always recognize this. When the American Copy Editors Society presents workshops on structural editing... a troubling comment keeps surfacing among the participants: "I wouldn't be allowed to raise questions like that at my paper."

Although copy editors' jobs charge them with evaluating stories, their concerns sometimes go unheeded; forces that Shoemaker and Reese identify as stronger "influences on media content" sometimes limit copy editors' authority. Nonetheless, Hank Glamann, former assistant managing editor for editing at the Cleveland Plain Dealer, urged members of the American Society of Newspaper Editors to "create a climate in your newsroom in which any member of the staff can ask any question about any story and expect to be heeded. To restrict who can ask about what is inefficient-and a real waste of talent."

This survey of copy desk workers sought to determine how they perceive their role as "final guardians" of journalistic ethics, and whether there are conflicts between what they think their role should be and what they perceive it actually is. The research is important for two reasons. First, copy editors constitute a significant proportion of the newsroom workforce-nearly 20 per cent in 200517-and are often difficult to hire second, how they see their jobs is important because, as Shoemaker and Reese wrote, journalists' role conceptions affect the content they produce: "[T]hese roles may determine how they define their jobs, the kinds of things they believe should be covered, and the ways in which they cover them." Copy editors do not cover news, of course, but they produce content as they condense news into headlines, elements that can have a bigger impact on readers' impressions of the news than the words written by reporters. In addition, they may select or help select wire stories for publication and help determine story play as they design pages.

Although there has been an explosion of scholarly interest in journalistic ethics during recent decades and much of the resulting literature describes the ethics, values, responsibilities, or roles of particular types of journalists, almost no work has assessed copy editors' values or how they perceive their role in upholding ethics standards. Other research on copy editing, however, suggests that technological innovations, as well as copy editors' perceptions of how others in the newsroom view them, may have implications for how copy editors think of their ethics roles.

During the past half century, newspaper copy desks have coped with at least four job-altering waves of technological innovation, each forcing copy editors to spend time adapting and some permanently reducing the time available for substantive editing. First, during the 1950s, newspapers introduced teletypesetting (TTS) equipment, which tran-smitted wire-service stories via hole-punched paper tape used to automatically activate linecasting machines.

This allowed quicker typesetting but forced some copy desks to adopt new style rules, so that local style would match wire-service stories, and was blamed in one study for an increase in errors.

Second, during the early 1970s, some newsrooms began using optical character recognition (OCR) equipment to produce perforated tape versions of local stories. This required copy editors to edit stories with a special pen and have their changes input by a corrections typist, changes that one study found led to an increase in published errors. Then, in the late 1970s and early 1980s, newsrooms introduced video-display terminals, which made updating and comparing stories easier but also introduced physical problems, such as eyestrain and headaches, and, some researchers reported, led to newspaper management deva-luing editing in favour of production tasks.

Perhaps the most significant technological change was the introduction in the 1980s and 1990s of electronic pagination, which shifted page makeup responsibilities from composing room staffs to copy editors. It gave editors greater control over page appearance, but also cut into the time copy editors had for substantive editing. In 1994, Russial reported that electronic makeup of a page took on average fifteen minutes more than drawing a paper "dummy." This time drain, which can be exacerbated by malfunctioning pagination equipment, persisted after newsrooms became familiar with the technology. In many cases, pagination turned the desk "from a centre of editing to a centre of production," and it made some copy editors feel they had become computer technicians or proofreaders.

Meanwhile, there are indications that a significant number of copy editors have felt a lack of respect for their work. A1984 report noted that a survey of forty copy editors had "raised disturbing questions about their treatment by senior editors and the lack of respect they got in their newsrooms." Three years later, a survey of 630 copy editors at fifty newspapers found that although 63 per cent said that their work was supported by senior editors, respondents were evenly split on whether the copy desk had "clout within the newsroom." A 2003 survey found that respect remained a problem, with 47 per cent of 337 responding copy editors disagreeing that "most copy editors feel appreciated at my newspaper" and 40 per cent disagreeing that "copy editors at my paper are held in the same esteem as reporters."

It is understandable, then, that copy editor job satisfaction has lagged behind that of other journalists. In 1989, ASNE reported that 43 per cent of 191 responding copy editors said they would be unhappy if they held the same job in five years, compared with about a third of other journalists. Four years later, Cook, Banks, and Thompson found that 39 per cent of fifty-nine copy editors in a study planned to leave journalism within five years, and Cook and Banks reported that copy editors in a sample of newspaper journalists were more likely to be burned out than reporters.

Similarly, in 1997, Voakes reported that 37 per cent of nearly 200 copy editors in an ASNE-sponsored study thought their current job had not met their expectations, compared with 22 per cent of non-copy editors. Finally, a survey of copy desk workers conducted in 2002 showed that although more than 70 per cent agreed at least somewhat that they were satisfied with their jobs, fewer than a fourth agreed strongly, this during a year when Weaver et al. found that about a third of U.S. journalists in general were "very satisfied" and 81 per cent were at least "fairly satisfied." Intriguingly, the 2002 copy editor job satisfaction study found satisfaction correlated with copy editors' opinions about the ethics standards of their newspapers.

THEORETICAL PERSPECTIVES

Studies of copy editing have not always made good use of theory, but three perspectives from sociology and mass communication appear useful in considering how copy editors perceive their ethics role. First, as Russial and Brill have proposed, some technological innovations may have resulted in the sort of "de-skilling" of copy editing that sociologist Harry Braverman observed when industrial jobs were routinized by automation. Braverman theorized that the introduction of automation or other technology into an occupation could reduce the number of skills used by workers so much that a job became "de-skilled." That resulted, he suggested, in a loss of power by workers, their supervisors, and the occupation itself.

Although pagination initially required copy editors to learn a new skill, one result of having copy editors paginate "may be a limitation in the discretion journalists have in deciding how much time to spend on traditional [editing] tasks." Thus, some copy desks may have lost, if not the skills of editing, then at least some discretion in how much time they can spend on serious editing concerns, such as story fairness and balance. Indeed, 53 per cent of copy editors surveyed in 1987 for ASNE perceived they did not have time to edit well. Such changes could also routinize copy editing so much that the job consists of little more than writing headlines, running spell checkers, and moving copy-very nearly what Bleske found copy editors doing at one 60,000-circulation daily. If routinization results in a loss of copy desk power, as Braverman's theory suggests, then it could rob copy editors of the ability to be ethical "backstops."

Power is also a consideration in Shoemaker and Reese's hierarchy of influences. They suggest that content is affected by "environmental factors" or influences, modeled as a series of concentric circles. The media worker at the centre is subject to forces in the outer circles-media routines, organizational influences, extramedia influences, and ideology-which are, in turn, subject to the forces in circles beyond them.

Although ethics does not play a large role in the model, the question of whether copy editors can be final guardians of ethical standards can be viewed in terms of the model. According to Shoemaker and Reese, the judgements of an individual journalist possessing sufficient power can influence content if there is no higher-level factor-such as a strong routine or organizational influence-covering the task at hand. As Shoemaker and Reese note, "institutional position greatly determines the power vested in a role," so copy editors may lack the authority to effectively call into question the actions of writers or assigning editors.

Relevant theory also comes from the sociological study of professional ethics, which generally posits that all professions share certain characteristics: a systematic base of knowledge, community sanction, a code of ethics, a distinctive culture maintained by associations, and a high degree of autonomy and authority conferred by clients. Although some writers have viewed journalism as either a profession or a professionalizing occupation, it has often been seen as lacking several prerequisites of professionalism. For example, Shoemaker and Reese note that journalists are not required to follow specific standards or obtain specific schooling. In addition, their autonomy "is limited by organizational constraints."

Copy editors appear to lack even more of these attributes of professionalism than other journalists. Although copy editors generally possess a broad base of knowledge that is systematic in the sense that it includes detailed information about language, they do not have a great deal of autonomy, they do not have a separate ethics code, and they did not have an association until the American Copy Editors Society was founded in 1996. Moreover, in many newsrooms, copy editors lack both "community" approval and authority conferred by "clients." The fact that copy editors are hired to be evaluators frequently sets up an adversarial relationship between them and their intra-office "clients," reporters and assigning editors. Copy editors also have external clients, the readers for whom they are pre-publication advocates. However, those reader-clients cannot confer authority upon copy editors, for they generally are not aware that the newsroom's most invisible workers exist.

HYPOTHESES

Even if copy desk workers think they should be guardians of ethics standards, they may not feel support in their newsrooms for such a role. As a result:

- *H1a*: Most respondents will report that identifying and seeking to eliminate potential ethics-related problems in stories should be integral parts of copy editors' jobs.
- *H1b*: Respondents will be significantly more likely to say that finding and eliminating errors and identifying and eliminating potential legal problems, such as libel, should be integral parts of copy editors' jobs than they will be to report that identifying and seeking to eliminate potential ethics related problems in stories should be integral parts of copy editors' jobs.
- *H2*: Respondents will be significantly more likely to perceive that eliminating errors and eliminating legal problems actually are integral parts of their jobs than they will be to say that identifying and seeking to eliminate potential ethics-related problems in stories actually are integral parts of their jobs.

- *H3*: There will be no significant differences between respondents' perceptions of what copy editors' roles in eliminating errors and potential legal problems should be and are, but there will be significant differences between perceptions about what copy editors' ethics roles should be and are.
- *H4a*: Respondents will be more likely to agree that copy editors should be encouraged to take questions to managers than they will be to say that copy editors at their newspapers are encouraged to take questions to managers.
- *H4b*: Respondents will perceive more support for taking potential ethics-related concerns to immediate supervisors or assigning editors than they will for taking unanswered concerns to senior managers.
- *H5*: Respondents who perceive that copy editors' actual ethics role differs from what it should be will report lower levels of job satisfaction than respondents whose ideal and real perceptions of their ethics role match.
- *H6*: Respondents whose perceptions of copy editors' ideal and real ethics role do not match will be less likely than others to rate their newspapers' ethical standards favorably.

Data were gathered via a survey sent in fall 2002 to journalists at 105 U.S. daily, English-language newspapers listed in the Editor and Publisher International Yearbook as having average weekday circulations greater than 25,000. Because copy editors' names generally do not appear in their newspapers, a two-step process was used to identify recipients. First, a scientifically selected sample of 105 newspapers was stratified into the five largest circulation categories used by ASNE.

The names of copy editors were obtained from newspaper Web sites, industry contacts, and the newspapers. Then a random sample of 803 copy desk workers was drawn, using a sampling frame designed to match ASNE's estimates of the distribution of copy/layout editors across the five circulation classes. The study used multiple contacts to improve response rates, and allowed recipients to fill out the questionnaire on paper or online; 470 usable responses were received from 100 newspapers for a 59 per cent response rate. Nearly 81 per cent of respondents identified themselves as copy editors or copy editor/page designers, though the sample contained copy desk chiefs, page designers, news editors, reporter/copy editors, and others who worked part-time on a copy desk.

H1a, which predicted that most respondents would view seeking to eliminate potential ethics-related problems from stories as an integral part of a copy editor's job, was supported. Nearly 95 per cent of copy desk workers agreed with a statement that made ethics part of copy editors' ideal roles, and more than two-thirds strongly agreed.

Testing other hypotheses involved wading into a long-running methodological debate over how ordinal and quasi-interval data can be analysed. Ordinal responses to statements about copy editors' roles in eliminating errors, legal problems, and potential ethics-related problems ("strongly agree," "somewhat agree," "undecided," "somewhat disagree," and "strongly disagree") were converted to quasi-interval data by assigning a number to each response so that mean responses could be calculated and compared using f-tests. Although this practice has the support of some scholars, some purists believe that only non-parametric statistics should be used with such ordinal data. So, while i-test results are reported in the text below, results from the sign test-a conservative, non-parametric test often considered appropriate for non-normal and non-symmetric, paired-measurement data like these-are provided in endnotes.

Both statistical tests offered only partial support for H1b, which held that errors and legal problems in stories would be more likely to be viewed as copy-desk concerns than would ethics-related problems. There was a statistically significant difference between the way respondents viewed copy editors' ideal roles in eliminating errors and potential ethics problems. But there was not a statistically significant difference between support for eliminating potential legal problems and potential ethics-related problems.

H2 predicted greater agreement that eliminating errors and eliminating potential legal problems actually were parts of copy editors' jobs than agreement that seeking to eliminate ethics-related problems was. H2 was supported. There were statistically significant differences between responses to statements about copy editors' actual roles in eliminating errors and in eliminating ethics-related problems, and between responses to statements about copy editors' actual roles in eliminating potential legal problems and in eliminating potential ethics-related problems.

H3 predicted that respondents would perceive that copy editors' ideal roles matched their actual roles when it came to eliminating errors and potential legal problems but not when it came to identifying and seeking to eliminate potential ethics-related problems. Contrary to expectations, there were statistically significant differences in respondents' perceptions of what copy editors' roles should be and what they are related to all three tasks: identifying and eliminating errors, identifying and eliminating legal problems and identifying and seeking to eliminate potential ethics-related problems.

H4a, which predicted that respondents would be more likely to agree that copy editors should be encouraged to take ethics-related concerns to managers than to say that they actually are encouraged, was supported. First, there was a significant difference between responses to statements, suggesting copy editors should be and are encouraged to bring concerns about ethics-related problems to their supervisors and/or assigning editors. Second, there was a significant difference between responses to statements about whether copy editors dissatisfied with those front-line managers' responses to potential ethics related problems in stories should be encouraged and are encouraged to carry the concerns to senior editors.

H4b, which asserted that respondents would be less likely to support and perceive encouragement for raising questions about ethics-related problems with senior managers than immediate supervisors or assigning editors, was supported. Respondents were significantly more likely to agree that copy editors should be encouraged to take ethics-related concerns to their immediate supervisors or the assigning editor for the story than they were to support taking subsequently unresolved concerns to senior managers. Respondents were also significantly more likely to say encouragement actually existed in their newsrooms for approaching immediate supervisors or assigning editors than for carrying concerns to senior managers.

H5, that copy desk workers would be less satisfied if they thought their ideal and real ethics roles differed, was supported. Independent samples f-tests showed that among respondents with opinions, those who perceived their ideal and actual ethics roles differed were significantly less likely to agree with five of seven statements about job satisfaction. The editors whose responses revealed a disconnect had significantly lower mean scores on statements about overall satisfaction, the prospect of doing the same work in five years, their prospects for advancement, and satisfaction with supervisors. In addition, respondents whose responses showed the disconnect had significantly lower scores on intending to remain at their newspapers for the next two years.

H6, predicting that respondents whose perceptions of copy editors' ideal and real ethics roles did not match would be less likely than others to rate their newspapers' ethical standards favorably, was supported. Respondents rated the ethics standards of their newspapers lower if their ideas of what copy editors' ethics roles should be did not match their perceptions of reality.

The copy editors think they should be the final guardians of journalistic ethics but perceive little newsroom support for that role. For example, almost three-fourths strongly agreed that addressing ethics related problems in stories should be part of copy editors' jobs, but only about 40 per cent said that was the case in their newsrooms. Similarly, although all but three respondents agreed copy editors should be encouraged to take concerns about ethics problems to their immediate supervisors and/or the assigning editors, only about 55 per cent said such a simple step was "always" encouraged in their newsrooms.

There was even less perceived support for pursuing ethics-related discussions to a higher level: 90 per cent agreed copy editors should be encouraged to take unresolved concerns to senior managers, but fewer than 15 per cent said such encouragement is "always" given. This suggests that newsrooms are constraining employees willing to serve as ethical backstops from using their niche in the production process to do so.

CONSTRAINED COPY EDITORS

Comments written in the margins of some returned questionnaires or in answer to two open-ended questions suggested how these constraints may be working: some come from deadlines, workload, and technological pressures. For example, a news copy editor at a newspaper with 500,000+ average weekday circulation wrote:

If for example there are 35 stories appearing in the paper, more likely than not, 25 of the stories move to the copydesk in the last 45 minutes before the paper is slated to lock up everything (or much of it) pops near deadline. That puts a strain on the ability to check facts, weigh fairness, check spelling and grammar, rectify inconsistencies, write a good headline and trim the story to fit the hole.

A features/lifestyle copy editor at a major metropolitan newspaper echoed Braverman's de-skilling theory, writing that with the [newspaper's] conversion to CCI [a proprietary electronic editing and pagination system sold by CCI Europe] the "art" of copy editing is being overtaken by the need for copy editors to act as typographers. This is compounded by a recent redesign that is adding a layer of mumbo-jumbo. It's less and less about journalism and more and more about production.

That copy editor's concern may be telling: 58 per cent of respondents designed pages using electronic software; 28 per cent worked for newspapers that changed editing or design software during the previous year; and 52 per cent worked for newspapers or sections that had been redesigned during the previous year.

At Issue: Power. Other comments suggested that the issue is power, a central notion in Braverman's de-skilling theory and Shoemaker and Reese's theory of influences on media content. A copy editor at a newspaper in the 25,001-50,000 weekday circulation group wrote: "We're grammarians and headline writers and only rarely deal with the substance of a story except to return it to [the assigning editors] if there's a problem in that area." A copy editor/page designer at another small newspaper described a similar situation: "The way our system is set up, the city desk determines content and balance on stories, and we merely lay out the pages, write headlines, and edit for AP style. We are not allowed to cut local stories, and not encouraged to question content and balance." Another wrote, "We're not allowed to change local copy."

In those cases-which may be particularly representative of small dailies with beginner copy editors, a powerful city editor, and no highly placed advocate for copy editors (*e.g.*, an assistant managing editor for copy desks)-the ability of copy editors to be ethics advocates may be constrained by their place in the newsroom hierarchy. Shoemaker and Reese suggest that media routines trump the individual's ability to influence media content, except in areas where there is no established routine. At some newspapers, not only is the routine for dealing with potential ethics-related problems in stories well established, but it also ends at the assigning desk. As a result, assigning editors do not grant to copy editors the sanction or approval they need to serve as even backup guardians of ethics standards.

Constraints on copy editors extend beyond ethics-related concerns. Although the largest difference between copy editors' views of their ideal and actual roles involved identifying and eliminating potential ethics-related problems, there were also significant differences between their ideal and real roles in eliminating errors and potential legal problems. Newspapers may also be wasting the talents of key employees by not supporting their efforts to find and eliminate errors and potential legal problems, such as libel. An assistant copy desk chief at a small daily wrote:

The other departments sometimes forget that we are not trained monkeys drawing boxes on the computer. We sift through wire copy and photos to select the most relevant and compelling items for our readers. When it comes to decisions about local copy and photos, however, comments from the copy desk are often pushed aside. The next afternoon we are the ones questioned about any confusing information, mistakes or questionable remarks. "Why didn't the desk change that?" "How did that get by the desk?" Limits have been placed on our authority as copy editors, yet we are still held responsible for the decisions we cannot make.

One effect of a disconnect between ideal and real roles is a lack of job satisfaction. The nearly one in five respondents reporting that disconnect was more likely to be dissatisfied with aspects of his/her job and to have a lower opinion of the ethics standards of his/her newspaper. However, it is impossible to tell which came first, the disconnect or the discontent.

How should newspapers tackle this situation? If newspapers want to enlist all journalists to help preserve ethical standards and, thus, credibility, managers should encourage copy editors to raise questions when stories with potential ethics-related problems reach them. This encouragement should be delivered in a public way so that newsroom staffers who have traditionally controlled the routine of dealing with substantive questions can see that newsroom policymakers want those routines to include copy editors. In addition, copy editors who still have concerns after talking with their supervisors and/or assigning editors should be encouraged to approach senior editors. A procedure for doing this should be made public, which could help reduce the perception that copy editors who take concerns to senior editors are acting maliciously, rather than merely doing their jobs. Meanwhile, both copy editors and senior managers should make increased efforts to get to know each other. As The

Poynter Institute's Karen Brown Dunlap has noted, one factor that can make copy editors' position in the newsroom precarious is that "their day begins as many reporters and editors prepare to end the day, keeping copy editors out of the flow of newsroom conversation." Greater connections between copy editors and senior editors would give the former access they need to raise concerns informally and offer the latter a better sense of what is going on in the trenches. It also might introduce senior editors to copy editors with reporting experience (of which there were many in this study) who would be good candidates for assigning editor positions. Considering them would help address two problems reported by this study: a perception that copy editors are not respected and the dissatisfaction of more than half with their prospects for advancement.

Further research might look beyond the copy desk to consider what reporters, midlevel managers, and senior managers consider their ideal ethics roles to be and how those stack up against what newsroom routines allow them to question or take responsibility for. Although media ethics research has often asked journalists "What behaviour do you consider ethical?" it has less often asked "What part of ethical journalism do you consider yourself responsible for?" A large body of work has tried to determine what influences the behaviour of journalists and other media practitioners. Those studies generally have assumed, though, that media workers will do what they think they should do. This study revealed a disconnect between the "ethics backstop" role some copy editors thought they should have and the roles they perceived they did have. Other journalists may similarly be disconnected from roles they believe they should fulfill.

8

News Gathering and Processing

Many journalists are just beginning to use computers as tools for newsgathering. How can it be done successfully? Many novices may not be quite sure how the process works. To get things going, let's consider the successful nature of these two case studies. Philadelphia's public schools had been judged by experts in 1994 to be failing their educational mission. But why? And how? Reporters and editors for *The Philadelphia Enquirer* sought to find answers and explanations. The newspaper's team of reporters began by collecting information about the performance of the schools in the School District of Philadelphia.

Staff writers found data and other forms of information in a variety of places. They obtained much of the data from the school district itself, but also found useful information from the Pennsylvania Department of Education, the University of Pittsburgh, the U.S. Department of Education, and a variety of other public sources. Led by Borowski, who is director of computer-assisted reporting (CAR) for his newspaper, the group worked with sociologists and other experts from Temple University to analyse data and uncover trends about the schools and their students.

Borowski (personal communication, November 17, 1995) explained: Tom Ferrick has been with *The Enquirer* for years. In the early 1980s or late 1970s, he did, in essence, a project just like this with yellow sheets of legal paper and a calculator, books, and he did it by hand. This time, we did it with a computer. The other interesting thing is that the city school district, through the 1980s, would not release a lot of data. They did not want to have their successes or their failures measured in any way. Very, very little data trickled out. They got a new assistant superintendent who came down here with a different attitude. The old administration of the school district left. And they said, "We'll give you whatever you want. We can't give you studentlevel stuff, but we'll give you different groups and things like that."

The result of the investigation and analysis was an eight-page special section entitled, "A District in Distress," that told readers how the problems causing the district's poor performance in educating children were only becoming worse. It described how the city had two school systems: a mostly minority public system and a mostly White private and parochial school system. The reporters pointed to the facts: Students could not complete basic tasks, such as math and reading, and their academic performance was poor when compared to other schools on standardized tests.

Other data showed that students did not attend school and that they did not graduate. The schools were unsafe and remained deeply segregated. The district, overall, was not doing well compared to nearby suburban districts. The project also demonstrated how the public school system was growing after a period of decline, but that funding was dropping. In the end, the team of reporters and editors found some cause for hope in a new superintendent, a court order to restructure the district, and a public focused on seeking change in the schools.

Most of the special section consisted of tables, colour graphs, and charts of data gleaned from the vast collection of sources located by *The Enquirer* staff. These summaries were supplemented with short stories to explain data and photographs to illustrate points.

The help the journalists got from experts paid off, Borowski stated: We got all the data. We got someone from Temple University who was doing research. And we came out with the project. In a newspaper like *The Enquirer* that puts a premium on investigations and nailing the bad guys, it was embarrassing that the school district sent over its congratulations on this project and said they loved it.

We wondered: "What did we do wrong?" We didn't do anything wrong. It was probably the best summary of school district statistics in a decade, something, I'm told, the school board can use as a reference. The project won a National Education Writers award and other recognition from journalists.

NEWS GATHERING

State political reporter at *The Age,* Richard Baker, was enjoying a drink at the pub one evening when an "older bloke" told him a yarn about the seals in Port Phillip Bay. It seemed the state government had built an expensive covered platform out in the bay for the seals to loll about on. But the seals were unimpressed. They were snubbing the new platform and refusing to budge from an antiquated, tumbledown structure nearby.

The story had several fine elements for a news piece; among them, government extravagance and appealing marine mammals. After a few calls to check it out, and the dispatch of a photographer to provide a visual showing the old and new platforms, with the seals firmly ensconced on the old one, Richard had a front page story.

The next day it was covered widely by radio and television and had become one of Victoria's more memorable human interest stories of the year. Journalists call the process of finding and developing an original item "breaking a story" and for most reporters it's what journalism is all about. Richard describes breaking news as "the most fun part of the job". It means "doing something no one else is doing and going home at night knowing that tomorrow it is going to be all over the radio and TV and at this stage you're the only person who knows about it". (Interview with Richard Baker.)

This section is about finding and developing news stories, both those initiated by reporters themselves and those assigned by the news desk.

The news day: Every day in every newsroom begins with a series of story possibilities. During the day some of these will become items for publication or broadcast. Extra stories will emerge while some of the original ones will fall out of consideration. The way in which each day's news agenda is developed is complex and, like so many other features of the industry, varies from one medium and one newsroom to the next.For instance, in a large metropolitan newsroom, most of the day's news will fall into one of four categories:

- First, there will be the predicted events, which are known about in advance and filed in the newsroom's diary. These can include sittings of parliament, council meetings and court hearings, media conferences, the release of official reports, scheduled meetings or negotiations, all sports events, the release of official statistics, regular financial decisions and events, openings, previews and pre-arranged interviews.
- *Then there are watching briefs*: These are the monitoring activities that generate news, including the calls to the emergency services, monitoring other media, stake-outs (at a scene where a newsmaker might appear) and running stories (where new developments are expected in an existing story or where the story can be developed by journalists finding new angles).
- *There are unpredicted events*: These include accidents, fires, natural disasters, attacks; things no one suspected in advance would happen.
- Finally there are stories which might be termed initiated stories. Like the example at the start of this section, they fall outside the routine news cycle and begin with a reporter's observation or a tip-off from a member of the public.

Non-metropolitan newsrooms, and those that don't have a daily output, including suburban papers, metro weeklies and so on, are likely to have a different pattern of gathering news from metro newsrooms. They may place more emphasis on initiated stories and less on events such as stake-outs or daily emergency stories.

Reporters can be given assignments by the chief of staff or editor. But newsrooms also rely on their journalists to generate stories themselves, within the framework of the organisation's specific news agenda. For instance, agency reporters need to be able to think of ways to develop new angles to stories that are already part of the news agenda because news wire services tend to stick closely to the main events and issues of each day. Television and radio also usually stick closely to the main events of the day. This is because—with the exception of round-the-clock services— broadcast news programmes are of fixed duration. The first priority for a television bulletin is to touch all the main bases of the day's events. There's usually room for one quirky or lighthearted item at the end. Radio's priority is to continually update the main stories of interest to the station's audience.

Reporters who work in radio and TV know their programmes have "no back page"—in other words, there's nowhere to put the stories of minor significance that are useful fillers in newspapers. But because radio is a high rotation medium, it also has some room for stories of limited impact which can be run on a single bulletin. Online news services have the capacity to run unlimited numbers of stories. But experience suggests that the stories that receive most of the "hits"—that is, the stories accessed by the largest number of readers—are those placed at the top of the story list on the screen and which are therefore deemed to be the most significant stories of the moment.

TECHNIQUES FOR DEVELOPING STORIES

In the last section we looked at some of the sources of news. These include tip-offs (as happened in the story described at the start of this section), direct observation, official hearings, media releases and so on.

Sometimes the raw material from these sources can be turned into news stories with very little effort on the part of the reporter. But to generate more original stories, journalists need to know some of the techniques that can be used to develop observations into stories or to develop new angles for existing news items. Some of these techniques include:

- *Repercussions and reaction*: News generates more news. A story of any significance will lead to break-out and follow-up stories, so reporters need to consider where they might look for reaction to a particular event or issue and its repercussions. One obvious source of repercussions is in your own local area. National and international events often create ripples that spread out across the nation, even the world. When something happens somewhere else, one of the first questions a journalist will ask is "What's the local angle?". There are also stories to be found in considering the repercussions of government decisions and asking "Who benefits?" and "Who has been left out?".

Tip

Reporters need to go beyond the superficial and ask questions about the repercussions of issues and events. This applies to even seemingly low-impact issues.

These are just two examples: First consider the fad for D-I-Y home improvements buttressed by several television "infotainment" programmes and lifestyle magazines.

When it arose the fad itself was worth a "colour" (*i.e.* light-hearted) story. But there was also a more serious news story later on, when statistics on hospital admissions suggested an increase in injuries from more people using power tools, working on ladders and so on.

Likewise, when small, collapsible scooters first hit the market, they prompted stories about the fad itself. But again, there were more serious stories to be told about the repercussions of young children riding these scooters, often without proper protective headgear, and the number of accidents and injuries that caused. So stories can be generated from looking at events and issues and considering "What next?".

- *The other person's opinion*. Rightly or wrongly the Australian media thrive on conflict. Another way of looking at it is that they value diversity of opinion. So whenever a decision or announcement is made, there's bound to be a story in the way various groups in the community react. Try to canvass opinion widely. There are not just two sides to every story. There are usually more.
- *Going back*. Revisiting past events to see what has happened since is a regular way of generating stories, not least because it helps to fulfil journalism's role of keeping officials accountable.

It also helps answer the criticism that journalism is too concerned with the short-term news cycle and not sufficiently concerned with longer term repercussions of events. Going back might mean looking at how a community has coped with tragedy, such as bushfires. It might mean looking at how a community of refugees has settled in. It might mean interviewing war veterans. It might mean asking "Where are they now?" of people who were once well known.

And revisiting doesn't just have to revolve around people. What about changes to local traffic management or town planning? Did they work? Stories on past events need an angle to justify revisiting them. The most common angle is an anniversary of the original event, though it's not the only angle available. Some issues and events are worth tracking as they progress and these stories can be picked up at any stage along the process.

Smart reporters will keep a file of stories worth tracking. These can include the construction of prominent buildings or developments, public campaigns and so on. They can also include far more personal stories.

For instance, landmark medical procedures or emergencies often make the news at the time but are quickly forgotten. But the aftermaths of such events will often make stories just as interesting as the initial ones.

- Backgrounding events. One of the most regular, and fair, criticisms of the way news is presented is that it focuses on the *when* and *where* at the expense of the *why*. This leaves the audience unable to put events or issues into a context. So stories which investigate the reasons behind events in the news have an importance beyond their contribution to the daily news quota.

- Looking forward. Some news events are known of in advance—a dignitary will visit, a protest is being planned, a big sports event is forthcoming and so on. These are worth a preview story.
- The story behind the story. Behind many news stories there is another story waiting to be told. Sometimes that means finding a wider issue in a story that focused on an individual.

For example, an item on a single franchisee's business difficulties might lead to a broader story about problems within the company or that particular field of commerce. Conversely, big picture stories also lend themselves to items on the individuals involved. For example, consider the Olympic Games.

Of course the high profile, well-credentialled athletes will be covered. But dig a little deeper and there will often be far more interesting stories of athletes who struggled against considerable odds for their place at the starting line, even if they have only a small chance of finishing well.

It may infuriate sports fans but a disproportionate amount of attention at the Calgary Winter Olympics and Sydney Olympics went, respectively, to British ski jumper "Eddie the Eagle" (Michael Edwards) and swimmer "Eric the Eel" (Eric Moussambani) from Equatorial Guinea, neither best remembered for their sporting skill. There are other, if less quirky, stories behind almost every competition—from the craft and cooking competitions at every Easter show to junior chess titles, to the wine awards. And competitions don't just have competitors. They have judges, statisticians, former winners and so on, all potentially worth a story. Even media coverage itself can generate good story material, such as the camera operators who train for months to run up and down the field covering the players at the footy grand final.

There's also a human story behind many official statistics; the family of the road accident victim, the person making a recovery from an accident, the small business person forced to close down, the farmers coping with land degradation. Almost any time you are presented with statistics on an issue, there's a human story that deserves to be told.

- *Local heroes*: The media are regularly criticised for too easily dividing the world into heroes and villains, and journalists need to avoid the tendency to oversimplify issues and events or stereotype individuals or groups. That said, the elevation of people or things to heroic status can be a way of creating stories, which become both a selling point for the media and a focus for the community. Heroic status can be conferred on almost anyone or anything.

- When bushfires raged across parts of New South Wales at the start of 2002, a large American helicopter nicknamed Elvis was designated the hero of the fight to control them. It helped that the name lent itself to a lot of "Elvis sighting" jokes. The emphasis on the machine may have clouded some of the serious issues the fires raised, but it provided some "feel good" stories at a time when they were needed.

WARNING

Note that it's particularly important to take great care when writing stories of this kind, because there is no shortage of examples of individuals whose high profile and status in one area has been allowed to distract the media from properly scrutinising other areas of their lives, particularly their business or professional activities.

- Individualise. Stories about the big issues—from serious medical problems to the impact of the federal or state budget—are usually more accessible if they are told from the viewpoint of one person or a small group of people. This tendency to individualise issues and events is sometimes criticised by those outside journalism.

They argue it diminishes the scale of stories and overs-implifies issues. The counter argument is that individualising issues, such as poverty, cancer, drug abuse and so on, makes them much easier for audiences to understand.

And far from diminishing the scale of such stories, individualising can give them depth by giving presenting a human face. Homelessness is more than a set of statistics. It is the destruction of individual lives and hopes.

Focusing on an individual gives the audience a chance to see that. Focusing on the individual living with or recovering from serious illness has the potential to offer hope and useful information to others in the same situation.

It can be hard for the audience to empathise with people with whom they rarely come in contact—such as asylum-seekers.

Indeed, one of the easiest ways to ensure lack of a public empathy is to cast a group of people as a faceless mass. In these cases, presenting individual stories to represent the issue serves to cut through political and official rhetoric.

- *Free plugs*: One of the first things a journalist discovers is that there's no shortage of people wanting you to give them or their business free publicity. This is an issue that warrants a good deal of discussion and the way it's handled varies from one organisation to another. Reporters have the power to give people and institutions a free plug.

At its worst this can result in uncritical, promotional pap being passed off as news. But some of the promotional aspects of news can be seen as both fair and socially useful. When a retailer provides a destitute family with new household goods does the promotional element of the story matter as long as the story has its own value as news? Stories about an upandcoming new band or a local festival are the sort of items that are a tonic for viewers, listeners and readers. And they don't have to come across as free PR, as long as they're written with a light touch.

- *The follow-up*: We've said already that news creates more news. That's one of the reasons reporters should be avid consumers of the media—their own and their competitors". Some stories will lend themselves to one or more spin-off pieces. It's important not to simply rip off another reporter's story. Plagiarism is always unacceptable. But developing an existing item into a new one is an everyday event. It's called "doing a follow-up". This can amount to no more than a new version of an existing idea.

For example, if one of the Sydney papers runs a story on a significant increase in the number of young people serving on local councils, reporters in other areas are likely to check to see if the same can be said for their own region.

In other cases, the original story provides a starting point for a new and different item. For example, an item in the Brisbane media on the number of southerners relocating north might prompt an article in the Melbourne media on the long-term effects on Melbourne property prices of people moving interstate. It's also worth monitoring overseas media for issues and trends that might lend themselves to a story on the Australian reaction. For instance, overseas developments in road safety and education have both generated stories about the implications for Australian experience, to cite just two examples.

Tip

- *Keep a file of story ideas*: This should include original ideas as well as stories clipped from newspapers, magazines and the Internet, or other sources, which could be developed in new directions or which are worth following up after a specific period of time. A file such as this is particularly useful on slow news days. But note that if you plan to cover a story on a weekend, particularly Sunday, or a public holiday, or during traditional holiday seasons, you should organise it in advance to make sure interviewees will be available. This is particularly important for television where you need the image of interviewees, not just a voice on a mobile phone.
- If you come across a potential story, never assume that it has already been covered. Check. It's easy for a reporter to lose a story by assuming that another journalist has already written it. But no good idea should be dismissed on these grounds without first checking with the news desk.
- Subscribe to e-mailed news lists, particularly lists of events in your city.

These can be a good source of news about activities worth covering.

- A certain amount of news is cyclical. This includes coverage of the main national and religious observances (including ANZAC and Australia Day, Easter, Christmas, Passover, Ramadan, New Year, Chinese New Year and others). It also includes the changing of the seasons (including the start of the snow and bushfire seasons) as well as the first day of school and so on. In these cases, your story file should include potential new approaches to familiar material.

Case studies—using contacts and ideas to generate stories

- Jane Rocca is a freelance journalist who has written extensively on music and youth issues. Since she relies on her ability to generate her own stories to get commissions, working her contacts and coming up with new ideas are essential."I make sure I maintain contact with publicists who organise upcoming events and generally keep an eye out for story ideas. Look at the opinion pages in the newspaper and see what people are writing about. This can give you a good indication of what editors want. It's about being aware of what's going on in your community." When an anti-drug campaign featured television ads showing body bags as a scare tactic, Jane developed a story on the effectiveness of the ads on their young target audience. It was a simple idea, but it involved a contemporary news issue.
- A young reporter at *The Fraser Coast Chronicle* heard that a friend of her mother's had become upset after the electricity company refused to allow her to pay her power bill using coins. The reporter turned it into a story on what is legal tender. What made the story particular interesting was its implications for all those people, especially those on a budget, who keep piggy banks just so they can pay their bills.
- Freelance journalist and trainer, Jane Cafarella, used a friend's tale about losing veggies from her suburban garden to furry, four-legged raiders for a story idea on rabbit control. And when the store-owner who sold her a piano told her about a French polisher who worked for him, Jane wrote a profile of the craftsman in question. He was 91.
- Out for dinner with a couple of friends? You are never "not a journalist". What are your friends talking about? What are their problems at work? One very experienced reporter who was out for dinner found she had trouble hearing her friends talk. She ended up with a news feature on noise limits and associated problems in city restaurants. Another reporter ended up with a page 1 investigation into conditions in a local mental health facility after listening to a friend describe her working conditions over dinner.

INITIATING STORIES

At News Ltd in Sydney, pitching stories is seen as fundamental to each reporter's daily routine. If they're not walking in the door and greeting the chief of staff with at least one story idea, the day's already a failure. We tell them, if they're sitting at their desk waiting for the chief of staff to give them a story, they're not a reporter, they're a clever clerk. We expect people to come up with ideas constantly and to follow those ideas through.

One metropolitan newsroom tests its trainees" ability to find news using a series of exercises. In one exercise, they are made to head out onto the streets without their mobile phones and come back with a publishable Covering assigned stories—such as this opening of a public garden—is a standard part of many reporters" work story. What do they find?

One reporter doorknocked nearby brothels for her story. Another went no further than a local lingerie shop for a quirky piece on the most popular item of women's underwear (the thong) and another used her skills of observation to pick up signs of domestic life in a nearby commercial building. Investigating further she found young squatters had turned the top floor into a personal arts commune.

Not all newsrooms require reporters to generate so many of their own stories. Certainly there is an expectation that reporters with their own round will come up with original ideas and break news. But general reporters may be expected to spend most of their time following up story ideas given to them by the assignments desk. Newsrooms with smaller staffs—for instance those in non-metropolitan areas—may need all their journalists to both cover a large number of stories assigned by the chief of staff as well as find their own material.

Covering assigned stories inevitably leaves a journalist with less time to dig up their own material, but it's a truism in journalism that any reporter who can pitch good stories to the chief of staff on a regular basis will be given more time to follow their own leads and will spend less time chasing the chief of staff's ideas.

The story with which we began this section came about because the reporter was an approachable person who was prepared to listen to a stranger's suggestion and check it out. Had the reporter been out sailing in Port Phillip Bay rather than having a drink in the pub, he might have noticed the unused seal platform for himself and generated the same story from observation rather than a tip-off. News stories can come about in many different ways, which are covered in the previous section of this book. But once the original idea is formulated, the process towards publication usually follows the sequence outlined below.

- From story idea to publication
- Research (this can include calls to check the story and finding an angle)

- Story idea
- Publication
- Interviews Writing and checking Sub editing
- The news conference

No matter who initiates the story idea, at some point early on in the process, it will need to be discussed by the reporter and the chief of staff or someone else in the editorial process. The reporter, the chief of staff and the editor all need to have an idea of the direction the story will take so that it can be fitted into the daily news hierarchy which determines where it will run in the paper, programme or site.

Chiefs of staff and news editors take this information to the news conference so that the various stories on offer for that day can be weighed up against each other to work out the final shape of the paper or broadcast.

Most large newspaper and television newsrooms hold at least two news conferences each day. At the morning conference, the editorial staff (which may include the editor, foreign editor, chief of staff and so on, depending on the size of the newsroom) discuss the day's potential stories, how they might be approached, who will be reporting them, any potential problems such as legal ones, and what rival news outlets might be doing. They hold another conference in the afternoon, to review what stories they have and work out a more detailed version of where the various news items will appear in the publication or broadcast.

THE STORY BRIEF

If a story is assigned to a reporter by the news desk, the reporter will be briefed on the way they should approach it. The story brief may include instructions on the kind of finished item that is expected—that is a human interest story, or a hard news item.

The reporter may be given suggestions as to the angle to take and who to interview. Working to a brief means a reporter has far less autonomy about how to prepare and write their stories than those outside the news business might imagine.

But for young reporters it can provide a useful guide to the way the finished story should read. Reporters who fail to follow the initial story brief can find themselves criticised by their news editor if their story is subsequently dropped. Journalists who generate their own stories have more control over the direction their work takes than those working on assigned pieces. They usually have the opportunity to decide how to frame their pieces and who to talk to when gathering the information needed to write them.

Chiefs of staff and editors value reporters with a positive attitude towards assignments—that is, reporters who don't try to talk down or reject the stories they're given. That doesn't mean that all assignments are potentially good stories. It means that chiefs of staff and editors know that the publication or programme has to be filled.

So reporters who want to challenge their assignments will find the process easier if they have better ideas of their own to offer. Reporters who try to "kill" stories to which they're assigned will quickly gain a reputation for negativity and laziness. Assigning editors are more likely to accept a change to the story brief if the reporter offers an alternative way of approaching it.

FINDING NEWS STORIES

News stories can be found anywhere. But to turn observations, incidents and information into news, reporters need four skills:

- They need to be able to see the potential for a news story.
- They need to know how to pitch the story to their chief of staff or editor—particularly in large metro newsrooms where there is intense competition for space in the news pages.
- They need to know how to find an angle that will make the story interesting to their particular audience.
- And they need to be able to follow through on their pitch and deliver the story.

To find potential news stories, reporters need to develop a series of habits. First, they need to develop good contacts with people who are, or might become, sources of information. They need also to read, watch, listen to and browse as many media as possible.

That includes the local, metro and national press and broadcast media. It also includes high quality international publications, such as *The Economist,* and the most populist of media, the women's magazines, music press and mass-market magazines.

There's no point in being snobbish about which media to dip into, though a media diet consisting entirely of popular magazines is no grounding for a career in news reporting and it is important to bear in mind the different journalistic standards of accuracy and attribution that apply within different media. Consuming a wide range of media gives a journalist a better understanding of the interests of all sections of the audience.

Reading, viewing and listening widely allow reporters to put the information they use for their stories into a wider context. This is a particular issue for young reporters who inevitably lack life experience. A good general knowledge allows young journalists to add some depth to their reporting.

Journalists on daily news publications and programmes are usually expected to have read two papers, listened to the morning radio news, and watched the previous night's TV news and current affairs programmes in preparation for each day's work. But it's not just these daily news services that are useful to journalists. The specialist media, which cover topics as diverse as computers, health, consumer issues, motoring and so on, are a particularly good source of ideas. They can alert journalists to trends or developments in a particular field that would be of interest to a wider news audience. Advertisements, including the classifieds, are another source of potential news stories.

Second, journalists should be observant. They should notice things going on around them and ask "why?"

Finally, journalists need to talk to people—all sorts of people. They need to be interested in other people and the things that concern them.

The editor of the Queensland regional daily, *The Fraser Coast Chronicle,* Nancy Bates, tells her reporters the best way to be a news gatherer is to avoid mixing with other reporters. She believes journalists can become too caught up in agendas and intrigues that are of limited interest to everyone else.

I find a lot of journalists tend to get a slightly groupie mentality about politicians and VIPs. They just get a little bit lost about what is really important to the person out there and what they are interested in.

Chronicle reporters are advised to get out and mix with the rest of the community and ask what's happening. When the sports reporter plays golf, he comes back with stories. And when reporters go shopping, they listen when other shoppers talk to them in the aisles in the hope of picking up story tips with their groceries.

There's an apocryphal story about a Sydney metropolitan radio news director who told his reporters to take the train to the outer western suburbs every month or so and just listen to what people were talking about to give them a feel for audience concerns.

True or not, it's a reminder that journalists need to be aware of those issues that are important to their readers, listeners or viewers. Journalists also need to know how to frame issues so that audiences can best understand them.

TTIP A successful reporter:

- Is a "media junkie" (and watches, listens to and reads as much as possible).
- Is observant and curious and asks "why?".
- Is interested in people and their concerns.

DEVELOPING CONTACTS

There are a few core skills in journalism. One of them is being able to spot a story and develop an angle. Another is writing.

And developing and keeping good contacts or sources is another. Contacts are more important than writing ability and there are examples of reporters with a mediocre writing style becoming valued and highly paid members of a newsroom on the basis of their contacts and therefore their ability to dig out information.

After all, someone else can always polish the story. But without good information to start with, there's no story to polish. Journalist Ingrid Svendsen describes the idea that journalism is primarily about writing as "the most common misconception" about the profession.

It's not about writing, it's about people skills and researching and finding out stuff and having the curiosity to wonder why things are as they are and having the ability to find out why a certain thing is happening. It's about contacts and knowing what is really going on and not just the official version of what's going on. (Interview with Ingrid Svendsen.)

Developing contacts probably sounds more complex than it really is. A contact is simply someone who can provide information and *anyone* can be a contact.

One of the misconceptions about contacts is that they have to be highly placed people. In fact, the opposite is often true. People in high places may hold many secrets. But they're unlikely to divulge them. And if they do, there are often strings attached which may not suit the journalist. But ordinary people often have a story to tell or have access to information and may be far more prepared to share it.

To look at just one example of this in practice, let's go back to 1978 and the aftermath of "the dismissal" of 1975, in which then governor-general Sir John Kerr sacked the Labour government of Gough Whitlam and installed Liberal leader Malcolm Fraser as prime minister. Nearly three years later, Sir John Kerr was living in Britain and would be a prize interview for any reporter able to find him.

The journalist who did manage to locate Sir John was Network 7 political correspondent, Mike Peterson, who was in Britain as one of the media contingent with then prime minister Malcolm Fraser for the Commonwealth Heads of Government conference. Peterson won a Walkley Award for his news story on Sir John and Lady Kerr at their Surrey home. He found them, where others had failed, because, as fellow Walkley winner John Hurst wrote later, he "had always believed that ordinary people—doormen, drivers, lift attendants and the like—were good sources of information if approached in the right way". Peterson asked a driver outside the official pool to put out feelers to see if any other drivers had an address for Sir John. It worked.

Journalists need to become accustomed to viewing everyone as a potential source of information and filing their contact details. You never know when they might come in handy. For example, a reporter at a suburban newspaper met a local American couple at a social function one evening in 2001. Nothing unusual there.

But it was a week before September 11. In the aftermath of the attacks on New York and Washington, the paper wanted to know how American members of its community were feeling. The couple the reporter had met socially were the first ones she turned to. The process of building contacts can be difficult for a reporter new to the job. Where do you start? Brett Foley, a journalist at

The Australian Financial Review, suggests keeping a notebook by the phone and writing down the name and number of everyone you speak to for every story then regularly entering the details in a hard-copy contact book or a contact file in a computer programme, preferably one with a search function. He says when you're a very junior reporter you're not "establishing a network of deep throats".

What's important is just to keep track of everybody you speak to. You might not pick a particular person as a contact because you might be on a story which is about something which doesn't seem very consequential ... But it always happens that not very far down the track, especially if you're covering general news, something will come up in their field and keeping track of those things allows you to show a bit of initiative and say you know someone. It's always handy to know the widest number of people in the widest number of capacities for you to draw on.

Ingrid Svendsen of *The Melbourne Times* says if you're new to a round, find out who's who. It's a matter of finding out who are the influential lobby groups in that area and getting in sweet with them because they know everything. They're doing submissions to government on various subjects, they're meeting with bureaucrats on the issues they're lobbying on.

They're very clued in. So they'll be able to tell you what's going on. If you're new to a town, it's a similar process. It's figuring out who's who.

Who's pushing the decision-makers in the town and who are the decision-makers—and cultivating them. In any sphere there are always decision-makers and lobbyists. It's a case of figuring out who they are and reaching them. Richard Baker suggests a reporter starting a new round should go through articles written by the last reporter on the round and note the names of people interviewed.

There will also be certain people a reporter will have to deal with while covering a round. For example, state rounds reporters have to deal with press secretaries. Richard suggests calling anyone who's likely to become a regular contact, introduce yourself, perhaps meet over a coffee and ask about the issues and events worth looking out for.

Regular contacts will often tell a reporter about things that are not yet ready to be written about but are worth keeping an eye on. A reporter might call a regular source every fortnight or so simply to check what's happening. It's important not to hassle contacts unnecessarily but to build a good working relationship.

Journalists find that people they meet casually often want to share some piece of information they reckon would make a good story. Sometimes they're wrong and the "story" is no more than a rumour unworthy of serious attention. At other times—as with the bloke in the pub and Richard Baker—they're right.

Building contacts is a circular process. Once you know someone inside an organisation or department or field, they can help to point you to other people in the same area. And once a reporter becomes known for their work, they can expect to have potential contacts approach *them.* A reporter's friends may become sources, but it's unwise to treat sources as friends. That's because the relationship between reporters and their sources is a professional one, based on mutual interest. The reporter needs stories and information. The source wants to see stories and information used in the media. But not everything a source wants to see published or broadcast will be judged newsworthy by the journalist. And journalists can't simply take a source's version of a story at face value. They need to take in other, often rival, angles and opinions. So reporters need to maintain their access to the source without winding up in their pocket.

Ingrid Svendsen believes it's important to treat sources with integrity and to "set out the ground rules clearly at the start". The problem with making contacts is that people often feel the need to display loyalty to those contacts at all costs. And it's a balancing act between treating your contacts well and treating them with integrity and faithfully reporting what they've told you and at the same time ensuring the public's right to have the full story. Your first sense of responsibility is to your readers, not your contacts. I've had to "burn" contacts and it's really unpleasant when you have to do it. But sometimes you have to because the issue is so important that you have to tell it as it is, even if that entails "burning" a contact. But Ingrid also says the potential for damaging relations with a contact can be minimised if they are given the chance to understand how journalists work. "Most contacts will understand that your job is to tell the full story and that their views will be fairly and accurately represented but they might not be the sole focus of the story. The story might have other angles."

ROUTINE CONTACTS

Some news sources are routine contacts for newsrooms. The most obvious of these are the emergency services-the police, ambulance and fire brigade. A reporter rostered to the first shift of the morning will usually ring the local branch of each of these to find out what has happened overnight. Some newsrooms, especially radio with its rapid turnaround of stories, will call later in the day as well.

Keep a contacts book (or electronic organiser). List the name of every person with whom you come in contact who might be useful as a source. Collect their work, home and mobile numbers plus their e-mail details. Addresses are useful, too (for those days when your source isn't answering the phone).

WORKING WITH INFORMATION FROM SOURCES

A story can begin with information from a single source, but it's rare that it can proceed on that alone. Stories need to be given depth with confirmation from other sources and with a range of comment from different sides of an issue or argument. It can be far too easy for young reporters to place too much faith in individual sources, without considering why a person is giving them information or without putting information into a wider context. Editor of The Courier, Stuart Howie, says he tries to instill in his largely young reporting staff the point that every story has more than one dimension. He says that sometimes even experienced reporters will talk to one person for a story and wrongly think that's the story.

It's never the story talking to one person. It's one person's viewpoint. People will only ever tell you something for their own benefit. And they will only ever tell you something from their own point of view, which is just human nature.

Stuart's advice to reporters is to get lots of points of view and work out each source's motives for their information or comment. "If you're going out on a story, talk to lots of people. The more you explore and investigate, the better the story and the more thorough your research will be and that will be reflected in what you write."

Tip

One of the skills every reporter needs is, for want of a better term, a "crap detector". Much of what they are told will come coloured by the source's self interest. Reporters must be able to tell when someone is spinning them a line and report in as balanced a manner as possible.

Information supplied by the representative of an organisation is often considered more reliable than that supplied by an individual alone. But anyone can set up an organisation and sometimes organisations are no more than a front for one person or a handful of people. When dealing with information and comment from organisations, especially little known ones, reporters are advised to check the size and scope of their membership and for whom they actually speak. This can be done by speaking to other groups in the same field, though it's important to take into account that any opinion from other groups might be tainted by rivalry.

This need for caution applies to written and online sources as much as to personal informants. Journalists need to weigh up the veracity of every piece of information they work with. For example, the newspaper files or story archives that are a routine source of background information can include errors that will be perpetuated unless the information is reassessed and checked before reuse.

GETTING PEOPLE TO TALK

Not everyone a journalist wants to talk to wants to talk to them. People often need to be encouraged to share what they know. They may also need to be reassured about the way in which their information will be treated.

Encouraging people to talk is one of the skills journalists need to develop. Ingrid Svendsen says even people who are seemingly unwilling to grant an interview or provide information are often prepared to speak, providing they are given the right reasons.

Most people are desperate to tell you stuff. It's basic human nature. People can't keep a secret. Everyone wants to tell what they know. It makes them feel like they're really informed and influential. So really it's just a matter of giving them a good reason to. It's a matter of appealing to whatever it is that's going to press their buttons and make them want to tell you. Perhaps by raising this issue they can assist other people who are in a similar situation to them, or their organisation might get funding as a result of it. Or it might just make them look good and raise their profile. There's always a reason for people to want to talk.

Ingrid says it surprises her how free people are with information. But she also says good sources of information are often overlooked, and one of the features of journalism that concerns her is that often "people who are in the know are never asked".

In any story involving a dispute, the people or organisations involved should be given the opportunity to present their sides of the story. In these cases, reporters usually phrase their request for an interview in these terms—that is, "We'd like to present your side of the story." It would be churlish to pretend that this is not a form of pressure on people to cooperate.

On the other hand, not giving people on different sides of a dispute the chance to have their say produces one-sided reports. There are at least two sides to most stories and there are frequently more than two. Good journalism involves reporting as many different points of view as possible.

Some people will refuse to be interviewed no matter how the journalist phrases the request. They may have good reasons for not wanting to talk. In some of these cases the reporter simply has to find an alternative interviewee. In other cases the refusal is more problematic. The person sought may be particularly important to the story, either for the information they can provide or because their opinion is necessary to ensure the story is balanced. If they can't be persuaded, it's customary to include within the story the fact that an interview was sought, using words such as "Mr X refused to speak to ..." or "The minister was offered the chance to comment but declined."

Alternatively, the questions can be used in the story, even if there are no answers: "If Mr X had agreed to speak to us, this is what we would have asked ..." But a reporter who uses this technique needs to ensure that the questions do not contain any defamatory insinuations.

THE DENIAL

One of the difficult circumstances in which journalists have to seek out additional comment is when they have to put an allegation to a person about whom the allegation has been made. Many stories begin with a claim which must be throughly checked out before the story can be written. An allegation can be made by one side of a dispute or it can come from a disinterested party—that is, someone with information they believe should be put before the public but with nothing personal to gain from the outcome.

For example, a whistleblower might accuse a company of dumping toxic waste. Before putting the accusation at the nub of the story to the person or organisation about whom it is being made, the reporter needs to marshal as many of the details as possible.

One reason is to see if the story is worth pursuing. Another is to have a solid foundation for the questions that the reporter will have to ask the subject of the accusation(s). Eventually the reporter must call or confront the subject for their response.

What if they deny it? Denial is hardly uncommon. But it doesn't necessarily mean that the story is wrong. Indeed, sometimes a denial simply makes a story better. Perhaps the most famous denial of an allegation in recent times is former US president Bill Clinton's insistence that he had not had "sexual relations with that woman". Did the denial kill the story? One reason it did not was that among the media, among many politicians on Capitol Hill (both Republican and Democrat) and among the US public, the denial was not considered credible. On the other hand, the media have been accused of pursuing some stories to the point of zealousness, despite a denial which was subsequently found to be correct.

If one of the parties to a potential story denies that it is true, the reporter (and their chief of staff or editor) has a series of options:

- If the balance of evidence suggests the story cannot be substantiated, it should be dropped.
- If the journalist remains convinced the story is true but does not yet have enough evidence to substantiate it, it may be worth additional research to try to verify it.
- Finally, if the journalist (and their chief of staff or editor) already have enough evidence to substantiate the story, despite the denial, then the denial becomes part of the report. Lines such as "Mr X has denied the claim" are a routine way of covering this, as are "Mr X was unavailable for comment" or "Ms Y refused to comment". In such cases the issue of defamation is an obvious concern and the journalist needs to be sure of their facts and of their ability to defend them.

It's important to remember that someone denying a story does not make it untrue any more than someone telling you a story makes it true. Each option has to be treated on its merits, bearing in mind the other available evidence, and each circumstance has to be treated with care.

On the Record/off the Record

Journalists deal with information from their sources on three basic levels:

- On the record.
- Background.
- Off the record.

A problem for journalists and sources alike is that these terms have no legal or even fixed definition. In his book, *The Journalist's Guide to Media Law,* journalism academic and lawyer Mark Pearson says that "part of the problem is that Australian journalists have no accepted system for ranking information according to its level of confidentiality, no way of defining what expressions like "off the record" or "background only" really mean".

Of the three terms above, the first is unambiguous. If someone speaks to a journalist "on the record", it means the reporter can use the information in full and attribute it to the source.

There's less consensus about the other two. Some of the common understandings of the terms are that:

- If someone speaks to a journalist on "background" it means the reporter can use the information but cannot attribute it to the source.
- If someone speaks "off the record", it means the journalist may not use the information (and by implication they can't name the source). Some reporters take the view that if they obtain information "off the record" they can't use it at all, even if someone else subsequently gives them the same material "on the record". Others take the contrary view—that is, that they can use the information if they subsequently hear it from someone else. Journalists who take the first view often won't allow a source to tell them something "off the record", because it would prevent them from using the material if they heard it again later.

Part of the difficulty with the term "off the record" is that it is used differently by people with different levels of experience with the media. To media novices it may mean that they can speak privately, without what they say being used. But to media-savvy operators, including government officials and their minders, "off the record" can be a way of giving a reporter information that the source wants to see used, as long as they can distance themselves from it. Offering reporters information as "background" is another common ploy of politicians, who use it to try out proposed policies or positions to see how the public will react while maintaining enough "wriggle room" to bail out if the reaction is adverse.

PROTECTING SOURCES

Reporters walk a fine line between trying to get information out of people and maintaining their trust. In some cases, the source will be taking a risk, either legally, professionally or personally, by giving a reporter information. In these cases, clarifying the way in which the information is to be reported is particularly important, both to protect the source and because the reporter might want to draw on that person in the future. Brett Foley regards clarifying the issue of whether information can be used "on" or "off the record" as very important.

A lot of the time you're dealing with people where that understanding is tacit anyway. They're very media savvy and they're aware of what they're able to say without getting themselves into trouble.

Increasingly you deal with people who say "XYZ-but you didn't hear it from me", or who go so far as to say, "You could phrase it this way to keep me out of it." You'll also come across people who aren't as savvy with the media.

You'll ask, "Can we say this on the record?" and the person might have to think about it and will say, "I guess I could get myself into trouble." In those cases you'll tell them, "There are ways we can get around that." You can phrase it a particular way or it could be not attributed and so on. But you'd also want to check that information and corroborate it before committing it to print.

Ingrid Svendsen believes that the need to exercise some care with sources who are inexperienced in dealing with the media is even more important for reporters working outside the metro dailies.

I don't think there's anything to be gained by abusing people's trust and I don't think there's anything wrong with explaining to people how the system works.

Most people don't deal with journalists every day of the week. So you ask them, "Do you want your name used? Do you want us to identify you and your agency? If you don't then do you prefer us to say "a social worker working in the drugs field?", What form of words makes you most comfortable?" If I know they're inexperienced I try to explain to them quite fully beforehand what it all means. Wherever possible, journalists are advised to obtain information "on the record". This recommendation is enshrined in the Journalists" Code of Ethics, clause 3, which urges journalists to "attribute information to its source" wherever possible and to consider "the source's motives" before agreeing to use information supplied anonymously. Information is always more credible if it can be traced to its source. If someone offers you information as "background" or "off the record", you need to ask yourself why they are not prepared to attach their name to it.

That said, a journalist who agrees to accept information on a not-forattribution basis is bound to protect the source of that information. Clause 3 of the Journalists" Code of Ethics ends: "Where confidences are accepted, respect them in all circumstances." On rare occasions, journalists have been ordered by a court or enquiry to give up the names of confidential sources and have gone to jail or suffered other sanctions rather than do so.

Tip

Remember that many people are unaccustomed to dealing with the media and don't know the ground rules so you may need to explain these to them. This is particularly important for reporters working for local media where the relationship between media outlets and their audience is different from that in large metropolitan areas.

WORKING WITH CHILDREN

Journalists need to exercise special care when reporting on or seeking information from children. Children are often the subject of lighthearted stories where parents or guardians are present and able to give consent (*e.g.* stories of children at shows or similar events). In other circumstances the ethical issues can be less clear cut. The 1999 Journalists" Code of Ethics does not specifically refer to children. But the in-house guidelines of some media outlets do.

For Instance, the Age Code of Conduct Specifies

- Special care should be taken when dealing with children (under the age of 16). The editor must be informed when children have been photographed or interviewed without parental consent.

The Professional Conduct Policy at News Ltd cautions journalists not to interview or photograph children under 16 in regard to their welfare or their parents or siblings unless a parent or guardian is present and has given consent.

In addition, it says:

- Extreme care should be taken that children are not prompted in interviews, or offered inducements to cooperate.
- The News Ltd policy also instructs its journalists not to "approach children in schools" without the school's consent.
- The law requires that children involved in court cases not be identified.

GENERAL TIPS FOR ROUNDS

There was a time when being given your first round (*i.e.* a specific area such as courts, politics, police) to cover was a sign that you had left the incubation crib of journalism and were moving into the world of being a seasoned reporter. Nowadays, not only is it common to be given a round very shortly after arriving in a newsroom, it is equally common to have more than one round, or to be moved frequently from one round to another.

Being a good roundsperson of course requires the same skills as being a good general reporter with the added requirement of being expected to generate more stories. Because of the general pace of newsrooms today and cutbacks in staffing levels, specific preparation or training for rounds is rare. At best, in many newsrooms, the preparation may consist of being given some advice on contacts from the departing reporter and, if you are lucky, a brief introduction to some key people on the round. Other than that, good rounds reporters have to fall back on the two important qualities any journalist needs: initiative and the ability to build good contacts.

Rounds journalists are likely to spend longer with contacts than general reporters, and build up deeper relationships, which of course can create problems indrawing boundary lines between personal and professional relationships.

The journalist covering rounds needs to be vigilant about whether information being given by contacts can be used and attributed to them. For instance, police round journalists are often given background information that should not be used. Such background information, especially when based on mere speculation or opinion, can be a dangerous influence.

This chapter will look at some of the key rounds of police or emergency services, courts, local and state government, health and sport.

POLICE ROUNDS AND EMERGENCY SERVICES

Reporting emergency services, that is, covering the police, fire and ambulance services, is the bread and butter of many newspapers.

This round may conjure up images of car chases, drug raids and scoops about major crime figures but covering this round involves the same mundane routines as reporting on other areas.

The nature of police rounds varies a great deal depending upon the news organisation and the audience they are targeting. For example, tabloid and broadsheet newspapers will want different things from these rounds. Tabloids may place more emphasis on the bizarre aspects of violent crime than the more conservative broadsheet newspapers, which may be more interested in processes, structures and other organisational issues.

If you scan the pages of your local suburban or regional paper, you will be able to gauge where police reporting fits into each organisation's news priorities. Break-ins, robberies, vandalism and assaults are all the mainstays of the police round in this context.

In metropolitan areas, police are likely to hold a daily conference where they brief reporters on any newsworthy occurrences.

Regional and country journalists can use the Internet to quickly check any breaking stories with central media liaison to see if there is any relevance for their local areas. All state and federal agencies have web sites with useful background information as well as contact details for specific follow-ups.

Coverage of courts and police rounds can often reflect the wider culture within a news organisation as well as that of its audience. As we noted earlier, suburban and regional organisations are often more sensitive to immediate community reactions than bigger news organisations.

This may affect things like:

- The size of headlines and language used in reports.
- The use of photographs—for example, publication of a car accident scene where a local person has died—will have major impact in a smaller community.
- The amount of detail or explicit descriptions included in copy.

Roundspeople should always ensure they are aware of any internal style or taste guidelines on issues such as these.

Adam Pearce covers police rounds for a regional newspaper. He also covers sports and general stories. Adam checks "in person" with his contacts twice each day and while some of that time is spent going through the "daybook" with the sergeant, he also spends time wandering around the station just talking with officers in different sections. Just chatting with people is never wasted time for the roundsperson or any journalist.

Adam advises reporters on police rounds to keep their "ears open, especially at the scene of incidents". For example, on one occasion, he was covering a house fire and while chatting to people at the scene, he discovered a number of emergency calls had been made before there was a response.

By following up on-the-scene gossip, he got a major story on how the local emergency response system had failed. Nina Lees has worked on newspapers in Tasmania and Victoria and is an experienced police and court reporter. She says it takes time and effort to build relationships with contacts in the field, and that a reporter has to work to build a reputation as someone who's trustworthy and efficient. Police work within a particularly strong and complex subculture and a journalist needs to appreciate this.

When it comes to building contacts, Nina suggests asking other people in the office about local personalities and finding out all you can about the sources you are going to be dealing with. She also notes that it's important to show that you value your contacts.

Getting to know the police takes a lot of work and you need to be prepared to give them a lot of attention and visit the station every day just so you are a face there. It helps them feel comfortable with you. Talk to as many officers as you can. It doesn't always have to be about work, but at the same time they must know that that is the main reason you are there. Still, keep the visits friendly and professional.

But Nina also believes that is as far as a professional relationship should go. Early on in her career, Nina made a personal decision not to socialise with contacts at all and she says if you're covering police rounds, "don't date a police officer", because you could lose your credibility.

Both Adam and Nina believe it's important for reporters to develop a wide range of sources "around the round". That gives them alternative sources of information. For instance, Adam finds union sources useful in his work.

GENERAL WRITING TECHNIQUES FOR COVERING POLICE ROUNDS OR EMERGENCY SERVICES:

- Because of the very nature of emergency stories, there will always be two key things that you will want to know and they should always be the first things to be included in your intro.
  They are:
  - *Threat to life*: Have any people been killed or injured? Was there any real threat to life? Did people have a narrow escape?
  - *Damage to property*: How much, and can anyone put a specific value on it?
  - Do note that your concerns should always be in that order. You would never write the following intro:
  - A truck crash on the Newcity Highway yesterday led to the loss of a load of grain worth $50,000.

The 40-year-old driver was killed in the accident.

Obviously the loss of human life in this story would come before the damage to property.

- *Look for the unique angle*: That is, what is unusual about the fire or the accident. For example, non-fatal fires in buildings occur every day but if the fire was caused by a pet, a faulty appliance or a cigarette and so on, that would probably be the angle. A quick check of the back files or with more experienced colleagues in the office might reveal that a fire was the second at a particular location in a year, or that an accident happened on a notorious stretch of road and so on.
- *Remember to be specific*: In covering these rounds, it should never be a case of "many people" were hurt or there was "some" damage. Even if you can't get a specific, confirmed figure before your deadline, get as near as you can.
- *Use any drama high up in the copy*: Any acts of heroism, rescue attempts or eyewitness accounts should be included in the first three or four paragraphs.
- Avoid clichés such as "a fair cop", "the long arm of the law", "mercy dash", "rampage", "streets of fear", "tragedy struck", "trouble flared".
- Know the jargon ("multiple offenders forced entry at the rear of the premises") but avoid it in your copy.

WARNING

Covering this round you must be careful to check on the difference between speculation and fact. It is a constant danger, especially if you are close to contacts, to take material as verified. Never become dependent upon one source for your information.

- Just because you get information from a police officer, don't take it as fact.

- Take great care to avoid attributing blame. A story may *sound* all right, but think carefully about whether it in any way attributes blame to anyone.
- Be careful not to sensationalise.
- *Be legally alert*: The journalist covering police rounds must always be wary. Once someone has been charged with an offence, the reporter is very limited in what they can report. Once a charge has been laid, a criminal case is deemed to be "pending" or *sub judice*(literally, "before the judge") and a reporter publishing material which could affect a person's right to a fair trial (such as a suggestion that the accused has already confessed) could be found guilty of contempt of court. All journalists have to be very careful of publishing background material about the events or circumstances which led to an arrest.

SIEGES AND DEATHKNOCKS

There are two situations that are specific to covering emergency rounds and both involve situations of high drama and stress.

These are sieges and deathknocks. Both place immense pressure on the emergency services and journalists must recognise the crucial role they also play.

Some of the risks that journalists run into when covering sieges include:

- The risk of glorifying offenders.
- The danger of inspiring "copy cats".
- The risk of hindering police work by tying up phone lines, divulging details of police operations, or interviewing offenders.
- The risk of distressing relatives of those involved.
- The danger of prejudicing subsequent court proceedings.

In order to avoid these risks, reporters need to:

- Know their legal rights and responsibilities—that is, what you can and cannot publish.
- Rely on good contacts you can trust.
- Know the policies of your employing organisation.

"Deathknocks" or "intrudes", as they are sometimes called, are professional jargon for interviews with the relatives of someone who has recently died or been killed in newsworthy circumstances.

Justifications given for doing these interviews include:

- They help to maintain the public's interest in the story.
- The public's right to know if there is a public safety issue related to the story.
- The story may help to mobilise public awareness or support.
- Telling the public about the incident may act as a form of grief therapy for the family.

Those who object say it is an unnecessary intrusion into people's grieving. However, journalists do have to accept that much of their work is covering the events of life that others don't want to think about. This does not mean journalists are not aware of the problems associated with this kind of interview. These are often the assignments most feared by young reporters.

Some have refused to carry out such interviews on ethical grounds. Others have pretended to carry out the interview when actually they never got out of their car. Many journalists are just plain fearful of a violent reaction from distraught relatives.

But some relatives can also be quite willing to talk. In some cases, they feel a story will offer public recognition of their loved one. Others may want to warn the public about the circumstances in which the person died.

The Journalists" Code of Ethics gives journalists the right to refuse to conduct deathknocks. Clause 11 says:Respect private grief and personal privacy. Journalists have the right to resist compulsion to intrude.

Many individual news outlets also have their own ethical codes, which cover such issues.In addition to these professional guidelines, every journalist asked to conduct a "deathknock" will also consider:

- What any rival media outlets might be doing?
- Who is your audience and what are their expectations?
- What does your editor/management expect?
- What is your own ethical position?

The first three of these points may seem unfeeling, but they are part of the reality of covering news. If you do conduct a deathknock interview, there is one thing you should always take with you and that is your own humanity. Deathknocks don't have to be done in an uncaring and intrusive way. Journalists don't and shouldn't leave compassion at the door.

Stuart Howie, editor of the Victorian regional daily, *The Courier,* says his paper only conducts a deathknock when it is considered appropriate and if the public interest merits the story.

He says covering these types of stories is different for a regional paper than for a metropolitan one, because, when someone in the community dies, it is usually someone they know. Stuart says his staff are encouraged to take a "step back" from the immediate family and look for other ways of getting the information or pictures.

For example, if a young person has died in tragic circumstances, it may be less stressful all round to approach their school for information and pictures, rather than the immediate family. This same policy also suggests that journalists should always try to use an intermediary to contact the relatives. Stuart suggests funeral directors can be a good link to those intermediaries.

Remember:

- Take your humanity with you.

- Check that the people know why you are there.
- Be honest.
- Identify yourself and your purpose.
- Don't say "I know how you feel" or ask "How does it feel?"
- Keep the interview equipment to a minimum and out of sight.
- Start with simple questions.
- Remember that many people do want some form of tribute for their loved one.

Checklists for Covering Emergency Stories

Below are some useful checklists for the standard emergency services story. In each case you should always check first whether anyone has been killed or injured.

Fires (remember no "blazing infernos" please):

- Check the extent of property loss.
- What rescue operations were/are involved? Was any special equipment used?
- Were there any evacuations?
- Check the cause of the fire, if known.
- Check the number of personnel, units or volunteers involved.

Accidents (remember you must not attribute blame in the initial report—that is likely to be the subject of an enquiry.):

- Check the location and time of the accident.
- Check the vehicles involved.
- Check cause, if known, from an official source.
- Check names of the dead or injured and whether these have been released (*i.e.* have the relatives been notified?)
- Check where any injured have been taken and find out their latest condition.
- Ask the extent of injuries, if known.
- Were there any rescue attempts or any heroic acts?
- Check if there were unusual weather or road conditions.
- Get any eyewitness accounts.

Crime stories:

- Check victims" names and addresses. Usually these details will not be released until relatives have been informed. Check. Don't release such details until police have informed relatives.
- Check the time and location of the crime.
- Were any weapons used?
- Check whether any goods were stolen or damaged and, if applicable, get the total value.
- Check how entry to the premises was made.

- Check circumstances of discovery. For example, who found the body?
- Get police comments.
- Get comments from neighbours, friends or victims if possible.
- Check any unusual circumstances.

COVERING COURTS

It should go without saying that court reporters require a sound basic knowledge of the law. They also need to be aware of any specific state legislation that changes the way they can report in different jurisdictions.

The Australian legal system consists of both state and federal courts. There are different tiers of court, depending on the nature, importance or severity of the case. Court reporters spend most of their time covering criminal cases in state courts, specifically:

- The Magistrates Court (also known as Local Courts or Court of Petty Sessions).
- The District (or County) court.
- The Supreme Court.

At federal level you will find the Federal Court, Family Court and the High Court.

More than any other single area of reporting, court stories are likely to have a negative impact on the people involved who will be exposed to public scrutiny regardless of the eventual outcome of their case. The issues this raises demand particular thought and care on the part of reporters.

Many journalists, particularly in regional areas, have had experience of individuals (or their families) pleading that their court appearances not be covered.

Different news organisations handle this in different ways and these can include a policy that all court stories are covered or that none are or that certain types of stories are covered and not others.

Some papers have a policy that the names and addresses of people appearing in court should not be published. The sensitivities of reporting courts have also led some news outlets to adopt policies such as dropping honorifics like "Mr" for people found guilty. Reporters need to be aware of their own organisation's guidelines.

The sensitivities of reporting courts in a small community can have repercussions for reporters themselves, and Nina Lees, who covers courts in a regional area, suggests regional court reporters should have unlisted numbers and protect the details of their home addresses. She also cautions against talking about court stories in public.

Court reports must be fair, balanced and accurate. Reporting courts requires even greater attention to detail than in other reporting. The elements that need to be included in a court report of a criminal matter include:

The full name, occupation, age and address of a person charged with an offence—except in those cases where identification is not permitted. (These details are necessary to avoid confusion between the accused and anyone else with a similar name.)

- The nature of the accused's plea—either guilty or not guilty. Note that this is so sensitive that you should check and recheck that it appears correctly in the copy.
- Full details of the charge.

It is obviously important to check the name of the magistrate or judge in a case, and of any lawyers or witnesses involved. Court reporter Nina Lees suggests going back to the Clerk of the Court to check basic details such as the accused's name and other details before writing a report.

Testimony quoted from a court case needs to be reproduced faithfully. Even small changes in the words used can change the meaning of what was said and have unwanted repercussions.

Nina advises writing down everything you hear in court, but only expect to use a fraction of it. Leave out anything you are not 100 per cent certain of, unless it is vital to the report, in which case check it until you are certain.

The terminology that applies to some cases also needs to be used accurately.

For instance:

- Committal hearings are held to decide whether there is enough evidence to send an accused person to trial. They are preliminary hearings, not trials.
- At the conclusion of a committal hearing, the accused is either discharged (not "acquitted") or committed for trial (not "found guilty").
- Reporters also need to ensure they accurately report a convicted person's sentence. If several offences have been dealt with, the accused may be ordered to serve concurrent or cumulative sentences. Concurrent means that the sentences will be served at the same time; cumulative means they will follow one after the other. If the time the convicted person spends in jail may be shortened by parole, this will affect the way the report should be phrased.

Generally, anything said in an open court is protected by privilege and may be reported. But some things cannot be published:

- An accused person's previous criminal history cannot be reported until a trial is over.
- Evidence must not be published until it is presented in open court.
- An accused person's confession must not be reported until read out in open court.
- Information given to a court in the absence of the jury must not be published.

- Any material which the judge has ordered suppressed must not be published.
- The victims in sexual assault cases may not be identified.
- Children charged with offences or otherwise involved in court cases may not be identified, but note that the age at which someone ceases to be a child varies between states and territories. Reporters need to check this in their own area.
- Parties or witnesses to cases in the Family Court may not be identified.
- If the identity of the accused could be an issue in a case then you should not publish the image of the accused (and this includes photographs, video and also drawings).

Like other rounds reporters, those covering courts need to develop specific contacts—including clerks of courts, judges and their associates, barristers and solicitors, police prosecutors and police officers. That said, court reporters need to take care not to uncritically accept information offered by their contacts, especially police contacts.

Court reporting involves respecting court etiquette. This includes dressing in a businesslike manner and bowing or nodding at the judge or magistrate when entering or leaving the court.

It goes without saying that you should turn off your mobile phone before entering the court and that you should not check mobile phone messages or chew gum in court.

Some courts now allow reporters to use recording devices—but only to ensure accuracy, not for broadcast. Check with the judge's associate or court information officer.

GENERAL COURT REPORTING AND WRITING TIPS

- Remember to make connections on both police and court rounds. If there are 10 assault cases of a particular type on one day, find out why.
- Look for the "around-the-system" type stories—for example, the appointment of a new person to deal with indigenous issues could provide a good story. Alternatively, if there have been a number of similar cases then that might warrant a background feature. One reporter found one such story in detailing the problems of the slow processing of domestic violence cases.

WARNING

Stay away from any colourful language. Write it straight. In particular there is no room for descriptions like "the guilty looking man fidgeted in the dock".

Defamation

While contempt of court is a particular concern for police and court reporters, all journalists need to know what constitutes defamation and the defences available.

The generally accepted definition of a defamatory statement is that it causes a person or institution to be:

- Exposed to hatred, contempt or ridicule.
- Lowered in the estimation of right-thinking people.
- Avoided or shunned by their peers.
- Stated or implied to be unfit, unqualified or incompetent for their professions.

The defences to defamation are:

- That the report is true. In Victoria, South Australia, Western

Australia and the Northern Territory, truth alone is a defence. In New South Wales you need to prove truth and public interest. In Queensland, Tasmania and the Australian Capital Territory, you need to prove truth and that its publication was for the public benefit.

- That the report is protected by qualified privilege. This defence applies to accurate and fair reports of the proceedings of parliaments and documents published with parliamentary authority, court proceedings, judicial enquiries such as Royal Commissions and, in some states or territories, council meetings and some other forums.
- *Fair comment*: This allows reviews of films, televisions and plays and sporting events provided these are fair and based on facts which are either well known or set out in the report.

Two excellent guides to media law are listed at the end of this section.

COVERING COUNCILS/LOCAL GOVERNMENT

Councils may be the lowest tier of government but they do deal with issues of major concern to many people and their activities are a staple of reporting for local papers. The proceedings of open council meetings can be reported and, in some states, qualified privilege applies to reports of these meetings. Journalists need to check the rules applying in their own area.

Council rounds reporters need:

- A working knowledge of the state or territory's Local Government Act.
- To know which departments look after specific functions.
- To know how to read a council report (but don't reproduce the jargon).
- To cultivate contacts among council officers.

TIPS FROM A REPORTER

Mary Papadakis covered local government for *The Geelong Advertiser* for several years. She concedes that "council is not traditionally seen as an exciting or "sexy" round like police rounds". But, she says, it can be. The most distinctive feature in this round is the fact that, at one time or another, council decisions will affect everybody living in the municipality. This makes the council round very newsworthy.

The contacts you use on the council round are very diverse. Contacts could include local pressure groups and other interest groups, local real estate agents, the local chamber of commerce, progress associations and resident action groups as well as sports associations and clubs like Rotary.

Depending on the story, contacts can be made simply, for example, by door-knocking residents living near the site of a proposed controversial development, or through ratepayer action groups. Council officers and councillors are always good sources. But Mary warns that it can be difficult on this round to access information other than through official channels because many councils now employ professional public relations and media teams.

Mary's survival tips for the council rounds are:

- Don't be afraid to ask questions.
- Always ask for copies of reports referred to by councillors in or out of meetings.
- Keep in regular contact with councillors, council officers and council media departments.
- Read up on ongoing issues before attending a council meeting.
- Familiarise yourself with the formalities of council meetings.
- Don't take things on face value or regurgitate the information provided in meeting agendas.
- Do your research and always look for a better story.

Mary also warns that young reporters need to work hard to turn what are essentially informative stories into stories that are interesting or entertaining. She says it can also be difficult to keep abreast of all council meetings and outcomes and be aware of a wide-range of issues including those of an environmental, social, political or economic nature.

Council stories should essentially be treated like any other story, always look for an interesting angle and make sure you are short, sharp and to the point. There is a formula to a degree in the sense of discussing motions and amendments, who voted for what and whether a decision provides scope for public comment.

The trick with council stories is also to look for a human-interest element and expand your story. Take time out to consider how a council proposal or decision will affect ratepayers, particularly their hip-pocket.

Health rounds

Anyone consuming some sections of our media could be forgiven for thinking that there is a major breakthrough or a new miracle cure every day and herein lies the first two lessons for covering the health round:

- Be sceptical. You must ask *who* is making any claim and *why*.
- Avoid the clichés.

Because this round covers a vital issue of concern to most people, it is absolutely essential that journalists strive for high standards of responsibility and accuracy.

- Don't fall for the PR and certainly don't accept any claims made in a media release. Try and find the source of the information—for instance, the leader of the university research team (though the claims of researchers should also be checked with others in the field).
- Always question who is backing the research.
- Cut out all the jargon. If you don't understand what the medical language means then certainly your readers won't understand it. Keep digging until you find someone who can explain the issue in clear, understandable language.
- Beware the words "groundbreaking" and "miracle cure".

Anyone who has worked in a newsroom will be aware of the intense public interest in any story canvassing new medical treatments. The special responsibility this places on journalists is spelt out in the Professional Conduct Policy at News Ltd:

Reports of new drugs or medical treatments must be considered with great caution. It is easy to raise false hopes or alarm among readers. Cross check all claims with responsible and neutral sources.

Mary-Anne Toy was the health editor for *The Age* newspaper for four years and she has her own insider tips for this complex round.

- Get out and see people whenever you can. Don't stay chained to the desk. Show people that you are around and that you are interested. Go to the hospitals, go the conferences and go to the Minister's launches. This all builds goodwill and this is the foundation of the round. Every contact is important, from the Minister down to the support staff in a hospital.
- Bookmark key web sites, including those of the leading medical journals.
- You need to develop good scanning skills and be sceptical: there are a lot of quacks (however well intentioned) and misinformation out there. You have to be able to take in a lot of information quickly and then you need contacts who can qualify and interpret that information for you.
- *Think of your audience*: You need to be able to explain your stories in terms that you can understand and that the public can understand. This is not about "dumbing down", this is about writing well. Most

scientists and doctors are good at explaining things if you are prepared to keep asking them.

When it comes to writing health stories, Mary-Anne says reporters need to consider both the market or the audience and the timing of the story.

Some stories will lend themselves to a straight news format, like a fresh outbreak of legionnaire's disease. But a new insight from laboratory work with mice may lend itself more to a feature-style article. You need to make your judgement calls based on experience.

POLITICAL ROUNDS

John Ferguson covers the state round for the *Herald Sun* in Melbourne and has covered politics in various states for almost 10 years. He says the most important thing when covering politics in any form is to establish your credibility as a journalist and credibility comes with being accurate. The more credibility you have, the more people will want to talk to you.

John's advice to anyone starting a political round is to "learn quickly who are the most reliable sources of information" and "work out which MPs will tell you what's really going on". He says you soon learn that there aren't many. Often good sources are the backbenchers or sometimes it is the malcontents, people who may have missed out on a promotion. These are people with an axe to grind and you need to learn to balance their prejudices. When dealing with sources, you always need to know who they are and where they are coming from. You need to understand why they are telling you something.

John says that building your contacts requires "an element of lunch or coffee". He says, "You want to be able to build a relationship that has a bit of a relaxed atmosphere. If it is always going to be on the record, you can't really build a strong relationship."

John's survival tips for political rounds include:

- Be accurate and be fair but also learn not to swallow the official line.
- Learn to poke and to prod.
- Everyone in politics has an agenda and everyone has the capacity to lie.
- The higher up the chain the source, the better the info.

When it comes to writing news stories on this round, John says any kind of formulaic writing is out.

The days of formulaic news writing are gone. There is a real art to writing news properly. Clichés are to be avoided wherever possible. You have to present your news stories in different forms; you don't want to be predictable.

There are always a hundred different ways to write any story. To capture the essence of a story, I will always try to portray its urgency and I try to capture detail and build atmosphere. For example, if the Premier is making an announcement and his back is covered in sweat, then this is a sign of a man under pressure, which is something you should try and convey to your readers. I always try to include colour into my writing.

Like most seasoned reporters, John understands that journalism doesn't stop when you leave the newsroom for the night. One evening he was having dinner in an Adelaide restaurant and, looking across a crowded room he spotted a man he recognised. The man was a merchant banker associated with the collapse of the State Bank who had gone to ground and had been "missing in action" for several weeks. John didn't hesitate to get up from his dinner, phone work and arrange for a photographer to meet him outside the restaurant. He also didn't hesitate to leave his friends sitting in the restaurant for more than an hour while he waited outside. He did however get the scoop.

SPORTS REPORTING

Nothing fills as much space in Australia's newspapers and time on its radio and television news bulletins as sport. Nothing can throw politics, economics or crime off the front pages faster than the latest sporting achievement or scandal involving a sporting icon.

Australians are obsessed with sport—whether it's in the cricket or tennis or golf season over summer, or in the football season (whatever the code) in winter, or when one of our favourite sons or daughters (or teams) is winning on the international stage.

When Brisbane Broncos rugby league star Allan (Alfie) Langer (temporarily) retired in 1999, saying his heart was no longer in the game, both the Queensland Premier and the Prime Minister felt it necessary to eulogise Alfie's contribution to the game. Channel 9 said on the news that night that Queenslanders were in shock.

Mention "the first Tuesday in November" or "the last Saturday in September" and sports fans around the nation know you're referring to the Melbourne Cup (for which we're told "the nation stops") and the AFL grand final (on the "hallowed turf" of the Melbourne Cricket Ground).

Sport is big business, and not only in terms of what free-to-air and pay TV networks shell out to broadcast events and in sponsorship deals for naming rights to the big events and teams. There's also the amounts paid to the stars of the major sports in earnings, appearance money and winnings, as well as the sponsorship dollars the stars can command for endorsing products.

In winnings alone, a Leighton Hewitt, Pat Rafter or Greg Norman can take home more in a competitive week than most Australians will earn in 20 years. Overseas, the earnings of major sporting stars—like Tiger Woods and other top golfers, Formula One racing driver Michael Schumacher, the world's best soccer players, and the baseball, basketball and gridiron stars of the US—beggar the imagination. It's the hundreds of hours a week devoted to sports coverage on freetoair and pay TV that's a major problem for sports journalists.

Every time they sit in front of their computer terminal to compose a story about the latest exploits of the national cricket side, the Brisbane Lions AFL team, or the Wallabies rugby side, they know that most fans already know the result, and either saw the game in person or on TV.

The West Australian's David Marsh is a senior sports writer who's covered three Olympic Games and three Commonwealth Games and has been covering sport for his Perth paper for nearly 20 years. What can he write that the audience doesn't already know from watching TV?

The sports journalist can no longer simply chronicle facts in the form of a match report, with readers wanting and demanding more from their paper. For example, after Cathy Freeman won the Olympic women's 400 metres gold medal in Sydney, simply providing a description of the race was superfluous for most Australians.

To remain valid, the print journalist will need to ask the big questions: What significance her victory will have for Australian society? What will it do for Aboriginal rights? And what does the man or woman in the street say about the victory?

REPORTING AND WRITING TIPS

Reporting sporting contests, whether they're between individuals or teams, involves many of the basic tenets of good reporting on any round, like politics, business, the law courts or police rounds. But to put these stories in their unique sporting context, here are some tips for reporting and writing this important round.

- *Do your research*: Know how the game or contest is won or lost. If, as a novice sports reporter (and all reporters will at some stage have to cover sport, even if they loathe it), you are sent to a sport you know next to nothing about, do as much research as you can beforehand. While most know the basics of the major games such as cricket, golf, tennis, basketball, baseball and the various football codes—AFL, rugby union and league, and soccer—from schooldays or casual interest, there are many sports which will be unfamiliar. Ring the local association, check the sport's web sites, and establish the fundamentals before the game. If you're still ignorant of the basics, find someone in the game's administration who can fill you in before the competition begins.
- *Know the rules of the game*: Learn how points, goals or whatever are scored. Find out if the particular fixture has a referee or an umpire. Establish what constitutes a penalty, under what circumstances a player can be sent off, and how the particular sport's judiciary system operates to decide further penalties for on or off-field indiscretions. Nothing opens you to more ridicule—if only among the sub-editors

back in the office—than confusing the fundamentals of the game. For instance, both rugby league and rugby union have tries. In rugby league, a team gets four points for a try, two for a successful goal conversion or penalty goal, and one for a field goal. In rugby union, it's five for a try and two for a successful conversion. Much of the scoring in union comes from penalty goals—each worth three points. Teams have scored tries in union, and been beaten because they gave away too many penalties that were converted into points.

- *Learn the language of the particular sport*: Each sport has its unique language. In golf, for instance, they talk about sub-par rounds, of birdies, eagles, albatrosses and the much-prized hole-in-one. Yachties talk about spinnakers, tacking and beating to windward. If you don't know what they're talking about, ask. Make sure you can write your stories so that people who are unfamiliar with the finer points of the contest will understand what happened. In other words, avoid using sports jargon in your stories.
- *Cultivate contacts in every sport*: This is especially helpful in the early stages of your sports reporting career. These contacts are the sports administrators, players, coaches, trainers, physios and so on who can give you invaluable background before and after the contest that will help you to put the conflict into context. As with all rounds, you need to nurture contacts, and sometimes you also have to criticise them in the context of a story, which can lead to strained relations.
- Know the star performers in the particular sport. Know if they are carrying an injury, returning from suspension or, in the case of cricketing twins Steve and Mark Waugh in 2002, struggling to keep their places on the national team. In this context you also need to know something of sports medicine. What is involved in the various common sporting injuries, what effects will the injuries have on the champion's performance, and how long will they be out of the game? Watch the stars to see if they rise to the occasion (most do), or if they underperform. Watch for the rising star. How do they perform on debut?
- *Be aware of the context of the contest*: It might be a club game, but is an individual playing for a place in a state or national team? Are they playing just to stay in the team? Or are they making a come-back?
- Get the background on the major issues in sport. Drugs are a major issue in sport, from the rugby league star who tests positive to recreational drugs to the systematic use of performance-enhancing drugs in sports such as cycling and weight-lifting. In recent years, the big issue in international cricket was match-fixing. At the Sydney 2000 Olympic Games, the major issues were drugs (again), and also

the politics of international sport, ticketing foul-ups, and public transport. All provided major stories during "the most successful Olympics ever".

- *Know the history of the team or individual*: If it's a team sport, what's the record of previous clashes between the two teams? How have the teams or individuals performed in recent times?
- *Keep the statistics*: All sports have their statistics. It's a way of comparing performances over the years. Know the ones that pertain to your particular sport and keep them at hand. Remember the excitement when the Sydney Swans" Tony (Plugger) Lockett broke the AFL's long-standing record for the most goals kicked? *The West Australian*'s David Marsh keeps a large database of sports at home. He collects basic biographical information and up-to-date results, and has copies of the annual books that cover the major performances around the world. "At my first Olympics in Seoul in 1988, I took all of my records in several manila folders. But at the 1998 Commonwealth Games and 2000 Olympics, with the improvements in technology, where I took a PC, all my records were downloaded into two floppy disks, " David says.
- Give the "why" and "how" of the contest, but don't forget the result. What was the turning point in the event? Why did the team or individual win or lose? How did the winning team or individual exert their dominance over the competition? This is where much of your audience will have an opinion, so get it right. Did anyone break a record during the game? It's here and in post-contest interviews with participants, coaches and officials that newspaper journalists often find the story that hasn't been seen on TV or from the grandstand.
- Watch the body language of the individual or team. Did the opposition drop their heads after the third try in five minutes in a rugby league game, or after the sixth unanswered goal in an AFL match? At what stage did they appear resigned to defeat?

COVERING MAJOR SPORTS EVENTS

Covering major events, like the final game of a competition but more particularly events such as the Commonwealth and Olympic games, poses its own set of problems. In Kuala Lumpur in 1998, Sydney in 2000 and Manchester in 2002, teams of reporters were sent from all over Australia to cover the gold-medal aspirants.

The big media groups, like News Ltd, Fairfax, Australian Associated Press and the major television and radio networks, sent teams of reporters (and photographers and cameramen) to slake Australians" insatiable thirst for news on our competitors. The major broadcast organisations pay big money for the rights to cover these events, and not having "rights-holder" access to athletes adds to the problems of a journalist from a relatively small media group.

Such organisations may send one or two reporters (and possibly a photographer) for the sole purpose of covering the performances of competitors from their local area. Not every competitor is going to win a gold medal, but there's a story in how the local hero performs against international competition, something the news agencies and major media groups are unlikely to cover unless the competitor ends up on the medal podium.

So how do you cover local competitors? The organisers of major sporting festivals like the Olympic and Commonwealth games set up internal news services to provide officials and the visiting media with coverage of every event. While this helps the journalist who has to cover several sports at different venues at the same time, it rarely provides enough detail about "local" competitors for the local paper "back home".

David Marsh had to cover several sports on his own at the 1988 Olympic Games in Seoul and at the 1990 Commonwealth Games in Auckland, New Zealand. Being the only reporter from the organisation at the Games meant being selective about which events to cover—and that meant covering events from an Australian perspective. The main sports I covered in Seoul were the swimming in the early part of the Games, and the track and field, which started at the end of the first week.

There are times when the unexpected can happen, which results in the best-laid plans being shelved. Seoul is an example, when Canadian sprinter Ben Johnson tested positive to the anabolic steroid stanazol. I was taken off my scheduled duties at the Games for more than a day to follow the Ben Johnson story.

The regional journalist faces any number of problems reporting such events. Transport to the various venues that doesn't run to the pre-arranged timetable, telephone connections that are unreliable, events that are completed after the paper's deadline (because of time differences) to name a few. Covering local competitors for regional media starts for the sports journalists long before the actual competition begins. They make contact with the competitors local to their area before they leave for the event. They get the competitors" mobile phone numbers, and organise to meet them after their main event. In this way they get "their story".

It may be a story of success or disappointment, but it will be the story the locals "back home" want to hear. Sometimes it will be a "colour" story of what the local competitor did in the Games city after their event—how they enjoyed the atmosphere of such a major event, whether the family were there to see them, what it was like to live in the athletes" village, or simply a story about a shopping spree with local athletes. These are the sorts of stories that the network and major newspaper coverage cannot provide, but will be of intense interest to "local" readers, listeners and viewers. But, like everything associated with journalism in general, and sports journalism in particular, pre-planning, an abundance of background knowledge and reliable contacts are essential. Actually writing the story is no different to any other news story. It is your evaluation of the various commonly used news criteria that will decide how the story will flow. Proximity, for instance, will determine a major part of the lead.

While in Brisbane a win by the rugby league team, the Broncos, will be lauded as another victory to the local audience, in the "local area" of the defeated team it will be reported as a loss. At the Kuala Lumpur games, the audience "back home" was really only interested in the gold medal victories of the Australian competitors, and the rare defeats of the highly fancied, like the full-strength Aussie cricket team.

One of the main news criteria used in sporting stories is, of course, conflict. Sports events are almost always characterised as conflicts, with sporting reporters using language perhaps more at home in the "War on Terror" than in a "conflict" on the sporting field.

In team sports, for instance, unless a key player is injured, the lead will usually be who won, the score and possibly why.

Prominence is another news criteria used by sports writers in determining the angle for their story. If the star performs well—a century to a one-day cricket captain, or five or more wickets to a top bowler—they will often figure in a "double-barrelled" lead that combines the outstanding performance with the result.

Two of the other accepted news criteria, suspense and resolution, figure in every sporting story—suspense as the contest is played out (and covered progressively on radio, online or TV) and resolution when we know the result.

Other news criteria also figure in sports reports, like timeliness (it must be the latest result), interest (there is always public interest in sports results—the more public interest, the bigger the story) and clarity (your story needs to be understood by all readers regardless of familiarity, or lack of, with the sport). Human interest (the rising star), novelty (the outstanding performance or strange occurrence) and, of course, sensation (in any form) will all have a place when deciding how to construct a sports story.

Bibliography

Ajay Dash: *News Editing*, Sonali Publication, Delhi, 2008.

Anita Kaur: *Career in Electronic Media*, Abhishek Publication, Delhi, 2010.

Aris, S.: *Print Media And Broadcast Journalism*, ABD Publication, Delhi, 2010.

Aruna Zachariah: *Print Media Communication and Management : Elements, Dimensions and Images*, Kanishka Publication, Delhi, 2006.

Bhanu Pratap Singh: *News Editing*, Anmol Publication, Delhi, 2011.

Bhanu Pratap Singh: *Print Media*, Anmol Publication, Delhi, 2011.

Charles Nandi: *Print Media and Photojournalism*, Reference Press, Delhi, 2006.

D.R. Gupta: *Development of Electronic Media*, Pearl Books, Delhi, 2012.

G.C. Kundra: *Role of Print Media*, ALP Books, Delhi, 2011.

G.P. Rastogi: *Importance of Print Media*, Pearl Books, Delhi, 2012.

Gaurav Oberoi: *Electronic Media And Journalism*, Murari Lal and Sons, Delhi, 2009.

Hemalatha Jain: *Techniques of Dyeing and Printing*, Ane Books, Delhi, 2010.

J.P. Ahluwaliya: *Modern News Structure in Print Media and Electronic Media*, Adhyayan Publication, Delhi, 2007.

Kunal Nagi: *Teach Yourself : Sprinting*, Sports Publication, Delhi, 2007.

M.H. Syed: *Encyclopaedia of Print Media (3 Vols-Set)*, Anmol Publication, Delhi, 2006.

Monita Singh: *Print Media and Photo Journalism*, Centrum Press, Delhi, 2010.

N Afaque Shamsi: *Electronic Media*, Anmol Publication, Delhi, 2006.

N. Afaque Shamsi: *Print Media*, Anmol Publication, Delhi, 2006.

N.K. Singh: *Print Media : Reporting Writing and Editing*, Arise Publishers, Delhi, 2012.

N.P. Sharma: *Play and Learn Sprinting*, Khel Sahitya Kendra, Delhi, 2005.

Pallavi Goswami: *Recent Trends in Indian English : A Linguistic Study of Print Media*, Readworthy, Delhi, 2010.

Prakash Shetty: *Science and Technology of Printing Materials*, MJP Publication, Delhi, 2008.

Priyanka Wadhwa: *Electronic Media*, Murari Lal and Sons, Delhi, 2007.

Rashmi Sharma: *Electronic Media : Issues and Innovations*, Regal Publication, Delhi, 2007.

S.C. Sharma and Sweta Bakshi: *Contemporary Electronic Media*, A.K. Publications, Delhi, 2009.

Sanjay Kaptan: *Advertisement in Print Media*, Book Enclave, Delhi, 2003.

Smruti S Pattanaik: *Elite Perceptions in Foreign Policy : Role of Print Media in Influencing India-Pakistan Relations, 1989-1999*, Manohar Publication, Delhi, 2004.

Subrata Ganguly: *Symbol, Script and Writing (From Petrogram to Printing and Further)*, Sharada Publication, Delhi, 2004.

Vandana Chauhan: *Dynamics of Electronic Media*, Sumit Enterprises, Delhi, 2010.

Vijay K Taneja: *Electronic Media*, Pacific Publication, Delhi, 2009.

Index